D0216698

# UNITED STATES
# IMMIGRATION

A Reference Handbook

Other titles in ABC-CLIO's
## CONTEMPORARY
## WORLD ISSUES
Series

Books in the Contemporary World Issues series address vital issues in today's society such as terrorism, sexual harassment, homelessness, AIDS, gambling, animal rights, and air pollution. Written by professional writers, scholars, and nonacademic experts, these books are authoritative, clearly written, up-to-date, and objective. They provide a good starting point for research by high school and college students, scholars, and general readers, as well as by legislators, businesspeople, activists, and others.

Each book, carefully organized and easy to use, contains an overview of the subject; a detailed chronology; biographical sketches; facts and data and/or documents and other primary-source material; a directory of organizations and agencies; annotated lists of print and nonprint resources; a glossary; and an index.

Readers of books in the Contemporary World Issues series will find the information they need in order to better understand the social, political, environmental, and economic issues facing the world today.

# UNITED STATES
# IMMIGRATION

## A Reference Handbook

E. Willard Miller
*Department of Geography*

Ruby M. Miller
*Pattee Library*

*The Pennsylvania State University*

CONTEMPORARY
WORLD ISSUES

**ABC-CLIO**

Santa Barbara, California
Denver, Colorado
Oxford, England

**Library of Congress Cataloging-in-Publication Data**

Miller, E. Willard (Eugene Willard), 1915–
    United States immigration : a reference handbook / E. Willard Miller, Ruby M. Miller.
       p.   cm.—(Contempory world issues series)
    Includes bibliographical references and index.
    1. United States—Emigration and immigration—Handbooks, manuals, etc.  2. United States—Emigration and immigration—Government policy—Handbooks, manuals, etc.  I. Miller, Ruby M. II. Title.  III. Series: Contemporary world issues.
JV6465.M55    1996                          96-19542
304.8′73—dc20                                CIP

ISBN 0-87436-845-6

02 01 00 99 98 97 96 95 10 9 8 7 6 5 4 3 2 1

ABC-CLIO, Inc.
130 Cremona Drive, P.O. Box 1911
Santa Barbara, California 93116-1911

This book is printed on acid-free paper ∞ .
Manufactured in the United States of America

# Contents

# Tables

# Preface

Immigration to the United States has played a major role in the development of the country's population since the first colony was established in 1607. More than 60 million people have immigrated to this nation as a result of a complex set of factors, particularly economic issues. America offered vast opportunities to improve the material well-being of millions of people and their descendants. But other factors have played a role, too. For instance, in the 1840s, famine in Ireland drove millions of people from the country. Many groups such as the Quakers, Amish, and Mennonites have sought refuge from religious persecution. In more recent times, immigrants to the United States have sought to escape from political persecution. The United States remains the sole nation where millions of people seek admission each year.

Chapter 1 of this book begins with a short analysis of the roots of immigration, followed by a historical account of how American immigration policy has evolved. Next comes an analysis of legal, illegal, and refugee immigration. Immigration can have significant effects on demographics, culture, education, welfare, and labor. The analysis of countries is regionally organized to give spatial coherence to the sources of immigrants.

Chapter 2 presents a chronology listing the evolution of laws and regulations governing the admission of immigrants to the United States. Because of the complex reasons immigrants have in coming to the United States, the federal government has found it difficult to develop a sound immigration policy. For example, it took seven years for the Immigration Reform and Control Act of 1986 to be passed by Congress. The chronology also provides a historical reference for the admission of major modern refugee groups.

Chapter 3 presents details of federal laws and regulations. It recognizes three major periods. The first covers the "open door" policy that extended prior to 1924, when there were essentially no restrictions on immigration to the United States. The second period extends from 1924 to 1965, when a quota system operated to restrict the number of immigrants who could enter the nation. The last period runs from 1965 to the present, when a set number of allowed immigrants has been established for each country. Because these limits do not always match the number of people who wish to immigrate to the United States from a particular country, a massive movement of illegal aliens has resulted.

As Chapter 4 reveals, a vast number of organizations handle different aspects of immigration. These organizations can be classified into four categories. The most comprehensive category includes the governmental and private general immigration organizations. Other types deal specifically with migrants, migrant labor, and refugees.

In recent years, there has been a tremendous increase in the amount of literature on immigration. Chapter 5 presents an annotated bibliography of books dealing with a variety of related topics, as well as over 600 articles from journals and government publications. The references are arranged topically, and the chapter includes a list of selected journals that publish articles on immigration.

Chapter 6 presents an annotated list of films, and the book concludes with a glossary and index.

The immigration and refugee statistics in this volume are from: U.S. Immigration and Naturalization Service, *Statistical Yearbook, Annual Report*, 1930–1992, Washington, DC: Government Printing Office; and U.S. Bureau of the Census, *Census of Population*, 1790–1990, Washington, DC: Government Printing Office.

# Immigration: A Perspective

Immigration has played a major role in establishing today's American society. Since the first English settlers arrived in 1607, successive waves of immigrants have come to the United States. Of the 60 million people who have relocated from Europe since 1600, more than two-thirds have come to the United States. American culture, economic life, political structures, and religion have all been influenced by immigrants over time.

For more than 300 years, the United States welcomed, with few restrictions, all peoples. This "open access" policy changed in the 1920s when free land was no longer available and industrial growth slowed. Strict limitations were then placed on the numbers of immigrants and their ethnic origins. These restrictions have gradually become less strict since 1965. As a consequence, immigration has once again increased, with a major surge of immigrants from Third World countries.

A major debate is now occurring as to the type of immigration policy the United States should develop. This debate poses an unprecedented challenge to the United States. Deciding which potential immigrants should be admitted raises many questions that have not been resolved concerning economic capability and commitment to humanitarian goals. Further, in more practical terms, finding homes and jobs for millions of new families presents formidable economic, social, cultural, and political problems. A fundamental question in this process is, How committed is the United States to becoming a multicultural society? Finding a satisfactory answer to this question may be the most important challenge the United States faces in the twenty-first century.

## Roots of Immigration

People throughout the world immigrate to new areas for many reasons. When the movement is voluntary, these people are known as *immigrants*. When the immigration is involuntary and the immigrant is seeking religious freedom or protection from political persecution, the term *refugee* is used. In either situation, people move because their society fails to meet their fundamental needs and aspirations. An understanding of why people want to move provides insight into the immigration of refugees and immigrants.

### Immigration

The most compelling factor in voluntary immigration is economics. A lack of economic opportunities may compel people to look elsewhere to find a way to take care of their families. In many instances, jobs in one location may pay so poorly that people lack the buying power for necessities such as food and clothing. When economic conditions are better in other regions, whether near or far, immigration will result.

Resource poverty and environmental degradation often create scarcities that inspire people to move. Exhaustion of basic resources (such as firewood for heating and cooking), overcrowding in homes, and a lack of domestic facilities all plague poor nations. These combined scarcities create an atmosphere of despair that people hope to escape by immigrating elsewhere.

### Refugees

Political disempowerment is another cause of immigration. People who are unable to vote or participate in public life but are not in communist countries are normally considered refugees under U.S. immigration policy. Therefore, they must demonstrate that they are being persecuted as a group before they can receive U.S. governmental assistance. This has been a major problem for immigrants from such areas as Haiti and Central America.

Involuntary movements of people have increased greatly in recent years for many reasons. Political persecution has played a major role. Persecution may be based on race, religion, nationality, or political opinions. It may be quite subtle or it may be enforced by governmental decree. While there are millions of people who move because of persecution, there are vast numbers of others who have the desire to move to another country but are prevented from doing so.

War is one of the major disasters that leads to massive refugee crises. Hostilities may cause both internal and international displacement of persons. When national borders are redrawn, people may move to newly created countries or to other countries where they feel more secure. Refugee immigration may be forced by governmental decree, or people may be forced to move because of dire political or economic conditions.

Because the movement of refugees is involuntary, the U.S. government provides aid from a number of sources. Thus, assistance may come from international sources, particularly the United Nations; it may come from national governmental sources, such as the funds provided by the U.S. government for the Cuban refugees; or it may come from private sources, such as the Red Cross. In contrast, aid for voluntary migrants is limited if it exists at all.

# U.S. Immigration Policy

## Open Door Policy, 1607–1917

From the beginning of colonial settlement in 1607 until 1917, there were few governmental controls placed on immigration to the United States. Economic opportunity was the greatest incentive to immigrants. Land was essentially free for several hundred years. In the last half of the nineteenth century and the early twentieth century, the unparalleled industrial development of the nation provided a major incentive for foreign immigration. Unlimited immigration was a necessity for the development of the nation.

For the first century after colonies were initially established, the immigrants were largely from England. Governor William

Penn of Pennsylvania was one of the first leaders to recognize that settlement from European countries should be increased. He therefore encouraged German immigration to Pennsylvania, promising religious freedom and generous land allotments. This eventually led to the extensive German immigration to Pennsylvania in the early eighteenth century.

George Washington, in a speech in 1783 to newly arrived Irish immigrants, established a U.S. governmental policy that lasted for more than a century. He stated, "The bosom of America is open to receive not only the opulent and respectable stranger but the oppressed and persecuted of all nations and religions."

Although the United States generally recognized the need to increase its population in the nineteenth century, there was still some opposition to the increasing foreign immigration. By the early nineteenth century, the German population in Pennsylvania had grown so large that other residents began to resent the speaking of German. The Pennsylvania legislature, fearful that the colony might degenerate into a foreign state, passed legislation in 1829 that placed a heavy tax on all foreigners entering the state. Although the law was quickly repealed, it marked the first modest attempt to control the number of immigrants coming from a particular country to America.

There was also opposition to extending civil rights to free black Americans. This viewpoint was so strong, particularly in the South, that Congress passed the Naturalization Act of 1790, the first law dealing with immigration; it limited citizenship to "free white persons."

A number of groups that favored restrictions on immigrants became organized from time to time. Certain religions were frequently the target of opposition. Anti-Catholic feelings were sometimes particularly strong. As late as 1700, only in Rhode Island did Catholics enjoy full civil rights and religious freedom. In the 1840s, a four-day riot between Catholics and Protestants over the use of bibles in Philadelphia schools was able to be quelled only by military force. In the late nineteenth century, a group known as the American Protective Association (APA) was organized to protect the nation against a perceived Catholic menace. The APA charged that Catholics in the Northeast were gaining control of state governments to the detriment of the nation.

Of all the immigrants, none were opposed more bitterly than the Chinese. Because the Chinese worked for low wages, the opposition from organized labor was particularly strong. As a result, the Chinese found it extremely difficult to become a part of American society.

As immigration from southern and eastern Europe increased, the notion that these groups came from another culture became widespread. As a result, a number of organizations formed to attempt to control these peoples' admittance to the nation. Three parallel developments were particularly important in this movement: the growing popularity of eugenics, the influence of a school of thought called progressivism, and the rebirth of the Ku Klux Klan.

The eugenics movement was founded by late nineteenth-century intellectuals who believed that selection could improve the quality of the human race. These professional groups believed that individual intelligence and behavior were attributable to ethnicity and race. They believed that people from eastern and southern Europe, who allegedly represented an inferior race, reduced the intellectual quality of the nation.

The progressives, whose members were largely middle-class people, believed that urban problems were due in great part to immigrants who did not become a part of U.S. culture. Their belief was that no more aliens should be admitted until those who were already here were fully assimilated into U.S. society.

The Ku Klux Klan's opposition to further immigration was based on their hostile views on race and Catholicism. The group perceived immigrants to be the basic cause of the moral disintegration of the nation.

In the late nineteenth century, there were a few modest attempts to control immigrants. Literacy legislation requiring people to speak and read English was introduced periodically in Congress with backing mostly from southern and western states. President Cleveland vetoed this type of early legislation. The first restrictive immigration law, which prohibited "obnoxious immigrants," was passed in 1875. It included persons who were destitute, those engaging in "immoral" activities, and the physically handicapped. The 1875 Immigration Act was followed by additional acts in 1882, 1891, and 1903.

Until 1850, virtually all immigrants to the United States were from the United Kingdom, Ireland, and Germany. After 1850, increasing numbers came from Latin America, China, and Scandinavia. In the late nineteenth century and early twentieth century, they came from Russia and eastern and southern Europe. As the number of immigrants grew, strong opposition arose within the nation's labor groups. Racism and Americans' anxiety over the economic threat from cheaper immigrant labor were major factors behind the Chinese Exclusion Act of 1882. This act limited the number of Chinese who could immigrate to the United States. Later amendments to the 1882 act ultimately prohibited immigration from China.

Late nineteenth-century immigration laws increased the role of the federal government in monitoring and regulating immigration. The Immigration Act of 1891 created the Office of Immigration, which evolved into the Immigration and Naturalization Service (INS). The 1891 act was administered by the secretary of the treasury.

There was continued concern about Asian immigration. In 1907, a verbal agreement with the Japanese government restricted Japanese immigration. Such immigration was later formally and unilaterally prohibited by the U.S. government in the Japanese Exclusion Act of 1924.

## Restricted Immigration, 1917–1965

In the late 1880s, the source of European immigration began to shift from western and northern Europe to eastern and southern Europe, with more than half of the new immigrants coming from Russia, Poland, Greece, and Italy. There was a strong reaction in the United States. Several federal commissions in the 1910s recommended that the nation restrict immigration and add some sort of qualification for admission. For example, the Dillingham Commission recommended in 1917 that immigrants should be literate and that no eastern Asian immigrants be admitted from such countries as China, Japan, and Korea— known as the "barren zones." Thus, in 1917 Congress passed a law requiring a literacy test for immigrants, over President Wilson's veto.

While immigration decreased during World War I, it resumed at a high level in the 1920s. Labor organizations strongly opposed these large numbers of immigrants. They were concerned that the growing number of aliens would lead to strong competition for jobs, but more important, they were worried that the wage gains they had achieved in World War I would be lost as a result of cheap foreign labor. In addition to economic issues, there were also ethnic and racial concerns. The peoples from eastern and southern Europe were considered inferior by many Americans whose ancestors came from northern and western Europe. Large numbers of immigrants came to occupy entire areas of cities. In addition, as the Communist Revolution gained control of the government in the Soviet Union and the communist philosophy expanded to other countries, there was concern that the new aliens would be agitators for the overthrow of the United States' form of government.

As a response to the public opposition to new immigrants, Congress enacted the 1921 Quota Act. This act limited yearly immigration to only 3 percent of the foreign-born population, by national origin, already in the United States according to the 1910 census.

In order to strengthen control of immigration, the Immigration Act of 1924 made the national quota permanent and further limited yearly immigration of the people of any nation to 2 percent of their U.S. population as listed in the 1890 census. This act accorded the largest allowable numbers to the peoples of northern and western Europe, who were the dominant groups in the 1890 population. In contrast, the allowed immigration from southern and eastern Europe was sharply decreased. The 1924 act also barred completely all aliens from Asia. Thus, this act confirmed previous legislation that barred Asians.

The Immigration Act of 1924 did not limit immigration from countries of the Western hemisphere. Congressmen from the Southwest wanted to maintain their cheap source of agricultural labor, primarily from Mexico. Despite conflicting public sentiment in much of the United States, the southwestern congressmen prevented the quota system from applying to Latin America. Also, in the interest of maintaining friendly relations with Canada, the quota system did not apply to that country either.

The 1924 act also made significant changes in how the immigration laws were implemented. It provided funds to create a large Border Patrol. By the 1930s, the Immigration Bureau relied on the Border Patrol to apprehend, exclude, and deport illegal immigrants and to review the applications of immigrants at major ports of entry. In 1933, by executive order of President Roosevelt, the Immigration and Naturalization Service was created.

After World War II, there was a need to change the immigration laws of the 1920s. The Immigration and Naturalization Act of 1952 codified many of the previous laws. It also introduced a preference structure for potential immigrants, with separate categories for types of relatives and worker skills. This act also removed some barriers to naturalization, although it retained the restrictions on national origin that were enacted in 1924.

A report by an immigration commission in 1953 recommended that the national origin system be replaced by a selection system based on family reunification and employment skills. The Eisenhower administration supported this viewpoint, but there was no reform until 1965, as discussed later in this chapter.

Because World War II created a large number of displaced persons and refugees, the U.S. Congress passed special legislation to admit these people. The Displaced Persons Act, passed in 1948, permitted the admittance of 400,000 refugees. The new statute assumed that the United States had a responsibility to deal with the displacement of persons caused by World War II. This act was followed in 1953 by the Refugees Relief Act, which established a new category of persons who were persecuted because of their political beliefs. This act conformed with a national foreign policy goal of aiding persons who wanted to flee from communist countries. It also established preferences for skilled workers. Thus, the law recognized the economic benefits to be derived from selecting immigrants based on occupation. Although the number admitted under this clause was small, the principle of linking immigrants with labor skills was established.

## Revising the Restricted Immigration Policy: The Immigration Act of 1965

In the 1950s, politicians began discussing the need for basic changes to the 1924 immigration law. In 1958, John F. Kennedy, then a senator, wrote a book titled *A Nation of Immigrants*, which showed the many contributions foreign-born immigrants had made to the United States. As president, Kennedy requested that Congress repeal the 1924 act, but because of his assassination, the repeal came under the Johnson administration.

The reforms were enacted in the Immigration Act of 1965. Most important, this legislation abolished the old national origin system. Specifically, it abandoned the 1890 country-specific quota, including the zero quotas for Asian countries. These legal changes set the stage for two major shifts in the character of immigration that occurred in the subsequent decades. The first shift occurred because the need for Mexican workers continued in agriculture in the Southwest but a quota was insufficient to supply the required workers. This triggered massive illegal immigration. The second shift occurred because the quotas of immigration visas were increased to immigrants in particular from Asia and Latin America. The number of Asian immigrants living in the United States rose from about 150,000 in the 1950s to more than 2.7 million in the 1980s, while European immigration fell by more than one-third. These immigrants came seeking relief from overpopulation, limited economic opportunity, and the devastation of war. Already-existing Asian communities in the United States, particularly in California, provided the essential economic and social linkages to the new immigrants. Further, outside the United States, few nations were willing to accept Asian immigrants.

There was also a massive increase from Latin American countries. During the 1950s, the 600,000 immigrants who came from Latin America and the Caribbean accounted for one in four immigrants. Three decades later, 3.5 million immigrants came from the Americas, accounting for 47 percent of all admissions. If illegal immigrants are included, far more than half of all immigrants to the United States came from the Western hemisphere.

The 1965 Immigration Act also had a major influence on the types of immigrants coming to the United States. With a preference given to skilled workers, the door was opened widest to Asians. To illustrate, in 1973 only about 25 percent of all immigrants had professional or technical backgrounds, but 54 percent of the Asian immigrants fell in this category.

In recent years, many scientists, engineers, managers, computer analysts, nurses, and doctors have been drawn to the United States by both high salaries and good working conditions. In the 1950s, the shortage of doctors in the United States was met by European and Canadian immigrants, but after 1965 the need for more doctors, partly as a response to the establishment of Medicare and Medicaid, brought 75,000 doctors to the United States within a decade. The largest numbers came from the Philippines, Korea, Iran, India, and Thailand. By 1974, foreign-born physicians made up one fifth of the U.S. total.

Besides its influence on the immigration of professionals, the 1965 law accelerated the immigration of other persons. The law's provisions for unifying families permitted legal relatives to come to the United States. This resulted in what has come to be known as "pyramiding." To illustrate, many immigrants entered the country with temporary work permits but did not leave after obtaining permanent resident status. This enabled them to bring in their parents as immediate family members. After becoming citizens, these individuals brought additional members of their family to the United States. It has been documented that one original immigrant could bring as many as 30 to 45 relatives. But it does not stop there. Since the children's spouse could, in turn, start a new pyramid, beginning with their parents, the final result could be hundreds of new immigrants.

## Modern Legislation

By the mid-1970s, Congress recognized that the 1965 act did not establish an effective immigration policy because it encouraged illegal immigration. In order to revise the existing legislation, a committee was appointed in 1979 to evaluate the existing laws and policies governing the admission of both immigrants and refugees. The committee's 1981 report culminated in two major new acts: the Immigration Reform and Control Act of 1986 and the Immigration Act of 1990. In addition to these two comprehensive acts, Congress passed the Refugee Act of 1990, which modernized the refugee policy and established guidelines for admitting refugees and handling aliens who declare themselves to be refugees.

The major purpose of the 1986 act was to reduce the number of illegal aliens by limiting their flow into the country and by legalizing the status of illegal aliens who had come to the United States before 1980. This act legalized the status of about 3 million aliens residing in the United States. A number of factors contributed to passage of the 1986 act. One key reason was the support of several influential Hispanic legislators who in the past had objected strenuously to the employee restriction provisions as discriminatory. These individuals reversed their position and now stated that the bill reduced the danger of discrimination. More important, Congress believed that the growing national sentiment against the amnesty provision would destroy the program if it were delayed further. In addition, rising unemployment in Texas due to the decline of the oil industry raised fear among some Hispanics that additional illegal immigration would hurt their own job prospects. In contrast, improved economic conditions in other regions allayed the concerns of workers there that aliens receiving citizenship would represent additional competition for jobs. The powerful agricultural lobby was placated with special provisions allowing entry of sufficient numbers of Mexican workers to meet the labor needs of the Southwest. The act gave these workers some protection against exploitation. In the past, organized labor and civil rights groups had vigorously opposed such a concession but now agreed to the new provisions. Finally, to placate states and localities fearful that the bill would saddle them with added expenditures for services rendered to legalized immigrants, the measure provided for compensatory payments from the federal government.

The Justice Department, which linked the entry of illegal aliens to the rise in drug traffic from Mexico, favored the 1986 legislation. Congress had just passed a tough anti-drug measure, and members would have found it difficult to vote against an immigration bill that was perceived as offering a new weapon in the war against drugs. On November 6, 1986, almost six years after the Select Commission on Immigration and Refugee Policy had submitted its original report, President Reagan signed the new bill into law. Although the Reagan administration questioned the legislation, a veto would have been unpopular given the public sentiment and bipartisan support in Congress.

In retrospect, the 1986 act has not been effective in controlling the entrance of illegal aliens to the United States. The illegal movement of Mexican aliens into this country has increased in the 1990s.

As soon as the 1986 Immigration Act had been passed, Congress began debating revisions culminating in the Immigration Act of 1990. This act made a number of changes, including a restructuring of the immigrant selection system; a revision and addition of a number of existing categories such as reorganization of the grounds for exclusion and deportation; and the creation of new procedures for protecting aliens who were fleeing civil unrest in their own countries. The 1990 act also dealt with family reunification, allowing for an unlimited number of visas for immediate relatives of U.S. citizens. It also placed restrictions on the number of visas to unskilled workers and increased the number of visas allowed for workers who had special skills and professionals. An additional 10,000 visas were to be granted to immigrant entrepreneurs who had $1 million or more to create employment for at least ten U.S. residents. Previously underrepresented nationalities were given more visas, with 40 percent of new "diversity" visas reserved for Irish applicants from 1992 to 1994. The 1990 act also included specific provisions legalizing some Central American refugees who were residing in the United States and offering naturalization to certain Filipino veterans of World War II.

## Future Considerations

Since 1921 when Congress passed the first modern legislation regulating the numbers of immigrants admitted to the United

States, it has been generally recognized that the United States cannot support a completely open door policy to millions of immigrants annually. In an attempt to develop an orderly immigration policy, Congress has established an overall ceiling of quotas for most types of immigrants.

A difficult and unanswered question concerns how to control illegal immigration. In the past decade the numbers of illegal aliens coming to the United States have been staggering. The present legislation to control these numbers has not been adequately enforced. A fundamental question is, is the nation capable of controlling its borders in the face of this invasion of illegal aliens?

The problem of illegal immigrants not only has economic and social implications, but also evokes highly emotional responses from the general public. The nation is at a crossroads in terms of changing from a secondary economy (one based on manufacturing and construction) to a tertiary economy based on services and communications. Given the present unprecedented forces that are shaping the occupational structure and geographic patterns of employment, new immigrants in the labor force play a greater role than in the past.

Immigration policy can influence not only the quantitative size of the labor force but also its qualitative characteristics. Present immigration policy does little to respond to changes in occupational needs. Although there is currently no labor shortage in the United States, the U.S. Department of Labor has indicated that a potential labor shortage could develop after the year 2000. These shortages will be most critical in the occupations that require extensive training and education. Therefore, serious consideration must be given to the types of immigrants who will fit into the economic system of the United States if the nation is to prosper.

## Immigration Trends

### Number

From the time of the first English colony in 1607, America has been the adopted homeland of many diverse peoples (Table 1). During the colonial period, the numbers were quite small. In the period from 1790 to 1830, the young nation provided few economic or cultural incentives to attract large numbers from Europe.

**Table 1   Number of Immigrants to the United States from Different Regions, 1820–1990**

| Time Period | Europe | Asia | Latin America | Africa | Australia, Pacific Islands | Other Countries |
|---|---|---|---|---|---|---|
| 1820–1940 | 32,468,776 | 1,074,926 | 4,401,486 | 26,080 | 65,526 | 253,683 |
| 1941–1950 | 621,147 | 37,028 | 354,804 | 17,367 | 14,551 | 146 |
| 1951–1960 | 1,325,727 | 153,249 | 996,944 | 14,082 | 12,976 | 12,491 |
| 1961–1970 | 1,128,432 | 427,642 | 1,716,324 | 28,954 | 25,142 | 93 |
| 1971–1980 | 800,368 | 1,580,178 | 1,982,785 | 80,779 | 47,242 | 12 |
| 1981–1990 | 705,630 | 2,066,455 | 3,580,828 | 182,212 | 41,230 | 196 |
| 1820–1990 | 37,484,028 | 7,171,986 | 15,064,901 | 439,512 | 211,867 | 272,243 |

Source: U.S. Bureau of the Census, *Census of Population*, Washington, DC: Government Printing Office.

## Table 2  Immigration to the United States, 1820–1990

| Time Period | Number of Immigrants (thousands) |
|---|---|
| 1820–1990 | 52,520 |
| 1820–1830 | 152 |
| 1831–1840 | 599 |
| 1841–1850 | 1,713 |
| 1851–1860 | 2,598 |
| 1861–1870 | 2,315 |
| 1871–1880 | 2,812 |
| 1881–1890 | 5,247 |
| 1891–1900 | 3,688 |
| 1901–1910 | 8,795 |
| 1911–1920 | 5,734 |
| 1921–1930 | 4,107 |
| 1931–1940 | 328 |
| 1941–1950 | 1,035 |
| 1951–1960 | 2,515 |
| 1961–1970 | 3,322 |
| 1971–1980 | 4,493 |
| 1981–1990 | 7,338 |

*Source:* U.S. Bureau of the Census, *Census of Population,* Washington, DC: Government Printing Office.

In the 1830s, however, the nation experienced its first mass immigration. The 1840 census reported 599,000 immigrants during the preceding decade. For the remainder of the nineteenth century and extending into the first two decades of the twentieth century, the available free land and the rapidly expanding industrial economy attracted more than 34 million immigrants to the United States. During this period, a peak of 8,795,000 immigrants came between 1900 and 1910 (Table 2).

In dramatic contrast, few immigrants came to the United States between 1924 and 1965 as a result of the Immigration Act of 1924. The Great Depression of the 1930s and the World War II period greatly reduced immigration to the United States. After World War II, however, the country opened its doors to a large number of political refugees.

In 1965, the 1890 quota system was abolished and a set immigration figure was established for different countries (Table 3). A ceiling of 170,000 visas was imposed on immigration from all the nations of the Eastern hemisphere. The totals for the Western hemisphere were set at 120,000. Thus, there was a yearly total limit on immigration to the United States of

Table 3   Legal Immigration to the United States, 1965–1990

| Year | Total |
| --- | --- |
| 1965 | 296,597 |
| 1966 | 323,040 |
| 1967 | 361,972 |
| 1968 | 454,448 |
| 1969 | 358,579 |
| 1970 | 373,326 |
| 1971 | 370,476 |
| 1972 | 384,685 |
| 1973 | 400,063 |
| 1974 | 394,861 |
| 1975 | 386,194 |
| 1976 | 398,613 |
| 1977 | 462,315 |
| 1978 | 601,442 |
| 1979 | 460,348 |
| 1980 | 530,639 |
| 1981 | 596,600 |
| 1982 | 594,131 |
| 1983 | 559,763 |
| 1984 | 543,903 |
| 1985 | 570,008 |
| 1986 | 601,708 |
| 1987 | 601,518 |
| 1988 | 643,025 |
| 1989 | 1,090,920 |
| 1990 | 1,536,483 |

*Source:* U.S. Immigration and Naturalization Service, *Statistical Yearbook, Annual Report,* Washington, DC: Government Printing Office.

290,000. The 1965 act also set a ceiling of 20,000 visas for any single country in the Eastern hemisphere. No ceiling was applied to any country in the Western hemisphere. Under the new law, the country of origin remained a basic component of immigration policy.

Modern immigration trends reflect a number of factors. First, the general upward trend of legal immigration reflects U.S. policy changes that allow visas for a larger number of immigrants. Second, changes throughout the world have provided important incentives for refugees to immigrate to the United States. A large number of refugees originate from countries to which the United States has a special obligation, such as Cuba and Vietnam. Congress has enacted special legislation that favors admission of these individuals. Third, legislation passed in the 1980s permitted over 3 million illegal aliens to become permanent residents of this country. Because the quota was too small to meet the desire of many Mexicans to migrate to the United States, the legislation forced them to enter the United States as illegal aliens, adding millions of people.

## Location of Immigrants

Almost 70 percent of the present-day foreign-born immigrants have settled in six states: California, New York, Florida, Texas, Illinois, and New Jersey, with 40 percent in California and New York alone. Three cities—Los Angeles, Miami, and New York— have populations that are more than 25 percent foreign born. Each of these three cities, however, has its own distinctive ethnic groups. Miami is the least varied. Its immigrants are over-whelmingly Hispanic, mostly Cuban. Los Angeles is more cos-mopolitan, with large numbers of Iranians, Salvadorans, Armenians, Chinese, Koreans, Vietnamese, Filipinos, and Arabs. However, in Los Angeles, more than two-thirds are Hispanic, with Mexicans easily the largest group. In New York City, the ethnic mix is remarkably broad, with no one group dominating. For example, more Dominicans live in New York City than in any city but Santo Domingo; more Haitians live there than in any city but Port-au-Prince; more Greeks live there than in any city but Athens; and the city has more Jamaican, Russian (mostly Jewish), and Chinese residents than any city outside Jamaica, Russia, and China. In addition, there are tens of thousands of New York City residents who were born in Ireland, Korea, India, Colombia, and Ecuador.

As is traditional with new immigrants, most of the modern immigrants have settled in cities, usually in a single district. Filipinos have concentrated in Honolulu, Los Angeles, and San Francisco, where there are longstanding Filipino connections. Chinese tend to settle in cities with Chinatowns, especially New York, San Francisco, and Los Angeles. Koreans are most highly concentrated in Los Angeles but are also in New York and Chicago. Arabic-speaking groups are located in the Detroit met-ropolitan areas, especially Dearborn. Jewish immigrants have concentrated in New York. Asian immigrants have concentrated in older and frequently run-down neighborhoods and have improved them.

Each of the Latin American and Caribbean groups have had distinctive settlement patterns. Each group has attempted to maintain its ethnic identity and culture and has had limited interaction with other groups. While most of the Hispanic immigrants come from rural areas, nearly all have become urban dwellers in the United States, with the largest concentrations in Los Angeles, Miami, and other Florida cities. Many of the immigrants, particularly from Mexico, Jamaica, the Dominican Republic, and Ecuador, continue to travel between their homeland and the United States.

## Ancestry of Modern Immigrants

In 1990, foreign-born people accounted for about 8 percent of the total U.S. population. Among the countries that receive numerous immigrants, Canada—with a 16 percent foreign-born population—is the only nation that exceeds the United States. Most European countries have less than half the U.S. percentage of foreign-born population.

Immigrants to the United States come from virtually every country in the world. In 1990, the U.S. Census Bureau indicated that there were 19,767,376 foreign-born persons in the country (Table 4). Of this number, Mexico accounted for nearly 22 percent of the total. Filipinos were the second-largest group, consisting of 4.6 percent, followed by Cubans and Canadians, each with 3.7 percent, and Germans with 3.6 percent. These five groups made up about 37 percent of the total.

The 1990 U.S. census also lists the ancestry of 222,608,247 persons (Table 5). Of this number, 23 percent of the population listed German ancestry, followed by Irish with 17.4 percent, English 14.6 percent, and Italian 6.6 percent of the total. These three groups accounted for about 47 percent of the specified ancestry of the U.S. population.

## Cultural and Economic Diversity

Because the United States has had such a massive flow of immigrants in recent decades, it has evolved into the world's largest multicultural society. As a result of the diverse countries of origin, the immigrants possess wide cultural and economic backgrounds.

Asian immigrants coming from such countries as the Philippines, South Korea, China, India, Vietnam, Cambodia, Saudi Arabia, Israel, and Japan have a richly diverse ethnic and cultural background. The native tongues include Tagalog (Filipinos), Korean, Khmer, Vietnamese, Hindi, Urdu, Gujarati, Faisi, Arabic, Yiddish, and Japanese, as well as scores of dialects. Next to language, religious diversity characterizes the Asian immigrants. The Filipinos as well as Vietnamese are generally

Table 4   Country of Origin of Foreign-Born Persons in the United States, 1990

| | |
|---|---|
| **Europe** | **4,016,678** |
| Germany | 711,929 |
| United Kingdom | 640,145 |
| Italy | 580,592 |
| Poland | 388,328 |
| Portugal | 210,122 |
| | |
| **Soviet Union** | **333,725** |
| | |
| **Asia** | **4,979,037** |
| Philippines | 912,674 |
| Korea | 568,397 |
| Vietnam | 543,262 |
| China | 529,637 |
| India | 450,406 |
| Japan | 290,128 |
| Taiwan | 244,102 |
| Laos | 177,577 |
| | |
| **North America** | **8,124,257** |
| Mexico | 4,294,014 |
| Canada | 744,830 |
| Cuba | 736,971 |
| El Salvador | 465,433 |
| Dominican Republic | 347,858 |
| Jamaica | 334,140 |
| Guatemala | 225,129 |
| Haiti | 225,393 |
| | |
| **South America** | **1,037,497** |
| Colombia | 286,124 |
| Peru | 144,199 |
| Ecuador | 143,314 |
| | |
| **Africa** | **363,819** |
| Egypt | 66,313 |
| Nigeria | 55,330 |
| | |
| **Oceania** | **104,145** |
| Australia | 42,267 |
| | |
| **Total** | **19,767,376** |

*Source:* Table 14, Place of Birth of Foreign Born Persons. U.S. Bureau of the Census, *1990 Census of Population,* Part 2, Social and Economic Characteristics, Washington, DC: Government Printing Office.

Table 5  Ancestry of the Foreign-Born Population of the United States, 1990

| Ancestry | Population | Ancestry | Population |
|---|---|---|---|
| German | 57,985,595 | French Canadian | 2,167,127 |
| Irish | 38,739,548 | Welsh | 2,033,093 |
| English | 32,655,779 | Slovak | 1,882,897 |
| Italian | 14,714,939 | Danish | 1,634,669 |
| American | 13,052,277 | Hungarian | 1,582,302 |
| French | 10,320,935 | Czech | 1,300,192 |
| Polish | 9,366,106 | West Indies | 1,155,490 |
| Dutch | 6,227,089 | Portuguese | 1,153,351 |
| Scotch–Irish | 5,617,773 | British | 1,119,154 |
| Scottish | 5,393,581 | Greek | 1,110,373 |
| Swedish | 4,680,843 | Swiss | 1,045,495 |

*Source:* Table 26, Ancestry. U.S. Bureau of the Census, *1990 Census of Population,* Part 1, Social and Economic Characteristics, Washington, DC: Government Printing Office.

NOTE:  **Ancestry specified**              222,608,247
       Single ancestry                148,836,940
       Multiple ancestry               73,771,307
       Ancestry unclassified or not reported   26,101,626

Catholic, and the Koreans are mostly Protestant, drawn from a minority in a nation that is mostly Confucian or Buddhist. Some of the Chinese immigrants are Christian, but like the Cambodians and Laotians, most are either Buddhist, Taoist, or Confucian. The immigrants from India are mostly Hindus, but there is a substantial minority of Sikhs, as well as Muslims, Jains, and Zoroastrians. The migrants from Pakistan and the Arab countries are overwhelmingly Muslims. Finally, the people from Israel are Jewish.

Many of the recent immigrants, especially from India, Korea, the Philippines, and Japan, are well educated and speak English. Nevertheless, all immigrants have to adjust to a wholly different culture. While certain highly qualified professionals— such as doctors, attorneys, bankers, accountants, and others— were able to enter the United States because of their skills, many have had difficulty in applying them immediately, partly because of strict licensing requirements. As a result, some immigrants have had to take semiskilled or unskilled jobs. Nurses have usually been employed immediately because of the demand for their skills.

Many of the immigrant groups have concentrated on particular occupations and businesses. The Chinese have become prominent in restaurants, food stores, laundries, and the garment industries. The Koreans, who are noted for their desire for economic independence, are known for their greengrocery stores in some cities. The Indians have concentrated on grocery stores, newsstands, and motels. Asians have climbed the economic ladder with extraordinary speed. Census data show that, on average, Asians have a higher salary than white Americans and much higher than African-Americans and Hispanics.

The immigrants from Latin America and the Caribbean have been less diverse than those from Asia but are far from homogeneous. The great majority of Hispanics are of Spanish origin and speak Spanish. However, the Brazilians speak Portuguese, the West Indians speak English, the Haitians speak French or Creole, and the Surnamese speak Dutch. These groups are also socially dissimilar. The immigrants from Mexico and parts of Central America are of Spanish and Indian ancestry and are known as mestizos. Those from the Dominican Republic, Honduras, and Panama are chiefly mulatto. Colombian costenos are black, as are nearly all from Jamaica and Haiti. Aside from a small black minority, all immigrants from Cuba have been of Spanish descent, as are those from Argentina, Chile, and Uruguay. Racial origin has affected the acceptance of Latin Americans into U.S. culture. The nonwhites have normally been unskilled and have obtained the lowest-paying jobs. They have also been subject to discrimination.

# Illegal Immigration

## Early Trends

Illegal immigration to the United States began on a small scale in the 1870s when the first restrictions were placed on open immigration. The Immigration Act of 1924 placed strict limitations on a large group of potential immigrants, but even then the number of illegal immigrants remained small. In the 1930s, the world economic depression discouraged immigration, as did the World War II period. During the 1940s and 1950s, there were only about 12,000 to 15,000 illegal immigrants annually. Mexicans accounted for the largest number of illegal immigrants, but an agreement between Mexico and the United States on contract labor (known as the bracero program, because such laborers were called braceros) provided a legal means for Mexicans to come to the

Table 6   Aliens Apprehended and Deported out of the United States, 1961–1990

| Year | Number | Year | Number | Year | Number |
|------|--------|------|--------|------|--------|
| 1961 | 88,823 | 1971 | 420,126 | 1981 | 975,780 |
| 1962 | 92,758 | 1972 | 505,949 | 1982 | 970,246 |
| 1963 | 88,712 | 1973 | 655,968 | 1983 | 1,251,357 |
| 1964 | 86,597 | 1974 | 788,145 | 1984 | 1,246,981 |
| 1965 | 110,371 | 1975 | 766,600 | 1985 | 1,348,749 |
| 1966 | 138,520 | 1976 | 875,915 | 1986 | 1,767,400 |
| 1967 | 161,608 | 1977 | 1,046,215 | 1987 | 1,180,488 |
| 1968 | 212,057 | 1978 | 1,057,977 | 1988 | 1,008,145 |
| 1969 | 283,557 | 1979 | 1,076,418 | 1989 | 954,243 |
| 1970 | 345,353 | 1980 | 910,361 | 1990 | 1,169,939 |
| 1961–1970 | 1,608,356 | 1971–1980 | 8,321,496 | 1981–1990 | 11,883,328 |

*Source:* Immigration and Naturalization Service. *Statistical Yearbook, Annual Report*, 1961–1990, Washington, DC: Government Printing Office.

United States; this agreement made it easier for Mexicans to enter into the country legally. During the bracero era, the Immigration and Naturalization Service patrolled the border between the two countries (as part of what was called Operation Wetback) and kept illegal immigration to a minimum.

## Effects of the Immigration Act of 1965

After passage of the Immigration Act of 1965, illegal immigration soared (Table 6). The act placed a ceiling of 20,000 immigrants annually from Western hemisphere countries; this provision became effective in mid-1968 and was extended to 1976. However, Mexican agricultural workers returned to the United States as illegal aliens to continue their farm work.

A massive backlog of potential immigrants grew immediately, most of whom were excluded. The only way they could qualify for legal immigration was (1) to have a relative who was already a U.S. citizen or a permanent resident alien, (2) to have the specific skills, education, or work experience needed by U.S. employers, or (3) to be a political refugee.

When a single ceiling on the total number of immigrants to the United States throughout the world went into effect, no non-preference visas were available. As a consequence, the only means available for people who wanted to immigrate to the United States and did not meet any of the legal criteria was to enter illegally.

By the mid-1970s the problem with illegal immigrants was generally considered to be out of control. Between 1965 and 1970, the number of illegal immigrants apprehended rose from 110,371 to 345,353; by 1980 the number had increased to 910,361. There are no data on the actual numbers of illegal aliens entering the country annually who were not apprehended.

Many of the world's people regard the United States as a sort of mecca. This attitude encourages immigration from countries plagued with such problems as poverty, overpopulation, unemployment, and political corruption. But these factors alone cannot explain the scale of illegal immigration to the United States. After all, there are other prosperous nations nearer to the homelands of the illegal immigrants.

One important explanation concerns the immigration laws enacted by Congress, which have provided little or no deterrent to illegal immigration. Other industrial nations have typically implemented a work permit system and a national identification system. In the process, they have quickly applied legal sanctions against employers who hire illegal immigrants. In the United States, however, it was illegal for aliens to enter the country without visas, but it was not illegal for an employer to hire such persons. Indeed, such hiring was encouraged by the Immigration and Nationality Act of 1952 as a concession to Texan agricultural employers; the act included a provision that exempted agricultural employers from restrictions on harboring an illegal immigrant.

Initially the United States did not make any changes to account for the dramatic increase in the number of illegal immigrants. In fact, for ten years after the enactment of the Immigration Act of 1965, Chairman James O. Eastland did not convene a meeting of the U.S. Senate Subcommittee on Immigration, where any new legislation had to originate. Thus, the attempts in the House of Representatives in the early 1970s to repeal the Texas proviso and to enact sanctions against employers who hired illegal immigrants failed.

## Immigration Reform and Control Act of 1986

When it was finally recognized that illegal immigration was reaching a crisis stage, President Carter, on August 4, 1977, sent a set of proposals to Congress "to help markedly reduce the increasing flow of undocumented aliens in this country and to regulate the presence of millions of undocumented aliens already here." The proposals included an employer sanctions program, enhanced funding for border enforcement, temporary legislation status for illegal immigrants who had been in this country for over five years, and a recommendation to increase the combined annual number of Canadian and Mexican immigrants allowed from 20,000 to 50,000.

These proposals were not enacted into law by Congress. Instead, in 1978 Congress established the Select Commission on Immigration and Refugee Policy to examine the immigration policy of the nation in its entirety. The commission released its final report on March 1, 1981. While it proposed significant changes to the nation's overall immigration policy, it focused mostly on illegal immigration. Most important, it called for civil and criminal sanctions against employers who hired illegal immigrants; identifying the aliens by name; increasing border enforcement to reduce illegal entry; and granting amnesty to those aliens who were in the United States as of some unspecified date, to be set several years prior to the enactment of employer sanctions.

The Carter administration was out of office when the commission reported, and the Reagan administration was wary of the topic. The Reagan administration set up its own commission that made less stringent recommendations. However, Congress did not accept the Reagan proposals and a new bipartisan bill was drafted. This bill accepted the key recommendations of the original commission. Once again, the portion that dealt with illegal immigration received the most attention. Employer sanctions and amnesty were the key points of debate. In general, those who supported one of these issues rejected the other, but both were vital to getting the bill passed. A number of amendments were added to the bill, including a foreign workers program for agricultural workers and new provisions to prohibit employment discrimination on the basis of a person's status as an alien. This bill was defeated in Congress in 1982 and defeated again after being revised in 1984.

As the problem of illegal immigration grew, U.S. politicians tried a new approach. Rather than proposing one bill that dealt with all aspects of immigration, they considered each individual item. Because illegal immigration was the most pressing problem, it was the first issue to be considered. Separate bills were introduced in the Senate and House. The Senate bill included the three central provisions: employer sanctions, amnesty, and expanded border enforcement. An amendment allowed 350,800 additional temporary workers to harvest agricultural goods; these workers were to be admitted every year for three years after passage of the bill. The amended bill passed the Senate in September 1985.

In the House, a similar bill was introduced in September 1985. A long debate centered on the issue of temporary foreign workers and the amnesty program. Finally, an amendment was passed as a compromise; it stated that the U.S. attorney general could grant lawful permanent resident status to any illegal immigrants who could prove that they had been working in perishable agriculture for at least 20 full days between May 1, 1985, and May 1, 1986. This amendment was known as the Special Agricultural Workers Program (SAWP). It was, in essence, an amnesty program.

There were many benefits for advocates of the SAWP. It overcame the southwestern growers' opposition to employer sanctions, which would make several hundred thousand of the growers' employees ineligible to remain in the United States. In due time, these aliens could become U.S. citizens. Moreover, the workers could seek better jobs in the United States, outside of agriculture, if they so chose. After long conferences between Senate and House committees, the Immigration Reform and Control Act (IRCA) was passed by Congress in October 1986, and signed into law by President Reagan on November 5, 1986. The act was the most comprehensive change in U.S. immigration policy since 1952, and it was the first to deal with illegal immigration.

This act was also the most extensive legislation in employment law in the United States in two decades. Among its multiple provisions were regulations designed to prohibit employers from hiring illegal immigrants. These regulations included an escalating series of penalties, including criminal penalties for employers who repeatedly violated the act's provisions.

The IRCA provided four separate amnesty programs that varied widely with respect to number of potential beneficiaries. The most important was the general amnesty program. It stated that any illegal immigrant living in the United States prior to January 1, 1982, and not classified in the excludable category could register within a 12-month period that began 6 months after passage of the IRCA. By December 1, 1991, 1,760,201 illegal aliens had applied for permanent residence under the general amnesty program.

The second amnesty program applied to those laborers who had worked in perishable agriculture for 90 days in the year ending May 1, 1986. The number of applicants to this program totaled 1,272,978, far more than had been expected.

The other two amnesty programs were similar in scale. One provided specific amnesty to Cuban-Haitian entrants who entered the United States in the early 1980s. The other program involved updating the legal registry dating from June 1, 1948, to January 1, 1972. This registry permitted the attorney general to adjust the status of persons who had illegally entered prior to 1948; they become permanent resident aliens without having to meet the various eligibility standards of the other amnesty programs.

In addition to the large number of persons who benefited directly from the amnesty programs, many families were able to travel to the United States to be be reunited with a family member who was granted resident alien status. However, the IRCA did not cover any persons who had entered the United States after 1982, so there was some concern that certain family members could be deported. In 1990, the Immigration and Naturalization Service changed its procedure in enforcing this policy to allow family members to remain in the United States.

The 1986 IRCA also included provisions that strengthened the existing law against employment discrimination on the basis of national origin. It expanded civil rights law by prohibiting discrimination on the basis of a person's status as an alien.

Finally, the IRCA included provisions to make it easier for employers to hire temporary agricultural workers. This feature applied specifically to workers needed when there was a real labor shortage to harvest perishable crops.

## Continued Illegal Immigration

While the objective of the IRCA was to control illegal immigration, there is little evidence that this has occurred. In contrast, there is every indication that illegal immigration is increasing. Between 1985 and 1991, the number of illegal aliens apprehended annually varied from 954,243 to 1,767,400. Some estimates place the total annual illegal immigration as high as 4,000,000. No satisfactory plan has been devised to enforce the immigration laws to control illegal immigration.

The 1986 employer sanction program contains major loopholes. The IRCA does not require absolute proof of identification to verify eligibility to work. Employers are not required to authenticate the documents offered by job applicants. Employers are required to make only a "reasonable effort" to make sure a document is valid. As a result, making counterfeit documents has become a thriving business. Further, additional funds to increase border patrols by the Immigration and Naturalization Service have not materialized. The number of applicants to the Special Agricultural Workers Program far exceeded expectations. In addition, the IRCA required the Immigration and Naturalization Service to prove that documents presented by applicants were not fraudulent, rather than having the applicants prove the documents were valid. As a consequence, control of the program has not been effective.

There were other ways in which the IRCA was ineffective in controlling illegal immigration. Prior to passage of the 1986 law, the INS could enter the open field of farm owners to search for illegal immigrants without first obtaining a search warrant from a court. As a result of pressure by agribusiness, however, the IRCA required the INS to secure a warrant before making a search. In rural areas far from courts, it is impractical to obtain search warrants and return to the search location. As a result, "field raids," which prior to 1986 had been highly successful, have essentially been abandoned.

## Routes of Illegal Immigration

Until the 1980s, about 90 percent of illegal immigrants entering the United States came from Mexico. Since then, illegal aliens have also been coming from the Far East, Middle East, Eastern Europe, and Latin America. Because the United States has exercised greater control over entrance from Mexico, the Caribbean is now a major point of departure. For example, the Dominican Republic has become a major center for illegal immigrants to begin their journey to the United States. These aliens enter the Dominican Republic through the capital, Santo Domingo. They are then transported to remote coastal areas to hiding places in safe houses and the surrounding jungle. Makeshift boats weighted down by rocks and submerged in streams await to take the travelers to the U.S. Commonwealth of Puerto Rico.

In the Dominican Republic, many of the small coastal towns transport illegal immigrants by boat 110 miles to Puerto Rico; this is a major Dominican industry. A relatively safe trip is extremely expensive. A Central American may pay as much as $4,000 for the whole journey to the Dominican Republic; someone leaving from China may spend as much as $35,000.

For those without much money, the 110-mile voyage is a brutal affair organized by about 100 boat captains who live along the Dominican coast. The boat captains sometimes do not permit hopeful immigrants to bring food aboard the boats for the two-day crossing; instead provisions are sold at exorbitant prices. It is not uncommon for passengers to be robbed before they disembark. However, the greatest peril is posed not by criminals but by nature. The Mona Straits, which separate the Dominican Republic from Puerto Rico, are among the most treacherous in the world for small boats to navigate. To avoid detection, poorly made boats usually set a course through the *desecho* (detour), a treacherous stretch of sea avoided by legitimate traffic. Experts estimate that in 10 to 20 percent of the trips the boats capsize and the passengers perish. A videotape taken several years ago by a Puerto Rican customs official shows some 50 refugees, their boat overturned, being devoured by frenzied sharks. There have been attempts to stop this practice, but it is too vital to the Dominican Republic's economy, so the immigration persists. Once the immigrant is in Puerto Rico, no passport is needed to enter the United States. An airline will transport the illegal immigrants to New York City, or some other urban area, where they blend into the life of the city.

# Migrants

## Mexico

### Early Immigration

The immigration of Mexicans to southwestern America dates from the earliest settlement of the region. The Spanish-speaking population in the territories the United States acquired by the 1848 Treaty of Guadalupe Hidalgo numbered approximately 100,000. The initial national border did not effectively separate the new U.S. possessions from land south of the border. The open door immigration policy of the United States placed no restrictions on Mexican immigrants.

A number of factors were important in the early immigration of Mexicans to the United States. With the discovery of gold in California, tens of thousands of Mexicans came to the gold fields in the 1850s. The use of Mexican labor in agriculture began in the late 1880s when the sugar beet industry was introduced into California. However, it was not until Congress passed the Dingley Tariff Act of 1897, which placed a heavy duty on imported sugar, that the sugar beet industry flourished in California. This law allowed the domestic sugar beet industry to become profitable by using inexpensive Mexican workers; American laborers refused to accept such backbreaking work. The industry became totally dependent on immigrants—mostly Mexicans but also some Japanese and Filipinos. Because this labor supply was available for other types of work, the entire economy of California was stimulated. Mexican immigrants were also utilized in U.S. cotton-growing regions, first in Texas but later in other southwestern states.

Just as important as having a cheap labor supply for agriculture was the construction of railroads in the Southwest. The trackmen and extra crews of the Southern Pacific and Santa Fe lines were nearly all Mexicans. Between 35,000 and 50,000 Mexicans were employed in the initial development of these railroads.

In the late nineteenth and early twentieth centuries, U.S. policy prevented legal Asian immigration from China and Japan. Mexican immigrants took the place previously held by Asian laborers.

Economic and political conditions in Mexico encouraged people there to seek a better life in the United States. In the period between 1877 and 1910, it is estimated that the population of Mexico increased by about 6 million. During this period, large Mexican haciendas (plantations) increased on average from about 12,000 to 20,000 acres. Some haciendas were as large as 250,000 acres. As a consequence, farmland available for rural families declined. In 1910, it is estimated that the total land held by rural families was no more than 7.7 percent of total agricultural acreage. As the population increased and available land declined, economic conditions became desperate. At the close of the nineteenth century, the purchasing power of an agricultural worker in Mexico was estimated to be one-fourteenth that of a farm laborer of the same class in the United States. In 1910, about 90 percent of the workers in Mexico were agricultural laborers.

The level of Mexican immigration between 1850 and 1940 demonstrated the advantages of work in the United States. Conversely, the Southwest also encouraged the migration to secure low-cost Mexican labor.

## Mexican Contract Laborers, 1942–1964

The Mexican Contract Laborers Program (also known as the bracero program) was devised so that Mexicans could be sent to

## Table 7    Bracero Program—Mexican Contract Labor Migration, 1942–1964

| Year | Mexican Workers Requesting Contracts According to Mexican Authorities[a] | Contracts Issued to Mexican Workers by U.S. Authorities[b] | Mexican Immigrants Legally Admitted to the United States[b] | Illegal Mexicans Apprehended[b] |
|---|---|---|---|---|
| 1942 | 4,152 | 4,203 | 2,378 | NS |
| 1943 | 75,923 | 52,098 | 4,172 | 8,189 |
| 1944 | 118,055 | 62,170 | 6,598 | 26,689 |
| 1945 | 104,641 | 49,454 | 6,702 | 63,602 |
| 1946 | 31,198 | 32,043 | 7,146 | 91,456 |
| 1947 | 72,769 | 19,632 | 7,558 | 182,986 |
| 1948 | 24,320 | 35,345 | 8,384 | 179,385 |
| 1949 | 19,866 | 107,000 | 8,083 | 278,538 |
| 1950 | 23,399 | 67,500 | 6,774 | 458,216 |
| 1951 | 308,878 | 192,000 | 6,153 | 500,800 |
| 1952 | 195,963 | 197,100 | 9,079 | 543,538 |
| 1953 | 130,794 | 201,380 | 17,183 | 865,318 |
| 1954 | 153,975 | 309,033 | 30,645 | 1,075,168 |
| 1955 | 398,703 | 398,650 | 50,772 | 246,608 |
| 1956 | 432,926 | 445,197 | 65,047 | 72,442 |
| 1957 | 436,049 | 436,049 | 49,154 | 44,451 |
| 1958 | 432,491 | 432,857 | 26,716 | 37,243 |
| 1959 | 444,408 | 432,643 | 23,061 | 30,196 |
| 1960 | 319,412 | 315,846 | 32,684 | 29,651 |
| 1961 | 296,464 | 291,420 | 41,632 | 29,817 |
| 1962 | 198,322 | 194,978 | 55,291 | 30,272 |
| 1963 | 189,528 | 186,865 | 55,263 | 39,124 |
| 1964 | 179,298 | 177,736 | 32,967 | 43,844 |

Sources: [a] *Anuario Estadistico de los Estados Unidos Mexicanos,* 1943–1964, Mexico City; [b] U.S. Immigration and Naturalization Service, *Annual Report,* 1943–1964, Washington, DC: Government Printing Office.
NOTE: NS = data not specified.

work in selected agricultural areas of the United States under a series of bilateral agreements between the two countries. The program was started in 1942, originally to provide agricultural workers during the World War II–era labor shortages in the United States (Table 7).

The contract system was administered by agencies in both Mexico and the United States. In Mexico, in order to secure workers, quotas were assigned to each Mexican state. The workers were then brought to the recruitment center (Mexico City from 1942 to 1944 and Guadalajara and Iraperato from

1944 to 1947). Those Mexicans who were accepted by their government as bracero program candidates were turned over to the U.S. Department of Labor, which acted as an agent for U.S. employers. This system of labor recruitment, with minor variations, lasted for 22 years.

As the program was implemented during World War II, the number of Mexicans wanting to come as contract workers to the United States far exceeded the number of U.S. contracts issued. For example, in 1945 the number of permits given by Mexico totaled 104,541, but only 49,454 contracts were issued by the U.S. Department of Labor. After World War II, however, the U.S. demand for Mexican workers increased greatly. Of a total of 4.6 million contracts issued during the life of the program, about 72 percent were printed between 1955 and 1964.

The program was not without controversy. Two related incidents are noteworthy. In 1948, the U.S. government pressured the Mexican government to allow recruitment along the border. Mexico reluctantly agreed and established a recruitment center at Mexicali and in several other border states. A labor shortage continued in the United States, and on October 13 and 18, 1948, the border was opened to several thousand undocumented Mexicans who wanted to enter the United States to work in the cotton fields of south Texas. The Mexican government responded by abrogating the 1942 Mexican Contract Laborers Agreement; it announced that it might consider filing claims for damages inflicted to the agricultural production along its northern border due to an uncontrolled exodus of border resident laborers. The U.S. government apologized and this incident ended.

In another incident on January 15, 1954, the U.S. departments of labor, justice, and state issued a joint press release indicating that braceros would be contracted unilaterally by the United States until a binational accord was reached. Mexico responded sharply by announcing that laborers could no longer be legally contracted to work in the United States; it asked Mexican laborers to stay at home. In spite of the Mexican request, hundreds of laborers gathered at the border cities expecting to enter the United States. Mexican local police converged upon the large groups, attempting to disperse them and prevent them from leaving the country. On the other side of the border, U.S. officials extended a helping hand to the Mexican laborers. As Mexican president Ruiz Cortines received reports that the international confrontation was turning into a domestic crisis at the border, he ordered Mexican troops to withdraw and instructed Mexican officials not to use any force against Mexicans desiring to go to the United States. During the crisis, the United States sent a number of signals to Mexico that it wanted to resolve the situation, and a new agreement was reached.

By 1955, the use of bracero labor was well established in the agricultural area from Texas to California. The substitution of contracted labor for domestic labor continued to grow throughout the 1950s. For example, in California between 1949 and 1959, the number of bracero laborers rose from 8,500 to 84,000. Gradually, however, the perception grew among agricultural labor organizations that importing this type of farm labor had an adverse effect on the wages of domestic labor. During the 1950s, it was shown that wages never got much higher than those paid to the Mexicans. It also became common to find domestic contractors and undocumented laborers in the same field crews. In addition, increased mechanization during the 1950s further decreased the demand for domestic labor. Domestic workers had little mobility between rural and urban occupations, and contract workers had no mobility. As a consequence, competition for the agricultural jobs increased.

In response to declining job opportunities, the National Agricultural Workers Union began a vigorous program in 1956 to stop the bracero program. In 1958, the Department of Labor improved the standard for bracero housing. In addition, a new formula for determining wages and ensuring a minimum hourly rate was established. As early as 1957, farmers in California began to sense that opposition to the bracero program was mounting and that contract labor was being seriously threatened.

Beginning in 1960, opposition to the bracero program arose in Congress. After acrimonious debate, supporters managed to extend the program six months. This was the first major attack on the program since its inception in 1942. In 1961, the program was extended another two years, and in 1962 the Kennedy administration openly opposed the program. In 1963, the program was extended a final year only after advocates indicated that the Mexican government strongly opposed an abrupt termination. The Mexican position was that the bracero program functioned as a substitute for illegal immigration.

The bracero immigration not only continued labor immigration to the United States but reaffirmed the concept that the northward migration is a continuous process. Termination of the contract labor program had a pronounced effect on Mexican policy makers. One result was the development of new jobs on

Table 8   Mexican Legal Immigration (thousands) to the United States, 1970–1992

| Year | Immigrants Admitted |
|------|---------------------|
| 1970 | 44.5 |
| 1975 | 62.2 |
| 1980 | 56.7 |
| 1985 | 61.1 |
| 1986 | 68.5 |
| 1987 | 72.4 |
| 1988 | 95.0 |
| 1989 | 405.2 |
| 1990 | 679.1 |
| 1991 | 946.2 |
| 1992 | 213.8 |

Source: U.S. Immigration and Naturalization Service, Statistical Yearbook, Annual Report, 1970–1992, Washington, DC: Government Printing Office.

the border area as part of what was called the Maquiladora Program. Through this program, U.S. corporations located manufacturing assembly plants in northern Mexican border towns, and production was exported entirely to the United States.

When the United States unilaterally abolished the bracero program, Mexican officials wanted to reestablish the program as a safety valve for growing unemployment. The braceros had acted to help control a growing problem of undocumented immigration. In 1975 Mexico recognized that its attempts to continue the program were unsuccessful. It declared that it no longer wanted a workers agreement, that such an agreement had never really succeeded and should not be considered. Although the Mexican government's goal was to develop new job opportunities, it soon recognized that even if it created new economic opportunities, its domestic employment problem would not be solved in the twentieth century.

### Evolution of U.S.-Mexican Immigration Policy

For most of the time between 1964 and 1980, immigration was not of major importance in foreign policy relations between Mexico and the United States (Table 8). Although questions concerning immigration remained one of the recurring themes of bilateral talks between representatives of both countries, no bilateral agreements were reached. By the late 1970s, largely as a response to the growing numbers of illegal immigrants from

Mexico, immigration once again became an important policy consideration for the U.S. government. U.S.-Mexican immigration policy became an item of intense political debate in the United States. Immigration matters have remained one of the most stable and crucial components of U.S. relations with Mexico. As a consequence, the North American media, U.S. officials, and the academic world have frequently identified immigration as the most critical issue in U.S.-Mexican relations. In 1977, a National Security paper of the U.S. government stated:

> Both in terms of the sheer number of people involved, and of the social, economic, and political consequences of this phenomenon for both the sending and receiving nations, illegal Mexican migration to the U.S. should be regarded as the most critical issue affecting relations between the U.S. and Mexico at present. It is of considerably greater importance than illicit drug traffic, prisoner exchange, Colorado River salinity, and other issues which have dominated discussions between the two countries for more than a decade.

Through the Immigration Reform Law of 1986, the United States attempted to gain some control over the illegal immigration of Mexican agricultural workers. This law provided a mechanism for admitting foreign workers to perform temporary labor where a shortage of domestic workers existed. While the law was not specifically directed at Mexico, it affected the flow of Mexican farm laborers most directly.

In order to secure Mexican workers, a U.S. employer must apply to the secretary of labor 60 days in advance to seek foreign workers and then try to find domestic workers for the job. The Labor Department must provide a certification decision within 20 days in advance of the need. The law provides for a quicker procedure if the Labor Department determines that qualified U.S. workers are not available at the appropriate time. The alien workers are guaranteed certain benefits, such as housing, worker compensation, travel, and subsistence costs. Access to U.S. government-funded legal services provides aid only for work-related matters.

The 1986 law recognized that there were a large number of illegal aliens working in U.S. agriculture. It was the first law to attempt to resolve this problem. This new agricultural program gave temporary resident status to a maximum of 350,000 illegal aliens who could prove that they had worked in perishable agriculture for at least 90 days in each of the last three years. After a year as temporary residents, they could become permanent resident aliens and were eligible for U.S. citizenship after another five years. Aliens who worked in agriculture for at least 90 days during the year preceding May 1, 1986, were also eligible to apply for temporary resident status, with adjustment to permanent status after two years. Workers in these two groups were not required to remain in farm jobs after they received temporary resident status. These workers were disqualified from receiving most welfare benefits such as health education after five years once they entered the program. The law also established the Commission on Agricultural Workers to study the availability of domestic farmworkers and the need for foreign workers.

The law also indicated that from 1990 to 1993, additional farmworkers, known as "replenishment workers," could be brought in as temporary residents if the Labor and Agriculture departments jointly determined that additional seasonal workers were needed. These workers were granted temporary resident status for three years but were disqualified for most types of public assistance. They had to perform at least 90 days of seasonal agricultural work in each of these three years. They were then eligible to seek permanent resident status and after another two years to apply for citizenship.

While this program provided some Mexican agricultural workers to the farms of the Southwest, it did not stem the tide of illegal aliens who continued to come to the United States. It therefore did not increase control over immigration from Mexico.

### Legal versus Illegal Immigration

The immigration of Mexicans can be distinguished as either legal or illegal (undocumented).

### Legal Immigration

In the 1920s, 459,287 Mexicans, accounting for 11.2 percent of all immigrants, were legally admitted to the United States. During the 1930s and 1940s, the numbers dropped sharply. In the 1950s, 298,811 legal Mexican immigrants were admitted. The absolute numbers grew to 453,937 (13.7 percent of the total) in the 1960s and 640,294 in the 1970s (14.2 percent). The U.S. decision to extend its quota system to countries in the Western hemisphere in 1970 did not appear to affect the number of Mexican immigrants. In the 1980s, the number of legal Mexican immigrants totaled about 1,600,000; this number reflected the growing proportion of Mexicans admitted under the U.S. preference system.

## Illegal Imigration

Although a lack of data has made estimating the increasing numbers of illegal immigrants difficult, U.S. officials need knowledge of these numbers to develop public policy. For example, in the 1980s the Office of Management and Budget estimated that granting citizenship to the illegal aliens at that time would cost the U.S. government several billion dollars.

A number of attempts have been made to estimate the number of illegal Mexican aliens. The earliest attempt was made in 1975 by Lesko Associates (Lesko Associates 1975). Based on the number of apprehended aliens, the report estimated that the undocumented alien population in the United States increased between 1970 and 1975 from 1.6 million to 5.2 million. The report's estimate was criticized as too high. Warren and Passel (A Count of the Uncountable. Estimates of Undocumented Aliens Counted in the 1980 Census) an estimated that 1,131,000 illegal Mexican aliens were included in the 1980 U.S. Census Bureau figures; of this number, an estimated 486,000 were female.

The number of illegal Mexicans in the United States appears to have increased steadily since 1980 because of worsening economic conditions in Mexico. Because the mass immigration is so spontaneous, there are few accurate estimates. Estimates of the number of illegal Mexicans in the United States in the 1990s have ranged from 3 million to 8 million persons. This figure fluctuates from season to season, since many Mexicans come to perform seasonal farm work.

## Mexican Population in the United States as of 1990

It has been estimated that in 1990 there were 12 million people from Mexico in the United States, accounting for about two-thirds of all Hispanics here. Of this number, only about 5 million are actually U.S. citizens. The remainder are permanent resident aliens or illegal aliens. Persons of Mexican origin make up the second largest minority group in the United States, exceeded only by the black population.

# Central America

## Modern Trends

The number of immigrants coming to the United States from Central America was quite small until the 1980s (Table 9). From

Table 9   Number of Legal Immigrants (thousands) to the United States from Central America, 1984–1992

| Year | El Salvador | Guatemala | Honduras | Nicaragua | Panama | Costa Rica |
|------|-------------|-----------|----------|-----------|--------|------------|
| 1984 | 8.8 | 3.9 | — | — | 2.3 | — |
| 1985 | 10.2 | 4.4 | — | — | 2.6 | — |
| 1986 | 10.9 | 5.2 | — | 2.8 | 2.2 | — |
| 1987 | 10.7 | 5.7 | — | 3.3 | 2.1 | — |
| 1988 | 12.0 | 5.7 | 4.3 | 3.3 | 2.5 | 1.4 |
| 1989 | 57.9 | 19.0 | 7.6 | 8.8 | 3.5 | 2.0 |
| 1990 | 80.2 | 32.2 | 12.0 | 11.6 | 3.4 | 2.8 |
| 1991 | 47.4 | 25.5 | 11.5 | 17.8 | 4.2 | — |
| 1992 | 26.2 | 10.5 | 6.6 | 8.9 | 2.8 | — |

*Source:* U.S. Immigration and Naturalization Service, *Statistical Yearbook, Annual Report*, 1984–1992, Washington, DC: Government Printing Office.

1979 to 1985, large numbers of persons fled Central America, mostly from El Salvador, Nicaragua, and Guatemala. Most of these immigrants were fleeing from political oppression and government violence. However, because they were fleeing from countries whose governments were fully supported by the United States, they were classified as migrants rather than refugees. It would have been embarrassing to U.S. foreign policy makers to provide official asylum for people fleeing governments supported by the United States.

Because the Central American governments were not communist, U.S. governmental aid was not provided to the migrants. The U.S. government nevertheless played an important role in a number of the Central American conflicts. For example, between 1979 and 1985, the United States provided over $2 billion in military aid to the governments of El Salvador and Honduras.

Nicaragua posed a significant problem for U.S. immigration policy. Although the U.S. government gave financial and military support to the groups opposing the Sandinista government, Nicaragua was not a declared communist nation and the United States maintained diplomatic relations with the Nicaraguan government. As a consequence, the Immigration and Naturalization Service would not regard the country's immigrants as fleeing from political oppression.

This interpretation resulted in a number of bizarre situations. In 1984, over 7,000 Nicaraguan draft dodgers fled to Miami illegally because their parents feared they would be killed. Under the Refugee Act of 1980, conscription was not considered political persecution. As a consequence, each case had to be considered individually. U.S. officials recognized that a dangerous precedent could be set if the 1980 refugee law was disregarded. Further, if the young Nicaraguans were permitted to remain in the United States, the Salvadoran migrants could complain of favoritism. In June 1985, the U.S. Congress approved $23 million to oppose the Sandinista government but failed to pass immigration reform. Therefore, many Central American immigrants continued their illegal status.

Because they perceived a lack of government action, many churches across the United States declared themselves to be sanctuaries for Central American immigrants escaping governmental persecution. This Sanctuary movement, as it came to be called, started on March 24, 1982, in the Southwest United Presbyterian Church in Tucson, Arizona. It was continued by the First Unitarian Church in Los Angeles, the University Lutheran Church in San Francisco, Luther Place Memorial Church in Washington, D.C., the Independent Bible Church in Long Island, New York, and many more. The Sanctuary movement encompassed a network of 75,000 religious people and more than 250 churches, synagogues, and Quaker meeting houses. The movement, outraged by the death toll of Nicaraguan civilians, decided to shelter undocumented Central Americans in their homes and churches regardless of the consequences.

The U.S. government responded to the Sanctuary movement by arresting 16 members and arraigning them in federal courts in Tucson, Arizona. These individuals were charged with 71 counts, including conspiracy and harboring and transporting illegal aliens. The charges were based on tapes made by paid Immigration and Naturalization Service informants who took recording equipment into the churches. Despite the political connotations of becoming involved with the situation in Nicaragua, the movement remained primarily religious and humanitarian in nature. Because the government's case against the group was unpopular and unpleasant, the charges were eventually dropped.

As political disturbances have become less frequent, the number of refugees from Central America has declined. However, the problem of the illegal status of these aliens in the United States has not been solved. The laws have not been changed and the illegal migrants have not been deported; they remain as illegal entrants with no possibility of becoming citizens.

Table 10   Number of Central American Nonimmigrant Visas Issued by the United States, 1961–1987

| Year | Costa Rica | El Salvador | Guatemala | Honduras | Nicaragua | Total |
|------|-----------|-------------|-----------|----------|-----------|-------|
| 1961 | 2,730 | 3,573 | 5,029 | 2,909 | 2,119 | 16,360 |
| 1965 | 4,873 | 5,740 | 9,969 | 4,775 | 4,626 | 29,983 |
| 1970 | 10,454 | 16,049 | 25,586 | 9,824 | 8,504 | 70,417 |
| 1975 | 14,409 | 14,791 | 18,800 | 16,017 | 11,217 | 75,234 |
| 1980 | 38,338 | 18,923 | 51,713 | 29,021 | 14,308 | 152,303 |
| 1985 | 27,156 | 29,912 | 40,512 | 28,206 | 15,206 | 140,812 |
| 1987 | 25,085 | 20,929 | 39,412 | 32,966 | 12,053 | 130,445 |

*Source:* U.S. Department of State, Bureau of Consular Affairs, Visa Office, *Report of the Visa Office*, Washington, DC: Government Printing Office.

## Nonimmigrant Visas to Central Americans

Nonimmigrant visas (outside the established visa quota) allow a foreigner to enter the United States for a specified, relatively brief period on the condition that he or she will return to the homeland (Table 10). The number of such visas issued to Central Americans has increased about tenfold since 1960. Each of the five consulates in Central America issues about 130,000 to 150,000 nonimmigrant visas each year. There are numerous reasons that foreigners can obtain these visas, such as the need for medical care, to visit families or friends, to conduct business, to study, and to travel as tourists.

The issuing of nonimmigrant visas is controlled by the Immigration and Nationality Act of 1982. The law is not precise as to what evidence is required to convince a skeptical consular office that an applicant has "compelling ties" to return to the native country; thus, the consular official must make reasoned judgments. In general, U.S. officers ask for a wide variety of documents that demonstrate the need for the immigrant's return. These include personal interviews as well as documents revealing employment, salary, bank account information, and other evidence that the migrant has definite reasons to return to the Central American country of origin.

## Haiti

Although the numbers of Haitians entering the United States is relatively small (Table 11), these immigrants present a particular problem as to how they should be classified. Since the Immigration and Naturalization Service has not established a

Table 11   Number of Haitian Legal Immigrants to the United States, 1970–1992

| Year | Number of Immigrants |
|------|---------------------|
| 1970 | 6,900 |
| 1975 | 5,100 |
| 1977 | 5,400 |
| 1978 | 6,500 |
| 1979 | 6,400 |
| 1980 | 6,500 |
| 1981 | 8,700 |
| 1984 | 19,800 |
| 1985 | 10,200 |
| 1986 | 12,700 |
| 1987 | 14,800 |
| 1988 | 34,900 |
| 1989 | 13,700 |
| 1990 | 20,300 |
| 1991 | 47,500 |
| 1992 | 11,000 |

Source: U.S. Immigration and Naturalization Service, *Statistical Yearbook, Annual Report*, 1970–1992, Washington, DC: Government Printing Office.
NOTE: Values rounded.

status for persons seeking asylum from a noncommunist country, Haitian immigrants are officially classified as having "no status." The illegal arrival of Haitians began in 1972 when the first boatload of Haitians landed in Florida.

Between 1972 and 1980, more than 1,000 people a month braved the rough, 800-mile voyage to south Florida in leaky wooden sailboats. By 1980, it was estimated that there were more than 60,000 illegal Haitians in the United States. These Haitian immigrants were very different from most of the migrants who came to the United States in the 1960s and 1970s. They were uneducated, unskilled, and overwhelmingly black, and they spoke Creole, a unique blend of French, Spanish, English, and several African dialects. These were the poorest people in the Western hemisphere. While they were allowed to remain in the United States, they received no government aid and had to depend on charitable organizations, churches, and Florida's black community for assistance. Nevertheless, they defied death at sea and on land to escape Haitian authorities and reach the "promised land," as they described the United States.

The open door immigration policy of the United States changed for Haitians on May 18, 1981, when the Immigration and Naturalization Service ended its policy of releasing Haitian immigrants into the community and began detaining them at Camp Krome, a former missile base in Dade Country, Florida. Detention was only part of the Reagan administration's plan to curb immigration from Haiti. On September 29, 1981, the president issued an executive order authorizing the Coast Guard to patrol the high seas and intercept vessels carrying "migrants" coming to the United States without necessary entry documents. The interdiction program was a joint U.S.-Haiti endeavor in which the United States provided all equipment and paid all expenses to patrol the 50-mile-wide Windward Passage between Cuba and Haiti.

This program had, at best, limited success. First, it was unable to stop all immigration from Haiti. Second, it was very expensive. Between October 1981 and December 1994, only 3,337 Haitians were turned back, at a cost of $116,670 for each Haitian returned. In addition, the policy triggered a loud outcry against U.S. immigration policy and practice.

While the interdiction debate raged, problems also arose at Camp Krome when the population rose to 1,200. By executive order President Reagan decided to move these 1,200 and an additional 1,300 in 14 other detention centers to Fort Drum in upstate New York. The Haitians, who were used to a tropical environment, were placed in a cold environment to which they were unaccustomed. This confused and traumatized them, and civil rights groups protested strongly.

As the Haitian plight gained national attention, court action began to permit the Haitians be removed from the camps and remain in the United States. In December 1981, the Haitian Refugee Center of Miami filed a class action suit against the federal government requesting the release of all detained Haitians. On June 18, 1982, the federal courts ruled that the detention of Haitians by the Immigration and Naturalization Service was in violation of federal administrative rules. As a result, the release of Haitians from the detention centers began.

This decision was immediately protested because the detention was declared illegal on a legal technicality rather than on ethical grounds. Then the decision was overturned on February 28, 1984, but the Immigration and Naturalization Service had already released most of the Haitians in its custody. Because the courts ruled that the U.S. government had the authority to control its borders, the INS increased its efforts to stop Haitians entering the country. Between 1982 and 1984, 425 Haitian boats were stopped on the high seas and 1,733 would-be immigrants were returned to Haiti.

In November 1984, the Immigration and Naturalization Service announced that the 125,000 Cubans who had entered the United States during the Mariel boatlift were eligible for legal status and U.S. citizenship under the Cuban Adjustment Act. This law did not apply to the 30,000 Haitians granted entrance status in 1980. Many groups felt that this decision demonstrated racism on the part of the INS.

Although the form of government has changed in Haiti with elections of officials, there is no evidence that the economic conditions have changed. As a consequence, Haitians have continued to immigrate illegally to the United States in small, unsafe sailboats. The United States is attempting to intercept these boats and send the people back to Haiti. For example, in November 1995, more than 1,100 boats were intercepted and the people returned to Haiti. There is no documentation on the boats that evaded the coastal patrols. As long as economic conditions remain desperate in Haiti, people will likely continue to attempt the perilous journey to the United States.

## The Philippines

Although a small number of Filipinos came to the United States in the nineteenth century, it was not until after the United States had taken control of the Filipino government in 1899 that any significant immigration began. Because there was a demand for educated people in the Philippines, President William Howard Taft in 1903 developed a program to send Filipino students to the United States. In 1903, 100 out of 20,000 applicants were selected to enter U.S. universities. This program continued until 1938, by which time 14,000 Filipino students received an education in the United States. An overwhelming number of this group returned to the Philippines.

The first sizable group of immigrants from the Philippines began to arrive in 1906. At this time, there was a demand for a large number of new agricultural workers in Hawaii and California. As a result of treaty agreements, the Japanese and Korean sources were no longer available. Filipinos became the major source for such labor. Between 1909 and 1914, an average of 4,000 Filipinos arrived each year in Hawaii. The Hawaii Sugar Planters Association (HSPA) actively recruited Philippine workers. Immigration slowed to about 2,000 annually between 1915 and 1920 but grew after 1920. During the 1920s, more than 65,000 men, 5,000 women, and 3,000 children immigrated to Hawaii with contracts from HSPA, which paid their passage. In addition, 1,000 Filipinos came on their own. By the mid-1920s, Filipinos accounted for 50 percent of all plantation workers in Hawaii and by 1934, 75 percent. Between 1909 and 1931, a total of 112,920 Filipinos went to Hawaii to work. Of this number, 38,946 returned to the Philippines and 18,607 moved to the U.S. mainland. In 1926, the HSPA stopped sponsoring workers. In the 1930s, because of depressed agricultural conditions, immigration declined greatly. In 1932, only 1,226 Filipinos came to Hawaii, whereas 7,300 were repatriated to the Philippines by the U.S. government.

The Filipino immigrants suffered from a number of unique problems. Of the 125,917 Filipinos who had been sponsored by the HSPA between 1909 and 1946, only 9,398 were women. Some men married women from other ethnic groups, but most remained single. Gambling, cockfights, and prostitution became major recreational activities for the single men. Filipinos coming to the U.S. mainland found even more acute problems. As the last Asian immigrants to arrive in the United States, they became victims of racist laws and discrimination. Most of the Filipinos stayed in California, but some migrated to Chicago, New York, and Philadelphia (Table 12).

Prior to their country's independence from the United States in 1946, Filipino immigrants encountered another legal problem. While they were considered nationals, they could not be naturalized as citizens, because a 1790 statute restricted naturalization to "free white persons." This law had been upheld in the courts. The problem was partially solved by the Immigration and Nationality Act of 1940, which allowed Filipinos who had entered as immigrants to apply for naturalization. However, the act did not apply to those who entered the United States as nationals prior to Tydings-McDuffie Act of 1934. Because the number of Filipino immigrants affected was small, the act was ineffective. The problem, however, was permanently solved by the Nationality Act of 1946. This act permitted all Asians who were permanent residents of the United States to apply for naturalization. Many Filipinos took advantage of this act to become U.S. citizens.

In 1946, when the Philippines became an independent nation, immigrants were admitted under the quota system. As

## Table 12    Filipino Population in the United States, 1920–1980

| Year | Mainland | Hawaii | California | Illinois | Total |
|------|----------|--------|-----------|----------|-------|
| 1920 | 5,603 | 21,031 | NA | NA | 26,634 |
| 1930 | 45,372 | 63,052 | NA | NA | 108,424 |
| 1940 | 45,876 | 52,659 | 31,408 | NA | 98,535 |
| 1950 | 61,645 | 61,062 | 40,424 | NA | 122,707 |
| 1960 | 107,669 | 68,641 | 64,459 | 3,587 | 176,310 |
| 1970 | 247,308 | 95,680 | 135,248 | 12,355 | 343,060 |
| 1980 | 640,712 | 133,940 | 357,432 | 43,857 | 774,942 |

*Source:* U.S. Bureau of the Census. *Census of the Population*, Washington, DC: Government Printing Office.
NOTE: NA = not available.

with all Asian nations, the Philippines immigration quota was set at 100 year. Two factors made this small number of little consequence in limiting the number of Filipino immigrants. First, because of two large U.S. naval bases in the Philippines, many servicemen married Filipino women, who later entered the United States as nonquota immigrants. Second, it was possible for newly naturalized Filipinos in the United States to petition for the admission of relatives, also as nonquota immigrants. As a consequence, between 1951 and 1960, 19,307 Filipinos were admitted to the United States. Of this number, 70.9 percent were women and 98.5 percent were nonquota immigrants.

The Immigration and Nationality Act of 1965, which placed all immigrants on an equal basis, provided for a great increase in Filipino immigration. The result is that Filipinos now account for the third highest number of immigrants to the United States, exceeded only by Mexicans and Cubans. The number of Filipinos doubled from 1960 to 1970 and doubled again over the next decade (see Table 12). By 1980, there were 774,942 Filipinos in the United States, 501,440 of whom were native born.

The character of the average Filipino immigrant has also changed. Originally, Filipinos immigrants were primarily rural workers with little education. Since 1965, they are more likely urban, many of whom are highly educated, including doctors, engineers, and teachers. Their geographic distribution has also changed. In 1950, the group was equally divided between Hawaii and California. Of those on the mainland, two-thirds were in California. By 1980, although Hawaii and California had the largest numbers, Filipinos were spreading out in the nation with a major concentration in Chicago.

# Korea

Prior to 1900, fewer than 100 Koreans immigrated annually to the United States. Sustained Korean immigration to the United States started in 1902. The Korean government set up an immigration office in Seoul because of the demand for sugar farm workers in Hawaii. Because of the chaotic political and depressed economic conditions in Korea, the numbers of immigrants grew significantly. In 1905, 2,500 Koreans immigrated to the United States. However, in November 1905, the Korean government stopped further immigration because of complaints that its people were being treated poorly on the Hawaiian farms.

Between 1907 and 1924, few Koreans came to the United States. Immigration to the United States essentially stopped in 1907 when the U.S. government refused to recognize Korean passports that had been issued to the workers by Korea's Japanese occupiers. During this period, the largest number of immigrants admitted were women coming to join their spouses in Hawaii. Until about 1920, the Korean immigrants remained on Hawaii's plantations, but in the 1920s they gradually drifted to Honolulu and began to work in the pineapple canneries. Because they could not become citizens, they remained laborers. A few entered business and worked in restaurants before 1940.

It was not until after the Korean War of the early 1950s that Korean immigration grew significantly. During the 1950s, the number of immigrants totaled 6,231, about 600 each year. In response to the Immigration Act of 1965, the number in the 1960s increased to 34,526; in the 1970s it increased again by nearly 800 percent to 267,638. In the 1980s, the number averaged about 30,000 per year (Table 13).

A number of factors have influenced this spectacular increase. By and large, post–Korean War immigrants tended to integrate well into U.S. society, not only because of their skills but also because they married U.S. citizens who had served in the armed forces in Korea. Between 1950 and 1975, 28,205 Koreans entered the United States as spouses of U.S. citizens. Another 7,000 came as nurses. Most were under the age of 40 and were from middle-class urban families. About half were Christians.

After the Korean War, the population in South Korea grew rapidly. As a consequence, immigration policies were liberalized in 1962, and a South Korean immigration officer was appointed. The greatest increase occurred in the 1970s, primarily because of

Table 13   Immigration to the United States from Selected Asian Countries, 1960–1992

| Year | Mainland China | Philippines | Korea | Vietnam | Laos | Cambodia |
|---|---|---|---|---|---|---|
| 1960 | 3,681 | 2,954 | 1,502 | 56 | 2 | 1 |
| 1961 | 3,213 | 2,738 | 1,534 | 83 | 2 | 4 |
| 1962 | 4,017 | 3,437 | 1,538 | 105 | 1 | 1 |
| 1963 | 4,658 | 3,648 | 2,580 | 140 | 4 | 4 |
| 1964 | 5,089 | 3,006 | 2,362 | 219 | 4 | 13 |
| 1965 | 4,057 | 3,430 | 2,165 | 226 | 9 | 9 |
| 1966 | 13,736 | 6,083 | 2,492 | 275 | 10 | 8 |
| 1967 | 19,741 | 10,865 | 3,956 | 480 | 8 | 8 |
| 1968 | 12,738 | 16,731 | 3,811 | 590 | 14 | 23 |
| 1969 | 15,440 | 20,744 | 6,045 | 953 | 15 | 27 |
| 1970 | 14,093 | 31,203 | 9,314 | 1,480 | 30 | 22 |
| 1971 | 14,417 | 28,471 | 14,297 | 2,038 | 24 | 27 |
| 1972 | 17,339 | 29,378 | 18,878 | 3,412 | 35 | 39 |
| 1973 | 17,297 | 30,799 | 22,930 | 4,569 | 48 | 66 |
| 1974 | 18,056 | 32,857 | 28,028 | 3,192 | 61 | 40 |
| 1975 | 18,536 | 31,751 | 28,362 | 3,039 | 96 | 98 |
| 1976 | 23,858 | 47,079 | 37,680 | 4,230 | 163 | 126 |
| 1977 | 19,785 | 39,111 | 30,917 | 4,629 | 237 | 125 |
| 1978 | 21,331 | 37,216 | 29,288 | 88,543 | 4,359 | 3,677 |
| 1979 | 24,277 | 41,300 | 29,248 | 22,546 | 3,565 | 1,432 |
| 1980 | 27,665 | 42,316 | 32,320 | 43,483 | 13,970 | 2,601 |
| 1981 | 25,893 | 43,772 | 32,663 | 55,631 | 15,805 | 12,749 |
| 1982 | 27,100 | 45,102 | 31,774 | 72,553 | 36,528 | 13,438 |
| 1983 | 25,777 | 41,546 | 33,339 | 37,560 | 23,662 | 18,120 |
| 1984 | 23,363 | 42,758 | 32,042 | 37,236 | 12,279 | 11,858 |
| 1985 | 24,787 | 42,979 | 35,253 | 31,895 | 9,133 | 13,563 |
| 1986 | 25,100 | 52,500 | 35,800 | 30,000 | 7,800 | 13,500 |
| 1987 | 25,800 | 50,100 | 35,800 | 24,200 | 6,800 | 12,500 |
| 1988 | 28,700 | 50,700 | 34,700 | 25,800 | 10,700 | 9,600 |
| 1989 | 32,300 | 57,000 | 34,200 | 31,900 | 12,500 | 5,600 |
| 1990 | 31,800 | 63,800 | 32,300 | 48,800 | 10,400 | 5,000 |
| 1991 | 33,000 | 63,500 | 26,500 | 55,300 | 10,000 | 3,300 |
| 1992 | 38,900 | 61,000 | 19,400 | 77,700 | 8,700 | 2,600 |

Source: U.S. Immigration and Naturalization Service, *Statistical Yearbook*, *Annual Report*, 1960–1992, Washington, DC: Government Printing Office.

immigration. In fact, in 1980, 81.8 percent of all Koreans in the United States were foreign born and 42.4 percent had arrived between 1975 and 1980. Therefore, at that time, more than two-thirds of all Koreans in the United States had been in residence less than ten years.

As the economy of South Korea has developed, a labor shortage has arisen there, so fewer people have wanted to immigrate to the United States in the 1990s. Whereas early Korean immigrants went primarily to Hawaii and California, their recent counterparts have tended to spread out to a number of states. By 1980, only one third of the Koreans resided in California. More than 33,000 were in New York, 25,000 in Illinois, 17,000 in Hawaii, and 15,000 in Maryland, Texas, Washington, and Virginia. Most of the Koreans in California lived in Los Angeles.

Most Koreans have adapted rapidly to U.S. culture. A large percentage of the Koreans started businesses. Most Korean businesses are concentrated in the retail and service sectors, including grocery stores, service stations, and liquor stores. Many of the businesses are located to serve not other Koreans but rather the underprivileged and minorities. Koreans, on average, have shown a strong desire to receive an education in the United States and have adhered to a strong work ethic.

## China

Chinese immigration to the United States has a long history. By 1790, many sailors had come from China to the United States as trade between the two countries developed, and a few remained. Immigration to the United States picked up after 1848, when gold was discovered in California. By 1850, it is estimated that there were 4,000 Chinese in the United States. Between 1850 and 1860, 41,538 Chinese entered the country, 64,759 came the following decade, and the number doubled to 123,201 in the 1870s. Yet by 1880, though a total of 229,045 Chinese had entered the United States, only 107,488 were counted by the Bureau of the Census. These numbers indicated that most Chinese had returned to China (Table 14).

There is evidence of little discrimination against the earliest Chinese immigrants. However, as the Chinese moved into the mining areas, resentment grew. In order to counter the adverse conditions they faced, the Chinese immigrants organized into secret associations. One of the largest of these was the Chinese Consolidated Benevolent Association, which helped Chinese immigrants deal with all types of problems.

The United States prohibited Chinese immigration in the early 1880s through the Chinese Exclusion Act of 1882. In 1892, the Gentry Act extended these provisions for ten additional years, and in 1898 the act was extended to Chinese immigrants

Table 14   Chinese Population in the United States, 1860–1980

| Year | Chinese Population |
|------|--------------------|
| 1860 | 34,933 |
| 1870 | 63,199 |
| 1880 | 105,465 |
| 1890 | 107,488 |
| 1900 | 89,883 |
| 1910 | 71,531 |
| 1920 | 60,639 |
| 1930 | 74,954 |
| 1940 | 77,504 |
| 1950 | 117,629 |
| 1960 | 198,958 |
| 1970 | 383,023 |
| 1980 | 812,178 |

Source: U.S. Bureau of the Census, Census of Population, Washington, DC: Government Printing Office.

seeking to enter the Hawaiian Islands. Finally, in 1904, the Chinese Exclusion Act was extended indefinitely.

Because of these laws, the number of Chinese legally entering the United States fell from 22,781 in 1876 to 10 in 1887. Until 1940, a few thousand immigrants continued to come to the United States each year, either as immediate relatives of U.S. citizens or illegally. Others came as traders, who were not excluded. Others came as U.S. citizens because their Chinese parents had been born in the United States. Between 1920 and 1940, the U.S. Immigration and Naturalization Service estimated that about 71,000 Chinese-born citizens were admitted to the United States.

During World War II, the U.S. attitude toward Chinese changed. Of the entire population of 80,800 Chinese in the United States, over 10 percent served in the armed forces. The Chinese Exclusion Act was repealed in 1943 and the Chinese were allowed to become citizens. However, the initial quota for Chinese immigrants was set at only 105 per year. Small numbers of Chinese came to the United States in the 1950s and 1960s, but it was only after the Immigration Act Amendment of 1965 that the numbers of Asian immigrants, including Chinese, rose dramatically. A total of 34,764 Chinese immigrants came between 1961 and 1970. The number rose to 124,126 in the following decade. There were 42,475 new Chinese immigrants in 1983 alone. By 1990, there were more than 400,000 Chinese immigrants in the United States.

Table 15    Refugee Admissions to the United States from Various Regions, 1975–1987

| Year | Africa | East Asia | Eastern Europe | Soviet Union | Latin America | Near East, South Asia | Total |
|------|--------|-----------|----------------|--------------|---------------|------------------------|-------|
| 1975 | 0 | 135,000 | 1,947 | 6,211 | 3,000 | 0 | 146,158 |
| 1976 | 0 | 15,000 | 1,756 | 7,450 | 3,000 | 0 | 27,206 |
| 1977 | 0 | 7,000 | 1,755 | 8,191 | 3,000 | 0 | 19,948 |
| 1978 | 0 | 20,374 | 2,245 | 10,688 | 3,000 | 0 | 36,507 |
| 1979 | 0 | 76,521 | 3,393 | 24,449 | 7,000 | 0 | 111,363 |
| 1980 | 956 | 163,799 | 5,025 | 28,444 | 6,662 | 2,231 | 207,116 |
| 1981 | 2,119 | 131,139 | 6,704 | 13,444 | 2,017 | 3,829 | 159,252 |
| 1982 | 3,326 | 73,522 | 10,780 | 2,756 | 602 | 6,369 | 97,356 |
| 1983 | 2,648 | 39,408 | 12,083 | 1,409 | 668 | 5,465 | 61,681 |
| 1984 | 2,747 | 51,960 | 10,285 | 715 | 160 | 5,246 | 71,113 |
| 1985 | 1,959 | 49,970 | 9,350 | 640 | 138 | 5,994 | 68,045 |
| 1986 | 1,316 | 45,454 | 8,713 | 787 | 173 | 5,998 | 62,480 |
| 1987 | 232 | 7,383 | 2,235 | 297 | 0 | 2,250 | 12,397 |
| Total | 15,295 | 816,725 | 78,271 | 105,481 | 29,420 | 37,382 | 1,090,374 |

*Source:* U.S. Department of State, Bureau of Refugee Programs, 1988, Washington, DC: Government Printing Office.

As prescribed by current U.S. law, the visa limit is 20,000 for China, 20,000 for Taiwan, and 600 for Hong Kong. Thus, technically 40,600 Chinese can come to the United States each year. However, a large number enter the United States as illegal aliens.

In the past, most Chinese came from the Canton area, but since 1968 immigrants have been coming from every part of mainland China. Chinese immigrants have primarily engaged in businesses such as restaurants and laundries. Although economic conditions have improved for immigrants, many Chinese still live in substandard conditions.

Once an American Chinese living abroad could establish that he was a U.S. citizen through a U.S. Court hearing, Chinese Americans began to return to the United States. For the first time, Chinese who were U.S. citizens born abroad could claim children who were allegedly born in China and were now eligible to come to the United States. In this manner, they established future U.S. citizenship claims for other Chinese. This scheme is known as "paper families." Because U.S. authorities are aware of this scheme, many Chinese immigrants are detained on Angel

Island in San Francisco Bay until their claim of legal admission can be authenticated.

# Refugees

As a result of U.S criteria concerning which immigrants can be classified as refugees, nearly all the refugees who have entered the United States since the 1940s have been from communist countries (Table 15). With the disappearance of communism in the Soviet Union and Eastern Europe, refugee immigration has declined. When the United States maintains diplomatic relations with a communist nation, such as China, it does not recognize political persecution and will not classify immigrants from that country as refugees. In 1995, Cuba and South Vietnam remain the major nations whose immigrants are recognized as refugees. A listing of principal refugee groups admitted to the United States is given below.

| Beginning Date | Group Admitted | Approximate Numbers Admitted |
|---|---|---|
| 1945 | Displaced persons from World War II: Germans, Poles, Soviets | 50,000 |
| 1953 | Cold War refugees: Eastern Europeans, Yugoslavs | 354,000 |
| 1958 | Hungarians | 39,000 |
| 1960 | Cubans | 664,603 |
| 1975 | Vietnamese | 880,000 |

## Hungary

The number of refugees fleeing political persecution increased with the spread of communism after World War II. The Truman administration responded to this problem by passing the Displaced Persons Act of 1948 and the Refugee Relief Act of 1953. However, these acts were directed at specific problems; no general U.S. policy on refugees evolved.

The modern U.S. refugee policy was developed by the Eisenhower administration in response to the invasion of Hungary in 1956 by the Soviet Union. In order to aid thousands of fleeing refugees, the United States established an emergency program.

On January 10, 1957, President Eisenhower, in his state of the union message, established the future U.S. refugee policy.

He stated, "The recent historic events in Hungary demand that all free nations share to the extent of their capability the responsibility of granting asylum to victims of Communist persecution." To implement the policy, the President's Commission for Hungarian Refugee Relief initially approved admission of at least 21,500 refugees. By the end of 1957, the total reached 38,000. Nearly every aspect of the Hungarian relief operation was founded on anti-Soviet and pro-U.S. rhetoric. For example, the *New York Times* reported the arrival of refugees with bold headlines. The Eisenhower administration encouraged the use of U.S. aid to lessen the plight of those suffering under communist domination. In the final report to President Eisenhower, Tracy S. Voorhees, chairman of Hungarian Refugee Relief, stated, "When Russian tanks were firing on Hungarians, the United States military planes and ships were carrying many thousands of them to the safe harbor of our free land." The plight of the Hungarian refugees attracted world attention, and the U.S. role in assisting them was lauded by much of the world community.

The criteria for selecting Hungarian refugees for admittance to the United States were not highly publicized. With the exception of hardship cases, only those best fitted for integration into the U.S. economy were granted asylum. The law stated:

> Those to be brought to the United States both from Austria and countries of second asylum will be refugees selected on the basis of hardship cases such as those involving broken families and special interest cases such as scientists, engineers, etc. whose skills will enable them to be integrated readily into the American economy.

The selection process was very effective in selecting adaptable Hungarians. The average level of education of the refugees was above the average for a U.S. citizen. Within months, the refugees were well integrated into U.S. society.

# Cuba

## Early Cuban Immigration

The United States first became a home for Cuban political refugees in the nineteenth century. The first major immigration occurred at the outbreak of the Cuban War of Independence in 1868. By 1869, it was estimated that over 100,000 Cubans had

## Table 16   Cuban Exiles in the United States, 1950–1959

| Year | Number who Immigrated | Number Naturalized |
|---|---|---|
| 1950 | 2,179 | 718 |
| 1951 | 1,893 | 775 |
| 1952 | 2,536 | 817 |
| 1953 | 3,509 | 982 |
| 1954 | 5,527 | 1,462 |
| 1955 | 9,294 | 1,921 |
| 1956 | 14,953 | 1,372 |
| 1957 | 13,733 | 1,344 |
| 1958 | 11,587 | 1,323 |
| 1959 | 7,021 | 1,319 |
| Total | 72,226 | 12,053 |

*Source:* U.S. Immigration and Naturalization Service, *Annual Report,* 1950–1959, Washington, DC: Government Printing Office.

sought refuge abroad. Key West became a significant Cuban community.

When Cuba became independent in 1898, many Cubans living in exile in the United States and Europe returned to their homeland. However, a very large group who had long been in the United States remained in Florida; returning to Cuba meant starting over in a war-ravaged country. This group established the cigar and sugar industries and were responsible for Florida's first labor union. What had begun as a temporary political oasis became a permanent community.

In the first half of the twentieth century, small groups of exiles came to the United States to escape political turbulence. In the late 1920s and early 1930s, a small group of political student activists during the time of President Gerardo Machado arrived. Similar movements took place during the presidencies of Fulgencio Batista (1940–1944 and 1952–1958), Ramon Grace San Martin (1944–1948), and Carlos Piro Socarros (1948–1952) (Table 16).

### Eisenhower and Cuban Immigration

Fidel Castro's insurrection ended in success on January 8, 1959, when his rebels marched into Havana. The initial response to this event in the United States was favorable. Castro was looked upon as a hero who had defeated the dictator Batista. Within a week, the United States recognized the government of Castro and expressed a desire to work with it. Although Castro was recognized as a communist, the United States was initially concerned more with the legality of Cuba's government than with the ideology of its leaders.

It is now recognized that the United States' concern over the political dangers from the Cuban revolution were so exaggerated and distorted that U.S. policymakers lost touch with reality. Contrary to popular belief, the Cuban-Soviet relationship grew slowly. In many ways, it was a response to events directly affecting Cuba and the United States rather than Cuba and the Soviet Union. Castro repeatedly insisted on Cuba's ideological independence. In reality, the Soviet Union had no part in the Cuban revolution's triumph. The revolution took place because of socioeconomic and political conditions in Cuba, which had been largely ignored by U.S. investors and policymakers. It was after Castro's triumph that the Cuban leaders had to face the realities of a bipolar world; their political philosophy inevitably led them to choose to develop relations with the Soviet Union.

As Castro gradually consolidated power in the 1950s, the former Cuban elite had little choice but to immigrate. Cuban immigrants had been a problem for the United States since the beginning of the Cuban Revolution, but their numbers rose rapidly from around 3,800 in 1953 to 14,950 in 1956.

As the number of potential immigrants increased, the Eisenhower administration developed a policy to handle them. This policy was based on (1) humanitarian concern, (2) the U.S. desire to overthrow the revolution with exiled forces, (3) the U.S. desire to embarrass the Cuban government, and (4) the recognition that most of the exiles could easily be assimilated into U.S. society. As a consequence, the U.S. had much to gain and little to lose by admitting these middle- and upper-class groups, who had professional training and skills. The mass movement of people from a communist nation to a capitalist nation made for great propaganda. The impact of this immigration was far greater in Cuba than in the United States. It is estimated that Cuba lost more than 50 percent of its doctors and teachers to the United States during the first two years of the revolution.

As the number of immigrants increased, relations with Cuba began to deteriorate after 1959. In June 1960 U.S. oil refineries in Cuba refused to process Russian crude oil. The Cuban government retaliated by nationalizing the oil refineries. On July 5, 1960, the Cuban government nationalized all U.S. property in

Cuba. In retaliation, the United States canceled Cuba's sugar export quota. This action amounted to an economic sanction against Cuba.

The final official break in diplomatic relations between the United States and Cuba came on January 3, 1961. The original humanitarian emphasis in the U.S. policy toward Cuban immigration changed so that the immigration was based on escape from the terror of communist oppression.

The diplomatic break also meant that Cubans seeking to immigrate to the United States would have to go through a third country (such as Spain) and acquire a visa there. Fortunately for the Cubans wishing to immigrate, this situation changed when the U.S. government dropped the visa requirement. After January 5, 1961, any Cuban who claimed to be "fleeing from Communist oppression" qualified for a visa in order to enter the United States. The basic policy that still exists today was thus established.

## Cuban Children's Program

The most striking episode of the early Cuban immigration to the United States came in 1960 as part of what was called the Cuban Children's Program. The program's advocates stated their desire to rescue Cuban children from being indoctrinated with communist doctrine. According to a Cuban decree issued at that time, the state had control of the nation's children. The decree stated:

> All children will remain with their parents until they are three years old, after which time they must be entrusted to the Organizacion de Circular Infantiles [state day-care centers]. Children from three to ten would live in government dormitories and would be permitted to visit their parents no less than two days a month....Other children would be assigned to the most appropriate place.

The Castro government declared that the decree was false and had been prepared by the Cuban underground opposed to Castro and the U.S. Central Intelligence Agency in an attempt to "save the children." An effort known as the Pedro Plan evolved to help Cuban parents send their children unaccompanied to the United States to avoid communism. Blanket authority was given to issue visa waivers to all children between the ages of 6 and 16.

This U.S. governmental program broke with traditional U.S. immigration policy. Previously, such undertakings had been supported by private groups, such as churches and individuals. News of the U.S. program spread rapidly throughout Cuba, and soon thousands of parents requested that their children be sent to the United States. On December 10, 1960, the first ten children were sent to Miami. Castro did not prevent the program from being implemented.

The program grew rapidly in 1961. Many Cuban parents did not want their sons and daughters raised in a communist state. On March 9, 1963, the *New York Times* stated:

> These parents would rather entrust their children to relatives, friends or strangers in the United States than to be indoctrinated with Communist ideas. Castro's Cuba Communist indoctrination starts in kindergarten and has to a great degree been substituted for education in all schools of the island.

A total of 14,018 children came to the United States during the program. Because the program had been politically motivated, there was little consideration of the effects on the children. The emotional problems of being separated from parents, arriving in a strange home, overcoming a language barrier, and adapting to a new culture were little considered. While originally it was thought that separation would last no longer than seven months, in reality many of the students were not reunited with their families for up to 20 years.

### The U.S. Invasion of Cuba: The Bay of Pigs

Attempts to free Cuba from Castro's regime began under the Eisenhower administration, and under the Kennedy administration, U.S.-Cuban relations continued to deteriorate. Less than three months after becoming president, Kennedy authorized an invasion of Castro's regime by Cuban exiles on April 17, 1961. Regrettably for the United States, the 1,500-man exile force was defeated in less than 72 hours. The invasion increased Castro's political power and popularity. As William Goodwin, a White House advisor, stated: "It made him even more of a hero as the man who had defended Cuba against the greatest power in the world."

The Bay of Pigs incident was Kennedy's most embarrassing foreign policy setback. The invasion shattered the hopes of returning to Cuba held by 116,000 exiles in the United States.

## 1960s Cuban Refugee Program

Upon assuming the presidency, Kennedy developed the Cuban Refugee Program. The program provided direct help to refugees. While direct federal assistance to Cuban exiles began in December 1960, the Kennedy program represented a commitment on a much larger scale. Both Cuba and the United States launched political attacks against each other. It was the Kennedy administration's plan not only to use the Cuban exiles as political weapons against Cuba but to drain the country of its best-qualified professionals.

Cuban immigrants to the United States included not only technicians but also professionals such as doctors, lawyers, and teachers. In addition to the shortages of consumer goods Cuba faced, the lack of doctors damaged Castro's plan for an expanded rural medical program. To prevent more professionals from fleeing, the Cuban government stripped those who had already fled of their citizenship and prohibited their return to their families. In addition, the Cuban government required flights to Miami to be paid in U.S. dollars; this way, many potential refugees were delayed in leaving Cuba by their lack of U.S. funds. Castro continued to downplay the immigration, dismissing it as misguided and declaring that the refugees would soon return to Cuba.

The Kennedy administration responded by offering free airlifts from Cuba starting in August 1961, at a cost of $350,000 to the United States. In addition, the administration asked Congress for $10 million a year to meet "unexpected refugee migration expenses." The budget continued to rise until it reached an all-time high of $136 million in 1972.

In 1961, the number of Cuban refugees totaled about 33,000. This number continued to rise; according to the Cuban Refugee Program, 447,738 Cubans entered the United States from January 1961 to December 1972. About two-thirds of this number settled somewhere other than Miami. Although humanitarian issues were always recognized as part of the program, the U.S. government never gave up its goal of removing Castro from power and forming a pro-U.S. regime.

### Camarioca Boatlift and Airlift

On September 26, 1965, the refugee program entered a new phase when Fidel Castro announced that Cubans who had relatives in the United States could leave the island if their relatives asked for them. By making this move, Castro demonstrated to the Cuban people that they had to choose whether they were willing to "struggle for the people" or leave the country. In order to relocate the potential immigrants, boats from Miami were to dock at Camarioca to pick up relatives. In addition, on September 30, Castro supplied two planes a day to carry passengers to Miami for free. Castro had three reasons for allowing thousands to leave: (1) to attempt to normalize diplomatic relations with the United States, (2) to ease internal economic problems, and (3) to provide a safety valve by letting dissidents go to the United States.

The Cuban government thus created a potentially massive refugee problem for the United States. The prospect of more than 200,000 refugees in a short period posed a serious dilemma for the Johnson administration. The number of Cuban refugees could double in just a few months. In response, the United States canceled daily flights between the two countries. Castro continued to blame the United States for its new policy, but he ignored Cuba's internal political and economic situation.

President Johnson chose to explain the potential influx of new refugees in strictly political terms. In a New York City address in 1965, he declared that the United States would welcome the refugees with the thought that "in another day, they can return to their homeland to find it cleansed of terror and free from fear." This had been the policy and philosophy of Eisenhower and Kennedy in opening the gates to all Cubans "escaping from Communism." However, both of those presidents had believed that the immigration would represent a short-term emergency rather than having long-range implications, with respect not only to Cuba but to the entire Third World.

On October 10, the mass migration began. Hundreds of vessels of all sizes arrived in the port of Camarioca. After about 5,000 immigrants made the journey, the transports stopped largely because of the season's weather. As the boatlift grew more dangerous, negotiations to end it and to establish a safer and more orderly process intensified. The Swiss ambassador who represented the United States developed the "Memorandum of Understanding" signed by the United States and Cuba on November 6, 1965. According to this memorandum, the government of Cuba agreed to permit the departure of Cubans who wished to leave for the United States, and the government of the United States agreed to permit their entry. Persons living in Cuba who were immediate relatives of persons living in the United States were to be given first priority in processing and movement. The government of the United States was to provide air transportation to carry persons permitted to depart Cuba from Varadero (70 miles east of Havana) to a point in the United States (Miami). The government of the United States agreed to provide transportation with such frequency and capacity as to permit the movement of 3,000 to 4,000 persons per month. The two governments agreed that the first movement under the terms of this memorandum of understanding was to begin no later than December 1, 1965.

The agreement triggered a powerful reaction in Cuba. Tens of thousands of Cubans applied for permits. The federally arranged migration of 4,000 refugees a month alarmed many U.S. agencies. Many Americans were concerned that many of the refugees would be communist spies. The black population in Florida was particularly disturbed about the potential for economic losses. In addition, they were concerned that they were not getting governmental assistance comparable in terms of quality to that received by the recent refugees. In addition, black Americans were concerned that Cuban children were being integrated into public schools while black children remained segregated.

The agreement to establish a regular air bridge between the two nations did not solve the political problems. The United States continued its policy of isolating Cuba. During the first year of the Cuban airlift, about 45,000 refugees were brought to Miami. It was estimated, however, that over 700,000 Cubans wanted to make the trip. The cost of the refugee situation continued to rise, and by 1970 the United States was spending approximately $100 million per year on the problem.

At times, the program did not proceed smoothly. There were cancellations of flights, and processing of applicants was sometimes slow. The people of Miami were worried that the ethnic and social character of the area was being altered. Finally, the two governments agreed to discontinue the flights. On April 6, 1973, after 3,049 flights by Eastern Airlines bringing a total of 260,251 Cubans to the United States, the flights ended.

The Camarioca boatlift and the subsequent airlift were conducted in the absence a clear U.S. immigration policy. Emergency guidelines were used to handle the situation, with decisions being made to meet the demands of the moment. The funds for transportation, food, housing, medical care, and so on were made available on a temporary basis. Neither the president nor Congress was able to produce a permanent solution.

## Mariel Boatlift

When Jimmy Carter became president in 1977, the United States indicated that it would be willing to normalize relations with Cuba. Negotiations resulted in a bilateral agreement that defined policy rights on overlapping offshore waters, a renewal of a bilateral anti-hijacking agreement, and, most significant, the opening of "interest sectors" in each nation's capital to conduct diplomatic business. It appeared that after two decades of hostility, the nations were on the path to reconciliation. President Carter personally believed that Castro had become disenchanted with the Soviet Union and that relations between Cuba and the United States could improve.

The first evidence of a change in the Cuban refugee movement came in December 1977 when a delegation of Cubans, known as the Antonio Maceo Brigade, went to Cuba. This group demonstrated that Cuban exiles were welcome to return to Cuba; it also demonstrated that the exile community was not uniform in its views on Castro's regime. Many Cuban exiles in Miami and other cities did not regard the brigade trip favorably. The exile press labeled the group traitors, Castro agents, and communists. Thus, it became clear that normalization would require much more effort.

In this political drama, the next step occurred on September 6, 1978, when Fidel Castro offered an opportunity for dialogue between the exiles and the Cuban government. Castro felt that this dialogue must include representatives of the community. The U.S. government was not invited to the talks. Opposition to the dialogue came mainly from the militant anti-Castro group in the United States. To begin discussion, a committee of 75 prominent exiles was organized in the initial meetings in November and December 1978. Castro lifted travel restrictions between Cuba and the United States, and 3,600 political prisoners were released from Cuban jails. However, when the Committee of 75 returned to the United States, another group of exiles, Omega 7, had formed to terrorize the 75 exiles who had gone to Cuba. The Committee of 75 continued to face assassinations, bombings, threats, and intimidation through 1979, but the exile trips to Cuba continued. From January 1979 to March 1980, decisions about which Cubans could travel to and from the United States were approved in Havana first and Washington later.

The next development began on April 1, 1980, when six people in a bus crashed through the gate of the Peruvian embassy in Cuba amid gunfire to secure political protection and ultimately freedom; one Cuban guard was killed. Cuba radio then announced that anyone could leave Cuba by going to the Peruvian embassy. Within a short time, more than 10,000 people entered the Peruvian embassy.

The problem of what to do with the 10,000 Cubans in the Peruvian embassy was solved in a most unique manner. Napoleon Vila Boa, a Bay of Pigs veteran, along with a group of exiles in Miami, proposed that Castro allow the exiles to transport the "Havana 10,000" to Florida. The Cuban government agreed, and a flotilla of 42 privately owned boats set out for Cuba loaded with food and medicine for the refugees. In a surprise move, the Cuban government also announced that not only could the refugees in the Peruvian embassy leave, but any Cubans whose exiled relatives would make the journey from the United States to Mariel could claim them. As a consequence, thousands of Cuban exiles rushed to Key West to rent or buy boats and then headed for Cuba to claim their relatives.

Within the first week of the boatlift in May 1980, more than 6,000 Cubans arrived in Key West, and throughout May, an average of 3,000 persons arrived daily. This massive immigration alarmed the U.S. government and posed a dilemma on how to handle the large number of aliens. On May 14, 1980, the U.S. government made an offer to the Cuban government and reiterated that the boatlift was illegal. The U.S. government indicated it would charter two large seaworthy vessels to go to Cuba to transport the refugees. Further, to ensure a legal and orderly process, all persons would have to be searched before departure from Cuba. The U.S. government proposal was immediately rejected by the Cuban government. Nearly 9,000 Cubans arrived in the United States in the first two days following the U.S. announcement. Fidel Castro was determined to turn the Peruvian embassy incident and subsequent boatlift into a personal political bonanza and to embarrass President Carter through defiance.

Because the United States was forced to cope with the massive immigration, on May 6, 1980, President Carter declared a state of emergency in Florida. To house the exiles, a tent city was erected in the Orange Bowl Stadium in Miami. Another tent city was constructed along Route 95, and thousands of refugees were flown to distant military bases: Fort Chaffee, Arkansas; Elgin Air Force Base, Florida; Fort Indiantown Gap, Pennsylvania; and Fort McCoy, Wisconsin. Many refugees became frustrated, and most of the criminals among the refugees are still in jail.

The U.S. government had to decide how it was going to respond to the illegal status of the refugees. On June 20, 1980, the Carter administration solved the problem temporarily when it created a new classification, "Cuban-Haitian entrant." Under this classification, the new entrants could stay in the United States and could become "permanent residents" after two years. Most important, the aliens were eligible for medical services, supplemental income, and emergency assistance benefits. State and local governments could be reimbursed for 75 percent of the costs.

Prior to the Mariel incident, Cubans immigrating to the United States had enjoyed a special status as political refugees from a communist country. However, the Mariel incident showed that the United States had no control over immigration from Cuba. From April 20 to September 26, 1980, Cuba directed the flow of immigrants to the United States. The Cuban government unilaterally decided when to open and when to close Mariel Harbor immigration, directed marine traffic to and from Mariel, and decided on each of the 125,000 Cubans who came to the United States. Under these political conditions, the Carter administration could classify the immigrants in any way it wanted, but it could not stop the immigration.

The Mariel immigration created many problems in the United States. It soon became evident that many of the immigrants came not to escape political persecution or even to reunite with families, but simply because the United States was considered the "land of opportunity." Castro had permitted the immigration to reduce unemployment and to make trouble for the United States. The magazine *U.S. News and World Report* described the Mariel immigrants (or Marielitos, as they were called) as "representatives of the most despised immigration in the nation's history." In Miami, the Marielitos were blamed for increased crime. Among the Marielitos, the United States classified 1,050 as excludable or undesirable. These individuals were detained indefinitely at the maximum-security federal penitentiary in Atlanta, Georgia. Under immigration laws, they were not recognized as having entered the country; instead they were placed in prison, not entitled to legal counsel or other constitutional rights afforded prisoners in the United States. Allegations, rumors, and stories about Castro's plan to remove these prisoners from Cuba made headlines in the United States. Many of the prisoners came to the United States with the understanding that if they had committed a crime in Cuba they would be welcomed as heroes in the United States.

The plight of the 1,050 Cubans in U.S. prisons did not receive attention until July 7, 1983, when a U.S. district judge ruled that the United States could not hold illegal aliens indefinitely without giving them the same constitutional rights as all U.S. citizens. The judge ordered that the Immigration and Naturalization Service begin new hearings for each of the Cuban prisoners. A decision was to be reached as to whether the prisoners could be paroled or returned to Cuba.

This ruling provoked mixed reactions. Civil rights groups hailed the decision because it granted limited constitutional rights to illegal aliens for the first time. Opponents noted that there was proof that these prisoners were criminals in Cuba; furthermore, there was suspicion that the Cuban government had infiltrated subversive agents into the United States disguised as refugees.

After long negotiations, on December 14, 1984, a pact was signed between Cuba and the United States that would allow the prisoners to be deported. This was the first accord of the Reagan administration. Cuba agreed to take back 2,746 mental patients and criminals who came to the United States during the Mariel boatlift. In return the United States would issue visas in 1985 to 3,000 political prisoners and their families, as well as to an additional 20,000 other Cubans. In the following year, visas would be issued at the rate of 20,000 annually.

Immediate deportation was declared illegal by a second court decision on October 15, 1984; this decision stipulated that the refugees officially classified as excludable were entitled to hearings as to their claim to political asylum. After due process, the first group of 23 were found ineligible for political asylum on February 21, 1985, and were flown back to Cuba. This initiated the beginning of a new chapter in U.S.-Cuban immigration history. For the first time since 1940, the United States agreed to return people to a communist country.

The December 1984 agreement was abruptly ended on May 20, 1985, when the U.S. government-controlled Radio Marti began broadcasting to Cuba. The Cuban government declared Radio Marti as subversive, insulting, and detrimental to future Cuban-U.S. relations. The Cuban government took the following actions:

1. It suspended all proceedings related to the implementation of the agreement on immigration questions agreed to by the United States and Cuba on December 14, 1984.

2. It suspended all trips by Cuban citizens living in the United States to Cuba, except those authorized on strictly humanitarian grounds.
3. It attempted to control communication between the United States and Cuba.
4. It reserved the right to reconsider the cooperation it had been unilaterally providing to the U.S. government in the struggle against illegal aliens.
5. It reserved the right to transport medium-wave radio broadcasts to the United States to make fully known its view on problems concerning the United States and U.S. international policy.

Cuba's cancellation of the immigration agreement affected thousands of Cubans in the United States. Most immediately affected were the remaining 2,345 excludables scheduled for deportation during the next two years. Without the agreement, the excludables could not be deported to Cuba; they were held in legal limbo. A similar uncertainly confronted 3,000 former political prisoners waiting in Cuba to immigrate to the United States. However, the United States continued its agreement to grant visas to at least 20,000 Cubans annually. Since then, the flow of Cubans has been orderly.

Although the Voice of America and other private radio programs had been accessible to Cubans for more than 25 years, the Cuban government did little to jam them. The Reagan administration, however, was committed to Radio Marti. The U.S. government justified the new Radio Marti on the grounds that the Cubans had been denied access to the free flow of information.

## Modern Policy Trends

Since 1985, the Cuban and U.S. governments have not been able to agree on an immigration policy. The number of Cubans entering the United States illegally has been modest. In August 1995, the Clinton administration abruptly halted the nation's three-decade open door policy for Cuban refugees, ordering the Coast Guard to intercept illegal boat people at sea and take them to the U.S. Navy base at Guantanamo Bay.

Castro responded to the measure by imposing a $750 visa service charge on Cubans who received legal U.S. immigrant visas. In an attempt to clarify some issues, including the severe changes resulting from the new regulations, the two governments met in New York in late November 1995. Consistent with long-standing U.S. policy, the officials did not discuss the trade

Table 17   Indo-Chinese Refugee Immigration to the United States, 1975–1982

| Year | Cambodia | Laos | Vietnam | Others | Total |
|------|----------|------|---------|--------|-------|
| 1975 | 5,571 | 108 | 124,108 | 5 | 129,792 |
| 1976 | 339 | 3,153 | 813 | 148 | 4,453 |
| 1977 | 44 | 213 | 3,333 | 128 | 3,718 |
| 1978 | 1,105 | 7,926 | 14,053 | 1,255 | 14,339 |
| 1979 | 9,422 | 24,414 | 63,020 | 6,472 | 103,328 |
| 1980 | 11,996 | 50,031 | 83,654 | 9,477 | 155,158 |
| 1981 | 31,945 | 23,966 | 57,673 | 6,870 | 120,454 |
| 1982 | 13,051 | 6,914 | 37,085 | 3,977 | 61,027 |

Source: Centers for Disease Control and Prevention, Office of Refugee Resettlement, *Indo–Chinese Refugee Immigration*, 1983, Washington, DC: Government Printing Office.

embargo or other political issues. The conference discussed the continued fate of the 1,280 Cubans who arrived in the United States in 1980 in the Mariel boatlift and have remained in federal detention centers. The governments also discussed allowing more Americans to travel in Cuba. In contrast, the labor policy law permitted about 100,000 Cubans to leave the island since 1988. Although the restrictions on travel to Cuba and on Cuban immigration to the United States have been relaxed somewhat, relations between the two countries concerning immigration remain strained.

## South Vietnam

### Vietnam War Refugees

The influx of Vietnamese refugees was a direct result of the Vietnam War of the 1960s and early 1970s. The refugee problem, however, began only after the conclusion of hostilities in 1975. Most of the Vietnamese refugees who live in the United States came in the short period from 1975 to 1983 (Table 17). The refugees were young to middle age. Because of their high birth rate, the Vietnamese will represent the third largest Asian American ethnic group in the United States by the year 2000.

The first mass movement of Vietnamese refugees— numbering about 128,000—occurred between 1975 and 1977 as a response to the end of the Vietnam War. These refugees primarily included U.S. employees and prominent members of the South Vietnamese military and government. They fled the country to avoid persecution by the North Vietnamese. While there was no bloodbath in Vietnam after the war, many South Vietnamese who remained in the country were incarcerated in reeducation camps for as long as 15 years. The rapid fleeing presented a number of problems. About two-thirds of the refugees had less than 24 hours to prepare for their departure, and over 80 percent had less than a week. While immediate family groups stayed together as they fled, many relatives were left behind.

From April to December 1975, the initial refugees were housed in camps in Camp Pendleton near San Diego, Fort Chaffee in Arkansas, Elgin Air Force Base near Pensacola, and Fort Indiantown Gap in Pennsylvania. The new refugees settled rapidly into permanent houses with their families. The funds for living expenses provided by the U.S. government were quite generous; the refugees received three years of such assistance. These refugees assimilated quickly because a large percentage were Catholics; they had some contact with Western culture and were well educated. By the mid-1980s, the Office of Refugee Resettlement reported that the salary of most refugees matched that of the larger U.S. population.

Because there was no sizable group of Vietnamese in the United States at the time, the refugees were initially widely distributed in the nation because they had been sponsored by churches and other organizations throughout the country.

## Boat People

The second group of Vietnamese refugees began to enter the United States with the outbreak of the Vietnam-China conflict in 1978. These refugees were generally known as "Boat People." They contrasted sharply with the initial group in that they were largely rural people with minimal education; most were farmers. Under the communist regime, many of them had been required to attend reeducation classes and live in new "economic zones." Fleeing involved making open sea voyages in leaky boats or long journeys by foot over difficult terrain in Cambodia to reach Thailand. Of those who escaped, many spent months in refugee camps. It is estimated that 50 percent of the Boat People died in their flight to freedom. Before reaching their destination in the United States, most spent months in refugee camps in Thailand, Malaysia, Indonesia, Philippines, or Hong Kong. The camps were crowded and disease was rampant. In most camps there were a variety of ethnic groups from Indochina.

Although the immigration was extremely difficult, about 800,000 Vietnamese came to the United States between 1975 and

1982. This number far exceeded the number of immigrants going to other countries such as Canada (126,000), Australia (122,000), France (108,000), and Germany (24,000). In addition, about 260,000 Chinese-Vietnamese returned to China by 1978. As late as 1989, 111,000 refugees remained in southeast Asian camps waiting to immigrate to other countries.

When refugees were selected by U.S. government officials to come to the United States, they received three months of education in the English language and U.S. culture. The Boat People had on average 7.05 years of total education in their home country, and half knew no English. After training, the refugees were flown to the United States, where they were met by U.S. representatives of resettlement agencies or sponsors and were given a place to live. Because of the danger of leaving Vietnam in the face of political controls, the number of males far exceeded the number of females. Many of these people found it difficult to find jobs in the United States. In addition, whereas many of the early refugees had been sponsored by Americans, the Boat People were frequently sponsored by Vietnamese families who had few connections with employers. Further, the later arrivals had to exist with less American aid, because in 1982 such assistance was reduced from 36 to 18 months and several other programs were eliminated.

### Ethnic Chinese from South Vietnam

The third group of Vietnamese immigrants to arrive after 1978 were members of Chinese ethnic groups who had been living in Vietnam. This group had long existed in Vietnam and its members were highly organized, often on the basis of dialect and region of origin. Many of the Chinese had been assimilated into Vietnamese culture, whereas others maintained a strong Chinese identity.

After the 1978 Vietnam-China War, the Chinese living in Vietnam were permitted, for a fee, to leave Vietnam. Their experience was in many ways similar to that of the Boat People in terms of the physical and psychological hardships. Relying on their business experience, many of these Chinese-Vietnamese were able to reestablish their roles as entrepreneurs in the United States. Because they were unfamiliar with Western customs and were often resented by other Vietnamese, the assimilation of Chinese-Vietnamese people into the United States has been slower than for ethnic Vietnamese. Further, the Chinese-Vietnamese have been divided by political and linguistic differences. Although it is difficult to determine, it is estimated that about one-third of all Vietnamese in southern California are of Chinese ethnicity.

## Immigration out of the United States

Although foreign immigrants far outnumber American emigrants (that is, those leaving the United States for another country), increasing numbers of native-born U.S. citizens are also emigrating. U.S. citizens can freely emigrate from the United States; there have been no restrictions on emigration since 1950. During the twentieth century, though the United States gained about 30 million foreign people, as many as 10 million of these people have left. Currently, more than 150,000 people, mostly former immigrants, leave each year.

Since 1900, there has been considerable variation in U.S. emigration. In total, immigration far exceeded emigration. Most significant is the fact that emigration of non-U.S. citizens was approximately 12 times greater than for U.S. citizens. With the passage of restrictive U.S. immigration laws in the 1920s, the numbers of immigrants declined and the numbers of emigrants proportionally increased. Data on emigrants were collected by U.S. Immigration and Naturalization Service from 1918 to 1950. Since 1950, the U.S. Statistical Office has prepared estimates of emigration. As the U.S. economy has become more integrated into the world economy, the numbers of U.S. emigrants have increased.

Although there are many countries to which U.S. citizens have emigrated, a few dominate (Table 18). In the period from 1960 to 1979, the receiving countries, in descending order of importance, were Mexico, Germany, United Kingdom, Canada, Japan, Australia, and Israel. These seven countries accounted for about 88 percent of total U.S. emigration. About half of the emigrants went to Mexico and Canada and about one-quarter to the Western European countries.

## Impact of Immigration

### Demographic Impact

There is an often stated perception in the United States that the nation, by accepting unprecedented numbers of immigrants, is altering its own ethnic character. It is correct that in the decade

Table 18 Emigration of Americans to Select Other Countries, 1961–1985

| Year | To Australia | To Canada | To Israel |
|------|------|------|------|
| 1961 | 1,033 | 11,516 | 1,871 |
| 1962 | 1,033 | 11,643 | 2,352 |
| 1963 | 1,109 | 11,736 | 2,850 |
| 1964 | 1,400 | 12,565 | 3,282 |
| 1965 | 1,805 | 15,143 | 3,227 |
| 1966 | 2,435 | 17,514 | 4,048 |
| 1967 | 2,472 | 19,038 | 6,216 |
| 1968 | 2,586 | 20,422 | 5,735 |
| 1969 | 3,190 | 22,783 | 6,424 |
| 1970 | 3,591 | 24,424 | 7,364 |
| 1971 | 5,447 | 24,336 | 5,515 |
| 1972 | 6,564 | 22,618 | 4,393 |
| 1973 | 3,828 | 25,242 | 3,089 |
| 1974 | 3,324 | 26,541 | 2,802 |
| 1975 | 3,192 | 20,155 | 2,700 |
| 1976 | 1,440 | 17,315 | 2,571 |
| 1977 | 1,180 | 12,888 | 2,921 |
| 1978 | 1,031 | 9,945 | 2,950 |
| 1979 | 1,079 | 9,617 | 2,312 |
| 1980 | 1,226 | 9,926 | 2,384 |
| 1981 | 1,607 | 10,559 | 2,693 |
| 1982 | 1,802 | 9,360 | 3,469 |
| 1983 | 1,920 | 7,381 | 2,750 |
| 1984 | 1,750 | 6,922 | 2,581 |
| 1985 | 1,540 | 6,661 | 2,175 |

*Source:* Australia: *Australian Government Statistics*; Canada: *Immigration Statistics, Canada*, and Israel: *Israel Central Bureau of Statistics.*

between 1980 and 1990 nearly 9 million legal immigrants arrived in this nation. With the exception of the decade between 1900 and 1910, this is the highest number in U.S. history.

Opponents of immigration argue that such a massive influx of immigrants is creating overpopulation problems. There is little question that selected regions of the country must integrate a substantial number of new immigrants into their economy. However, immigration advocates argue, if overpopulation is measured by number of people per square mile, the United States is among the least populated industrial nations in the world. In the 1980s, despite extremely high levels of immigration, the rate of U.S. population growth was lower than during any decade since the 1940s.

The U.S. immigration rate rose from 2.0 per 1,000 residents in the 1950s and 1960s to about 3.2 per 1,000 residents in the 1980s. The average annual number of new immigrants over the past 50 years has been about 5 per 1,000 residents. The actual immigration rate in the 1990s is estimated to be about 3.5 per 1,000 residents.

At present, more than 20 million U.S. citizens, or more than 1 in 12, are foreign born. This is a significant increase from the 1950s and 1960s, when immigration was at a fairly low level. However, this is much lower than in the first decade of the twentieth century, when 1 in 6 Americans was foreign born. The United States was much more a nation of immigrants a century ago.

The increase in immigration is significant in the context of the slow growth expected in the U.S. labor force in the next decade. It is predicted that if immigration totals 1 million persons per year, the labor force will increase at only half the rate of the 1970s. It appears that immigrants will be required for the United States to maintain a satisfactory labor supply.

Opponents of immigration note that the United States receives a greater number of migrants and refugees than other countries. In terms of the number of immigrants entering other industrialized countries relative to total population, though, the United States has not received a proportionately large number of immigrants. Of the three major immigrant-receiving countries—Australia, Canada, and the United States—the United States has the lowest immigration rate. For example, in 1985 the United States permitted entry of 3 immigrants per 1,000 population; Canada permitted 3.5 and Australia 12. Germany permitted 7 immigrants per 1,000 population, Switzerland 15, and the United Kingdom 4.

Some opponents of immigration have expressed concern about the ethnic composition of recent immigrants. The number of European immigrants has declined while non-European immigration has increased. There are some predictions that in the coming years non-Hispanics in Texas will be a minority. Ethnic composition is not only a cultural matter; it is also an economic issue in that, for example, many of the Latin American immigrants are unskilled laborers, whereas many of the Asians are highly educated.

There has also been a change in the number of female to male immigrants since the 1970s. In earlier waves of immigration, there was a predominance of males. Since the Immigration Act of 1965, preference has been given to immigrants who want to reunite with family members. Today about 80 percent of legal immigrants are family sponsored, about 15 percent are political refugees, and only 5 percent are chosen for special skills. As a response to legislation allowing spouses of immigrants to enter the United States, the gender composition of immigration has changed markedly as wives move to join their husbands (Moore 1989).

There is some debate over whether the change in ethnic composition has had a favorable or unfavorable impact on the culture and economy of the United States. There is strong evidence that Asian immigrants have adjusted to U.S. society. For example, the 1990 U.S. Census revealed that the earnings of Asians were higher than for any other ethnic group. The average household income of Asians was $36,000 in 1990, compared to $29,000 for all U.S. households.

The decline in the number of European immigrants since World War II is due not to immigration policy but to political conditions in Poland, Hungary, Russia, Romania, and Bulgaria. Immigration was largely forbidden from these nations between 1945 and the early 1990s. In the 1980s, only about 3 percent of U.S. immigrants came from these nations.

Predictions of population growth and estimated labor demands indicate that in the twenty-first century, increased immigration will be important in maintaining the economic growth of the United States. The domestic demographic change will be due to the aging of the "baby boom" generation and the low U.S. population growth in recent decades. In 1990, Peter Francese, president of the American Demographic Society, wrote in the *Wall Street Journal:*

> There are powerful demographic forces at work in the U.S. that vitally mandate federal policy be changed to permit more immigration than we have now. The rapid increase in the number of very elderly people combined with declining numbers of young adults and a record low population growth rate, will put this nation in a demographic vise.
>
> Paying for the income security and medical needs of the elderly while at the same time improving the educational opportunities and well-being of children will squeeze future U.S. workers in the grips of higher federal payroll taxes and local property taxes.
>
> The U.S. needs to admit more immigrants to get us out of the demographic bind.

Present-day statistics confirm these predictions. New entrants to the work force (age 20 to 29) are expected to decline in the coming decades. In addition, in 1970 there were three workers for every retired person; by 2000 there will be fewer than two. To provide promised federal health care and Social Security benefits to the present "baby boomers" will require nearly a 40 percent increase in payroll taxes based on current population trends.

It will be a challenge for U.S. immigration policy in the twenty-first century to reflect the changes in the population's demographics. Such a policy must recognize the changes in ethnic numbers and reflect the types of skills the new immigrants have. Many fundamental questions must be debated and resolved in the development of a sound immigration policy.

## Cultural Adaptation

All areas of the United States are faced with the challenges of social and cultural adaptation of new groups of immigrants. Although traditionally a new group may concentrate in a particular area of the country upon its initial arrival, these concentrations have for the most part been temporary. From the first American colony begun in 1607 up until the 1920s, immigrants could enter the United States without restriction. These immigrants demonstrated a desire to assimilate themselves into the dominant American society. The notion of the U.S. "melting pot" arose in the early twentieth century. Historian Frederick Jackson Turner probably did more than anyone else to popularize this concept when he wrote, "The frontier promoted the formation of a composite nationality for the American people. . . . In the crucible of the frontier, the immigrants were Americanized, liberated and fused into a mixed race."

Following the tremendous U.S. immigration since 1965, there has been much discussion concerning the advantages of cultural assimilation versus cultural separation. For instance, in conjunction with the massive numbers of Mexican immigrants in the Southwest, there are a few Spanish-speaking groups that aspire to "take back" the areas secured by U.S. military force over 140 years ago.

More than 80 percent of the immigrants since 1990 are Latinos or Asians. Cultural assimilation of these groups is likely to be more difficult than it was with the European immigrants of the nineteenth century and early twentieth century. The growth of large enclaves of these new immigrants in certain parts of the country precludes easy assimilation into the dominant culture of the nation. Furthermore, it is not clear that the new groups want to be part of a new "melting pot."

Immigration advocates note that the challenge faced by the growing multiracial U.S. society is to provide equal access for all peoples to all avenues of success and in the process to adapt to the shifts in culture. It is important for a form of cultural adaptation to be accepted that combines the best of the new ideas that immigrants bring to this nation and at the same time allows a distinct overall culture to develop and become accepted by all peoples.

## Education of Latin American Children in the United States

Many of the children of immigrants, particularly those from Latin America, are poorly educated. The problems of educating these children have become particularly acute in California. The number of Mexican students is growing at a remarkable pace. In the Los Angeles school district, the largest in California, 1990 enrollment was 63 percent Latino, up from 22 percent in 1970. During this period, the white, non-Latino student population declined from 50 percent to 14 percent. In the elementary schools, Latino students, mostly Mexican, accounted for 67 percent of the total in 1990.

Latino students have come to be characterized by poor academic performance. This appears to be the result of a series of problems. Few of the students speak or write English, so a language barrier exists. This problem was recognized in 1968 in the federal Bilanguage Act, which provided federal money to any state that did not already have a bilingual education program. This act has come under attack, and in 1987 California's governor George Deukmejan vetoed an extension of the state's native-language instruction requirements. Although the federal program remains in effect, 25 percent of its funds may now be spent in programs other than native-language instruction. Despite opposition, the bilingual program has become well established in California schools. Nevertheless, Latino students continue to experience difficulty.

Another, possibly more important cause of Latin American students' low achievement concerns the low socioeconomic status of the families. For example, a recent study of eighth graders found that 40 percent of those from advantaged families had academic scores in the top 25 percent, whereas only 9.3 percent scored in the bottom quarter. Among disadvantaged students, in contrast, only 8 percent were in the top groups, while 44 percent were in the bottom. Although low income is one indicator of student success, parental education and guidance appear to be more important. Better-educated parents teach their children the importance of an education in obtaining adequate employment. Educated parents help students with their homework and help negotiate educational bureaucracies. Further, educated people tend to have higher educational aspirations and expectations for their children.

Another significant problem is the overcrowding of Mexican minority schools in California and the general lack of equipment in their classrooms. Because of low budgets, new schools are not being built in adequate numbers. The overcrowded and poorly equipped schools in the Latino areas are a major factor in denying Mexican students equal educational opportunities.

## Immigration and the Welfare State

It has been suggested that liberal U.S. welfare policies have been a major factor in increased levels of immigration. For example, Governor Pete Wilson of California has stated that the state's chronic multibillion-dollar budget deficits are a result of expenditures on social services and the low incomes of immigrants. Many other population specialists have indicated that Calfornia's welfare policies have acted as a magnet to immigrants (Briggs and Moore 1994).

The level of welfare benefits for low-income families has increased rapidly in the United States in the past 30 years. Federal benefits include public housing, child nutrition programs, Medicaid, unemployment insurance, and others. In some states, notably California and New York, additional benefits are added. It is estimated that these federal and state benefits have a cash value of more than $14,000 annually (Bean, Lewis, and Taylor 1988).

Studies indicate that the use of services by all immigrants is similar to that of all U.S. citizens. For example, a study by the U.S. Department of Labor in 1984 revealed that 12.8 percent of the foreign-born U.S. residents received public assistance, compared with 13.9 percent of native-born Americans. Other studies also show that services to immigrants are quite similar to those for U.S.-born citizens.

There is a general perception that Hispanic immigrants are especially heavy users of welfare services. In a 1984 Urban

Institute study of California, it was found that the average California household receiving aid received $575 per month, whereas the typical Mexican immigrant household received less than half this amount, about $251. The one major exception was in the education of the children of Mexican immigrants. The cost per Mexican family was $1,966 annually, compared to $872 for the average California family. This was partly due to the larger size of the typical Mexican family, but more important were the extra educational requirements of students who spoke only Spanish.

There is evidence that Mexican immigrants have a high work ethic. Most are willing to work longer hours than U.S. citizens and are highly motivated. There is also evidence that Mexicans immigrate to find work and do not come to go on welfare. A study in 1990 by the University of California of Los Angeles found that 81 percent of Mexican immigrant men were in the labor force, compared with 76 percent of white men and 67 percent of black men.

In spite of this evidence, the welfare problem of financially distressed cities is a growing concern. The major problem is that a significant proportion of the services given to immigrants is paid for by local taxes. Thus, local U.S.-born citizens bear a disproportionate share of the burden for providing these services. Nevertheless, Urban Institute research found that even though the welfare payments made to immigrant families in California are greater than the amount those families pay in local taxes, the immigrants are still a significant economic asset to California's communities in terms of their purchases of goods and services. This fact probably outweighs the economic costs of these fiscal deficits.

There have been only a few studies on immigrants' use of welfare over a lifetime. In 1984, Julian Simon of the University of Maryland found that immigrants, in their early years in the United States, use fewer public services than U.S.-born citizens, but that in their later years they use about the same amount of services (Simon 1990). This is partly due to the fact that new immigrants are not eligible for many welfare programs, but in their later years they gain the right to such public welfare benefits as Social Security. There is evidence that immigrants, over the years, contribute substantially to the federal government but are a fiscal drain at the local level. One proposed solution to this disparity is for the federal government to reimburse local governments for a portion of the services being provided to immigrants.

In contrast to other immigrants, refugees present a special problem. Refugees in general use substantially more services than other immigrants. In addition, they may be unemployed for a considerable period after they come to the United States. To illustrate, in 1984, 64 percent of the U.S. population was in the labor force, but only 55 percent of the refugees were.

The most comprehensive study to date on refugees was conducted by Susan Forbes of the Refugee Policy Group in 1985. She found that in their first year in the United States, about 75 percent of refugees were on public assistance. This decreased to 50 percent in the second year and decreased rapidly afterward. For example, the Office of Refugee Resettlement reported that half of the Southeast Asian refugees who arrived in the United States in 1985 were unemployed at the end of 1985; 20 percent were unemployed in 1986, 9 percent in 1987, and 5 percent in 1988. Thus, the employment rate slowly reached that of most Americans. Nevertheless, the rate of dependency among refugees in their early years is problematic. Immediate access to welfare may be a deterrent to early employment and is costly to U.S. taxpayers.

In general, immigrants do not appear to create an economic problem over an extended period. Most want to earn a living and adjust to the U.S. economic system. In recent years, many immigrants have arrived with a good education and skills. Within a short time, their rising level of income provides taxes to all levels of government. Their dependence on welfare programs is thus relatively short.

## Labor Market

Because recent immigrants vary from unskilled workers to such qualified professionals as doctors and scientists, it is difficult to find simple answers on how immigrants affect the U.S. labor market (Table 19). An overwhelming percentage of recent immigrants find jobs using their skills within a few years. However, few have been screened in order to determine whether their skills are needed in the labor market of the United States. Potential legal immigrants face a preference system that, in accordance with the 1986 Immigration Act, favors family unification over U.S. work force needs. Of the 9 million immigrants who arrived in the 1980s, fewer than 4 percent were selected because they had a specific skill.

One of the most significant problems for the future is that the U.S. economy requires a labor force with increasingly

Table 19    Projected California Labor Force by Ethnicity, 1980–2030 (in thousands)

|  | 1980 | | 2000 | | 2030 | |
|---|---|---|---|---|---|---|
|  | Number | Percent | Number Projected | Percent Projected | Number Projected | Percent Projected |
| Non–Hispanic white | 8,198 | 69.5 | 9,576 | 54.5 | 8,610 | 37.9 |
| Black | 792 | 6.7 | 1,262 | 7.2 | 1,476 | 6.5 |
| Hispanic | 2,026 | 17.3 | 4,701 | 26.8 | 8,716 | 38.4 |
| Asian and other | 784 | 6.5 | 2,032 | 11.5 | 3,894 | 17.2 |
| Total | 11,800 | 100 | 17,571 | 100 | 22,698 | 100 |

*Source:* U.S. Department of Labor Report, Washington, DC.

greater skills, but that many of the immigrants lack these skills; this is particularly true for illegal aliens. In the 1980s, almost half of all immigrants performed lower-skilled work as laborers, service workers, and farmworkers. Only about one-third of all workers in the United States had these occupations.

There are three general viewpoints as to how unskilled immigrants affect the U.S. labor market. The first viewpoint says that unskilled immigrants will take jobs from unskilled Americans because they will work for a lower salary and will work harder because they need to keep the job. The second viewpoint is that unskilled immigrants do not compete with unskilled American workers, because the only jobs these immigrants can get are those rejected by Americans. The third point of view is that the labor market adjusts to the availability or unavailability of unskilled immigrants; thus, the disappearance of immigrants could force some employers out of business but would increase jobs with better pay for Americans.

To date, U.S. immigration policy in general has not been strictly linked to employment policies. For example, in the 1980s the United States legalized roughly 3 million immigrants who, on average, had less than a high school education, even though a number of recent reports warn that within a decade the number of jobs for persons with such a low level of education will shrink.

At the beginning of the twenty-first century, U.S. factories and farms will be the primary employers for the huge numbers of immigrants entering the country. However, economists speculate that the number of unskilled workers will exceed the number of jobs available. This situation has two likely implications.

First, when the number of unskilled workers dictates the labor market in certain areas, those areas will become low-cost manufacturing centers. However, these centers may not be able to compete with other centers worldwide because the U.S. economy is geared toward advanced industry. Second, and more important, there must be a massive retraining program so that the immigrants can obtain the technical skills needed to find jobs in the United States.

Because of the impending need for additional labor in the United States in the immediate future, there is an ongoing debate on whether additional immigrants will be a necessary part of the labor force. Immigration advocates argue that unskilled immigration cannot do harm to the U.S. labor market. They note that the unemployment rate in the U.S. Southwest is no higher than the national average. However, this viewpoint overlooks the fact that unskilled Americans are migrating out of the region. Massive levels of immigration into areas such as Los Angeles often drive unskilled Americans away, and the underclass that remains tends to drop out of the labor force, making the unemployment rate appear deceptively low.

## Immigration's Effect on Wage Rates

There is a popular conception that immigrants will work for lower wages and thus drive down the wage rate of all workers. Many studies have investigated U.S. immigration and wage rates in recent decades. Evidence indicates that immigration has had little influence on wages. To illustrate, a study of the effect of foreign-born manufacturing workers on manufacturing wages in 35 major metropolitan areas between 1970 and 1978 indicated that wages were lowered only after foreign workers made up more than 20 percent of the labor force. Other studies in individual industries, such as apparel, found a similar economic effect (Bean, Lewis, and Taylor 1988).

Similar studies of the 1980s found that, even under heavy immigration, wage rates were not reduced (Borjas 1992). It was also determined that low-skilled Hispanic immigrants, who competed with low-skilled Americans, had no effect on the wage rate for either group (DeFraitas 1988).

The massive influx of illegal immigrants has often been thought to be especially harmful to the wage rates of U.S. workers. However, one of the most comprehensive studies (Bean, Lewis, and Taylor 1988) found that employment of illegal aliens was economically beneficial, based on 1980 Census

Bureau estimates for illegal Mexican immigration in 47 metropolitan areas. The report concluded that the illegal workers probably complemented the labor of U.S. citizens. The 1986 Immigration Reform and Control Act was designed to keep illegal aliens from competing with American workers by imposing sanctions on U.S. employers who hired illegal aliens. However, this act has been relatively ineffective because of its poor enforcement policies.

In conclusion, research concerning wage rates reveals that immigrants have not lowered the wages of American workers. There is also little evidence that immigration raises the wages of low-paid American workers. Thus, studies reveal that increased wages for industrial labor are primarily a response to rising productivity. Immigrants have contributed to rising real wages for U.S. labor.

## References

Baker, Reginald, and David S. North. *The Vietnamese Refugees: Their First Five Years in America*. Washington, DC: New Trans Century Foundation, 1984.

Bean, Frank D., Lindsay Lewis, and Lowell, J. Taylor. "Undocumented Mexican Immigrants and the Earnings of Other Workers in the United States." *Demography* (February 1988): 15–19.

Borjas, George. *Friends or Strangers? The Impact of Immigration on the U.S. Economy*. New York: Basic Books, 1990.

Briggs, Vernon M. J. *Mass Immigration and the National Interest*. Armonk, NY: M. E. Sharpe, 1992.

Buchanan, Patrick. "The Immigration Bomb," *National Review* (April 1992): 18.

DeFraitas, Gregory. "Hispanic Immigration and Labor Market Segmentation." *Industrial Relations* (1988): 195–214.

DeFraitas, Gregory, and Adriana Marshall, "Immigrant and Wage Growth in U.S. Manufacturing in the 1970s." *Proceedings, Annual Meeting of the Industrial Relations Research Association*, 1984, pp. 148–156.

Forbes, Susan. *Adaptation and Integration of Recent Refugees to the United States*. Washington, DC: Refugee Policy Group, 1985.

Francese, Peter. "Aging America Needs Foreign Blood," *Wall Street Journal* (27 March, 1990), editorial.

Freeman, Richard B., and John M. Abowd. *Immigration, Trade and the Labor Market.* Chicago: University of Chicago Press, 1990.

Lesko Associates. "Basic Data and Guidance Required to Implement a Major Illegal Alien Study during Fiscal Year 1976." Report to U.S. Immigration and Naturalization Service, Washington, DC: 1975.

Los Angeles Board of Supervisors. *Impact of Immigrants on County Services.* Los Angeles, CA: 1992.

McCarthy, Kevin, and R. Burciago Valdez, *Current and Future Effects of Mexican Immigration in California: Executive Summary.* Santa Monica, CA: Rand Corporation, 1985.

Moore, Stephen. "A Pro-Family, Pro-Growth Immigration Policy for America." *Backgrounder.* Washington, DC: Heritage Foundation, 1989.

Papademetriou, Demetrious, and Thomas Muller. *Recent Immigration: Labor Market and Social Policy Issues.* Washington, DC: National Commission on Employment Policy, 1987.

Simon, Julian L. *The Economic Consequences of Immigration.* Cambridge, MA: Basil Blackwell, 1990.

Simon, Julian L., and Stephen Moore. "Communism, Capitalism and Economic Growth." *Backgrounder.* Washington, DC: Heritage Foundation, 1989.

Sorensen, Elaine, and Maria E. Enchautegin. *Immigrant Male Earnings in the 1980s: Divergent Patterns by Race and Ethnicity.* Washington, DC: Urban Institute, 1992.

Wattenburg, Ben J. *The First Universal Nation.* New York: Macmillan, 1991.

Warren, Robert and Jeffrey S. Passel, "A Count of the Uncountable: Estimates of Undocumented Aliens Counted in the 1980 United States Census." *Demography (Population Association of America)* 24 (August 1989): 375–393.

# Chronology 2

## Laws and Regulations

### Immigration Laws

| | |
|---|---|
| 1864 | Immigration Act (July 4, 1864, Chapter 246, 13 Statute 385) Revised 1882, 1871, 1903, 1907, 1917, 1918, 1920, 1921, 1924, 1937, 1940, 1942, 1944, 1945, 1946, 1947, 1948, 1950, and 1952. |
| 1917 | Immigration Act of 1917 (February 5, 1917, Chapter 29) |
| 1924 | Immigration Act of 1924 (May 26, 1924, Chapter 190, 43 Statute 153) |
| 1952 | Immigration and Nationality Act of 1952 (July 27, 1952, Public Law 414, 66 Statute 163) |
| 1965 | Immigration and Nationality Act of 1965 |
| 1986 | Immigration Reform and Control Act of 1986 (November 1986, Public Law 99-603, 100 Statute 3359) |

| | |
|---|---|
| 1988 | Immigration Technical Corrections Act of 1988 (October 24, 1988, Public Law 100-525, 102 Statute 2609) |
| | Revised 1991. |
| | Immigration Amendment of 1988 (November 15, 1988, Public Law 100-658, 102 Statute 3908) |
| 1990 | Immigration Act of 1990 (November 29, 1990, Public Law 101-649, 104 Statute 4978) |
| | Revised 1991. |
| 1995 | Immigration Reform and Control Act of 1986 (November 6, 1986, Public Law 99-603, 100 Statute 3359) |

## Naturalization Laws

| | |
|---|---|
| 1790 | Naturalization Act of 1790 (March 26, 1790, Chapter 3, 1 Statute 103) |
| | Revised 1795, 1798, 1802, 1808, 1821, 1870, and 1906. |
| 1940 | Nationality Act of 1940 (October 14, 1940, Chapter 876, 54 Statute 1137) |
| | Revised 1941, 1942, 1943, 1944, 1945, 1946, 1947, 1948, 1949, 1950, and 1952. |

## Refugee Laws

| | |
|---|---|
| 1948 | Displaced Persons Act of 1948 |
| 1953 | Refugee Relief Act of 1953 |
| 1962 | Migration and Refugee Assistance Act of 1962 (June 28, 1962, Public Law 87-510, 76 Statute 121) |
| 1980 | Refugee Act of 1980 (March 17, 1980, Public Law 96-212, 94 Statute 102) |
| | Refugee Education Assistance Act of 1980 (October 10, 1980, Public Law 96-422, 44 Statute 1799) |

## Special Legislation

| | |
|---|---|
| 1962 | Migrant Health Act (September 25, 1962, Public Law 87-692, 76 Statute 592) |
| 1978 | Migrant and Community Health Centers Amendment of 1978 (November 10, 1978, Public Law 95-626, Title I, part A 101 to 107, 92 Statute 3551 to 3562) |

1983        Migrant and Seasonal Agricultural Workers Protection Act (January 14, 1983, Public Law 97-490, 96 Statute 2583) Revised 1985 and 1992.

1986        Immigration Marriage Fraud Amendments of 1986 (November 10, 1986, Public Law 99-639, 1003 Statute 3537) Revised 1988.

1989        Immigration Nursing Relief Act of 1989 (December 18, 1989, Public Law 101-238, 103 Statute 2099)

# Legislative Process Leading to the Immigration Reform and Control Act of 1986*

1978        October 5. The Select Commission on Immigration and Refugee Policy is created under Public Law 86-412 to coordinate a study of immigration and refugee laws and to report its findings to the president and Congress. The 16-member committee consists of four senators, four representatives, four cabinet secretaries, and four public appointments, including its chair, Rev. Theodore N. Hesburgh, president of Notre Dame University.

1981        March 6. The Select Commission on Immigration and Refugee Policy issues its final report recommending "immediate action" on immigration reform. Key elements of the report include recommended employer sanctions, legalization of selected aliens living in the United States, and increased funding for border patrol. The report rejects any new temporary foreign agricultural worker programs.

             May 5–7. House and Senate immigration subcommittees hold joint meetings on the Select Commission on Immigration and Refugee Policy recommendations. This is the first joint committee meeting since 1951.

* Data from Montweiler, Nancy H., *The Immigration Control and Reform Law of 1986*, 1987, Washington, D.C.: The Bureau of National Affairs.

| | |
|---|---|
| 1981, *cont.* | June 30. President Reagan recommends new immigration legislation calling for sanctions, two-year guest worker programs, and increased border patrols. |
| 1982 | March 17. A joint immigration reform bill is introduced by Sen. Alan Simpson (R–Wyoming) and Rep. Romano Mazzoli (D–Kentucky), chairs of the Senate and House immigration subcommittees. Special features include the granting of permanent residence to aliens who have lived in the United States since January 1, 1978, and temporary status for those who have lived here since January 1, 1980; sanctions against employers who knowingly hire illegal aliens; and a broadened program for temporary foreign farmworkers. Opposition to the bill comes from employers, Hispanic groups, and western growers. |
| | August 17. Senate passes bill by a vote of 80-19 after three days of debate. |
| | December 16–18. Bill is debated on the House floor, with no vote taken. Bill dies at end of 97th Congress after more than 300 amendments are attached. |
| 1983 | February 17. Senator Simpson and Representative Mazzoli reintroduce legislation in the Senate and House. |
| | May 18. Senate bill passes a second time by a vote of 76-18. One major amendment creates a three-year transitional program for foreign agricultural workers. |
| 1984 | June 20. After seven days of debate, House passes bill by a vote of 216 to 211. Major amendments include establishing a guest worker program and the creation of an immigration board modeled after the National Labor Relations Board to hear charges of discrimination based on aliens' national origin or age. |
| | September 13. House and Senate begin a ten-day conference in an attempt to resolve differences between the two bills. Although there are many |

| | |
|---|---|
| 1984 | differences, the question of federal reimbursements to states is what causes a major disagreement. Differences are not resolved and bill dies with end of the 98th Congress. |
| 1985 | May 23. Senator Simpson reintroduces bill (S. 1200) similar to earlier bills. |

July 25. Peter Rodino (D–New Jersey), chair of the House Judiciary Committee, and Representative Mazzoli introduce H.R. 3080, combining both bills that were passed by the House in the previous Congress, along with some revisions approved by the conference committee.

September 19. Senate passes comprehensive immigration reform bill for a third time by a 69-30 vote. One of the major changes calls for a guest work program to admit 350,000 aliens as temporary farm workers.

September and October. House Immigration Subcommittee holds four days of hearings with testimony from 50 witnesses.

November 19. House Immigration Subcommittee clears bill for action by the full Judiciary Committee. Discussion on agricultural provisions is postponed for further negotiations.

| | |
|---|---|
| 1986 | June 25. House Judiciary Committee clears bill by 25-10 vote after adopting a narrow compromise amendment granting permanent resident status to illegal aliens who can prove they have been employed as farmworkers for at least 60 days during the 12 months preceding May 1, 1986. |

September 26. On procedural motion, House votes 202-180 not to debate bill on floor. Controversy centers on temporary farmworker provisions that have been added by the Judiciary Committee.

October 8. Bill is resurrected after negotiations lead to modification of farmworker program. House approves legislation by 250-166 vote.

October 14. House and Senate conferences agree to compromise legislation.

1986,          October 15. House approves conference bill by
*cont.*        238-173 vote.

               October 17. President Reagan supports legislation.
               Senate approves bill by 63-24 vote.

               November 6. President Reagan signs bill (Public
               Law No. 99-603) into law, declaring its objective:
               "to establish a reasonable, fair, orderly, and secure
               system of immigration into this country and not to
               discriminate in any way against particular nations
               or peoples."

# Chronology of Refugee Admissions

## Hungary

1956           October. Soviet Union invades Hungary.

1957           January 10. President Eisenhower, in a reference to
               Hungarian refugees, indicates that the free nations
               have a responsibility for granting asylum to victims
               of communist persecution.

               President's Committee for Hungarian Refugee
               Relief is commissioned to develop policies for the
               admission of Hungarian Refugees to the United
               States.

1957–1959      United States approves admission of 38,000
               Hungarian refugees and pays for resettlement by
               air or sea lift.

               Refugees are admitted to the United States through
               Joyce Kilmer Reception Center at Camp Kilmer,
               New Jersey.

## Cuba

1830s          Groups of laborers immigrate to Key West, Florida,
               to produce cigars, thus avoiding high import
               tariffs.

1868–1869      At the outbreak of war for Cuban independence,
               significant immigration begins. By 1869, more than
               100,000 Cubans have left the country to come to
               the United States. The largest group is made up
               of workers who come to New York and the

1868–1869    southeastern United States. A second group of professionals and business leaders come to New York, Philadelphia, and Boston, and a small group of aristocrats also moves to live in Europe.

1900–1950    Small groups of Cubans come to the United States to escape political turbulence in Cuba. In the late 1920s and early 1930s, a small group of political and student activists find refuge in Miami and New York. Many of these people return to Cuba when political unrest ceases. Similar groups leave Cuba during the presidencies of Fulgencio Batista (1940–1944 and 1952–1958), Ramon Gran San Martino (1944–1948), and Carlos Prio Socarras (1948–1952).

1950–1960    In the late 1950s, Cuban exiles begin to flee the country. The first 500 exiles of the deposed dictator enter the United States under political asylum. This opens the door for future immigration from Cuba.

1960    December 10. The Eisenhower administration begins a program to bring Cuban children to the United States in order to escape communism. By the conclusion of the program, 14,018 children have come to the United States.

1961    January 3. Diplomatic relations between the United States and Cuba are terminated.

January 5. The United States government indicates that any Cuban "fleeing from Communist oppression" is automatically qualified for a U.S. visa to enter the United States.

April 16. Castro proclaims the "socialist character of the Revolution."

Cuban Emergency Center in Miami makes a commitment to handle the refugee problem on a much larger scale and wider scope.

1961–1965    The U.S./Cuban Refugee Program leads both countries to level political attacks on each other. The program has the ultimate goal of destroying the Castro regime in Cuba. The Kennedy administration strategy to drain Cuba of its best-qualified professionals has a devastating short-term effect on the Cuban economy.

1965–1973   The Camarioca boatlift and airlift begin on
September 25, 1965. Fidel Castro announces that
Cubans with relatives in the United States can leave
Cuba if their relatives ask for them. In so doing,
Castro indicates that the people of Cuba have to
make a choice to stay in Cuba and make the revolu-
tion successful or leave the nation. The boatlift and
airlift end on April 6, 1973.

1980–1985   The Mariel open door policy begins with a program
to release about 10,000 political prisoners in Cuba.
Castro declares that any Cubans in the United
States can come to Cuba to get their relatives. As a
consequence, thousands of Cuban exiles in the
United States rent boats to go to Mariel, Cuba, to
secure their relatives. In the first week of May 1980,
more than 6,000 Cubans arrive in Key West.
Throughout the rest of May, more than 3,000 people arrive from Cuba every day. The Mariel open
door policy ends on May 20, 1985.

1985–1995   Over this period, the legal admission of Cubans to
the United States varies between 10,000 and 28,000.
The number of illegal Cuban immigrants is quite
small.

## South Vietnam

1975–1977   Vietnamese refugees begin heading to the United
States with the withdrawal of U.S. forces in
Vietnam. Many of these people had been employed
by U.S. agencies during the war.

1978   Vietnamese refugee immigration starts up again
because of the Vietnam-China War of 1978. These
refugees are generally known as "Boat People."
Most of them are rural people fleeing from the
effects of war.

1980   More refugees head to the United States from
Vietnam. Most of them are ethnic Chinese fleeing
from the effects of war.

# Illegal Immigration

## Haiti

| | |
|---|---|
| 1972 | December 12. First boat load of 65 Haitians lands in Miami to seek refuge from political persecution. |
| 1972–1980 | Between 65,000 and 75,000 Haitians have come to the United States in boats and have begun life in communities, mostly in Florida. |
| 1980 | More than 1,000 Haitians a month are arriving by boat in Florida. |
| 1981 | May 18. Under the executive order of President Reagan, the Immigration and Naturalization Service begins placing all new Haitian aliens in former military camps.

December. Haitian Refugee Center of Miami files a class action suit against the federal government for the release of all detained Haitians in the United States and Puerto Rico. |
| 1982 | June 18. A U.S. federal court rules that the Immigration and Naturalization Service has devised a policy in violation of federal administrative rules. |
| 1984 | February 28. Federal court decision is immediately protested because the detention was declared illegal on a legal technicality rather than ethical grounds. The decision is overturned, but by this date most of the Haitians have been released from custody.

November. The United States offers citizenship to 125,000 illegal Cubans, but the decision does not apply to Haitians. Many Americans feel that this decision is discriminatory, but the decision stands. |
| 1984–1994 | Haitians continue to come to the United States illegally by boat. |
| 1995 | The U.S. Coast Guard increases its ocean patrols to intercept illegal Haitian aliens. In November, 1,100 boats are intercepted and the Haitians returned to Haiti. There is no documentation on the boats that evaded coastal surveillance. |

# Laws and Regulations    3

C ongress passed its first immigration act in 1864 in order to encourage immigration to the United States. Although this fundamental law was revised a number of times, the concept of an "open door" to the United States prevailed until 1924. By the 1920s, economic and social pressures were developing not only to limit the number of new immigrants but also to control where they came from. The Immigration Act of 1924 established the philosophy of modern U.S. immigration.

This chapter lists the major immigration acts of the United States.

## Immigration

### Immigration Act of 1864

(July 4, 1864, Chapter 246, 13 Statute 385)

Revised 1882, 1891, 1903, 1907, 1917, 1918, 1920, 1921, 1924, 1937, 1940, 1942, 1944, 1945, 1946, 1947, 1948, 1950, and 1952.

The Immigration Act was enacted by Congress to encourage immigration to the United States. In order to implement the act, a commissioner of immigration was established in the Department of State. An immigrant could apply for aid to defray a part of the expenses involved. The contract with the immigrant stipulated that

1. In order to repay the expenses of coming to the United States, funds were guaranteed not to exceed one year.
2. This advance of funds, if so stipulated in the contract, was to operate as a lien upon any land acquired by the emigrant, whether under the homestead law (which provided land to immigrants) or on property acquired otherwise.

The law also provided that

1. No person could be a part of the immigration commission if he or she was directly or indirectly associated with a corporation that sold land to immigrants or transported immigrants.
2. The commissioner had to report annually to Congress the number of foreign immigrants admitted to the United States.
3. No male immigrant who arrived after the passage of this act could be compelled to provide military service in the Civil War unless he voluntarily renounced under oath his allegiance to the country of his birth and declared his intentions to become a citizen of the United States.

## Immigration Act of 1917
(February 5, 1917, Chapter 29)

The Immigration Act of 1917 was enacted to exclude certain types of aliens. These included

1. All idiots, imbeciles, the feeble-minded, epileptics, and persons with chronic alcoholism and tuberculosis.
2. Paupers, beggars, vagrants, and persons with physical defects that would prevent an individual from earning a living.
3. Polygamists.
4. Persons convicted or admitted of having committed (1) a felony or crime or (2) a misdemeanor involving "moral turpitude."

5. Prostitutes or "any other immoral person."
6. An individual of any organization who taught (1) disbelief in or opposition to organized government or (2) the unlawful distribution of property.
7. Contract laborers who had been encouraged or solicited to immigrate to the United States by offers or promises of employment.
8. Persons who came as a consequence of advertisements for laborers printed in a foreign country.
9. Persons who were likely to become public charges.
10. Persons who had been deported under one of the provisions of the act or were seeking readmission.
11. All children under 16 who were not accompanied by their parents.
12. Persons from Asia.
13. Other individuals who were "not assets to the United States."

The law also encouraged certain groups to come to the United States:

1. Skilled labor could be imported if there was no unemployment in the United States.
2. The law's restrictions did not apply to professional actors, artists, lecturers, surgeons, nurses, ministers, and college professor, and persons could be admitted as domestic servants.
3. The law did not apply to aliens returning after a temporary absence.

This law provided the foundation for later restrictive immigration policies.

## Immigration Act of 1924
(May 26, 1924, Chapter 190, 43 Statute 153)

The Immigration Act of 1924 was one of the fundamental acts limiting immigration of aliens into the United States. In order to enter the United States, the alien initially had to apply for a visa in his or her native country. The visa specified

1. The nationality of the immigrant.
2. Whether he or she was a quota or nonquota immigrant.

3. The date of expiration of the visa.
4. Additional information necessary to the proper enforcement of the immigration and naturalization laws.

The number of aliens admitted to the United States was
established by a quota system. The law stated the following:

1. The annual quota of any nationality was to be a percentage of the number of foreign-born individuals of that
   nationality residing in the continental United States as
   determined by the 1890 U.S. census. The minimum
   quota of any nationality was established as 100.
2. National origin was determined by the number of
   inhabitants in the United States in 1920 from a given
   geographical area. No immigrant could be admitted to
   the United States who had an expired immigration visa
   or had been born after an immigration visa was issued
   to the accompanying parents.
3. The number of immigration visas each year did not
   exceed the established quota of the nationality.

The law provided specific instructions for admittance to the
United States. The secretary of state had to report annually to the
president the quota of each nationality. The president reported
such quotas for all fiscal years.

The law specified that no immigrant could be admitted to
the United States unless he or she

1. Had an unexpired immigration visa or was born after
   the immigration visa was issued to the accompanying
   parents.
2. Was of the nationality specified in the immigration visa.
3. Was a nonquota immigrant (someone who has a visa
   because of special qualifications).
4. Was otherwise admissible.

# Immigration and Nationality Act of 1952
(July 27, 1952, Public Law 414, 66 Statute 163)

Revised 1954, 1956, 1957, 1958, 1959, 1960, 1961, 1962, 1964, 1965,
1966, 1967, 1968, 1969, 1970, 1972, 1975, 1976, 1977, 1978, 1979,
1980, 1981, 1982, 1983, 1984, 1985, 1986, 1987, 1988, 1989, 1990,
1991, 1992, and 1993.

This law provided the first fundamental revision of the initial
Immigration Act of 1864.

## Title I, General

Title I provided basic information on definitions, powers, and duties of the attorney general, the commissioner of immigration, the secretary of state, and the Bureau of Security and Consular Affairs.

## Title II, Immigration

Title II revised the 1924 law establishing quotas for immigration. It stated

1. The annual quota of any quota area was to be one-sixth of 1 percent of the number of inhabitants in the continental United States in 1920.
2. This number, except for the purpose of computing quotas for quota areas within the Asian-Pacific triangle, was to be the same number previously determined under the provisions of Section II of the Immigration Act of 1924, attributable to national origin of the same quota area.
3. The quota existing for Chinese prior to the enactment of the act was to be continued.
4. The minimum quota from any quota class was set at 100.

### Visas

The act established the procedures for issuing visas. No immigrant was to be admitted to the United States unless he or she

1. Had a valid unexpired immigration visa.
2. Was properly chargeable to the quota specified in the immigration visa.
3. Was a nonquota immigrant (i.e., was admitted outside the quota for special reasons, such as status as a professional) specified as such in the immigrant visa.
4. Was otherwise admissible under the act.

The U.S. attorney general was given authority to admit any alien at his or her discretion.

The following classes of aliens were excluded from receiving visas:

1. The feeble-minded.
2. The insane.

3. Persons with a psychopathic personality.
4. Drug addicts.
5. Patients with tuberculosis.
6. Patients with physical defects.
7. Paupers.
8. Persons convicted of a crime.
9. Polygamists.
10. Prostitutes.
11. Persons engaging in any immoral sexual act.
12. Persons engaging in unskilled or skilled labor unless approved by the secretary of labor.
13. Anyone likely to become public charges.
14. Previously deported aliens.
15. Stowaways.
16. Any alien misrepresenting facts.
17. Any alien without a visa.
18. Aliens ineligible for citizenship.
19. Persons engaging in illicit trade.
20. Citizens of selected countries.
21. Persons who cannot read some language.
22. Any person who may engage in activities prejudicial to the United States.
23. Anarchists or Communist Party personnel who advocate the destruction of the U.S. government.

This title specified that a valid visa was required for admittance to the United States. Each alien was registered at the time the visa was received. The visa had a specified date. An alien could be detained at the port of entry to check whether there was any reason he or she should not be admitted.

### Deportation

According to this title, any alien could be exported by the attorney general when the alien

1. Was excluded by U.S. law.
2. Entered the United States without inspection.
3. Was institutionalized at public expense.
4. Was convicted of a crime.
5. Failed to comply with the nation's laws.
6. Was a member of the Communist Party, was an anarchist, or attempted to overthrow the U.S. government.
7. Carried an illegal weapon.
8. Interfered with the function of the government.

### General Regulations

Title II also provided information on registration of aliens, general penalty provisions, and miscellaneous information.

### Title III, Nationality and Naturalization

#### Nationals and Citizens of the United States at Birth

According to Title III, nationals and citizens of the United States include

1. Persons born in the United States.
2. Indians, Eskimos, and Aleutians.
3. Persons born outside the United States but of U.S. parents.
4. Persons born in a possession of the United States.

#### Nationality through Nationalization

According to Title III, the following qualifications are necessary for a person to be nationalized:

1. The person must be able to speak and read English.
2. The person must have a fundamental knowledge and understanding of history and the principles and form of government of the United States.

Title III specifies that no person should be naturalized who

1. Wants to overthrow the U.S. government.
2. Advocates the economic, international, and governmental doctrines of world communism.

This title also provides regulations for residence, temporary absence for persons performing religious duties, married persons, children born in foreign countries, former citizens of the United States, adopted children of U.S. citizens, U.S. citizens who lose their citizenship because of serving in the armed forces of another country, naturalization through service in the armed forces of the United States, alien enemies, petitions for naturalization court hearings, certificates of naturalization, fiscal provisions, and loss of nationality.

## Immigration and Nationality Act of 1965

The Immigration and Nationality Act of 1965 amended the Immigration Act of 1924. It clarified some of the provisions of the 1924 act, especially the restrictive provisions of the national origin quota systems, which were discontinued. It made the following specifications:

1. It specified that the number of visas was not to exceed 45,000 in each of the first three quarters of any fiscal year and was not to exceed a total of 170,000 in any fiscal year.
2. During the period from July 1, 1965, through June 30, 1968, the annual quotas of any quota area were be the same as those that existed for the same areas on June 30, 1965.
3. Quota numbers not used in a specific year were to be transferred to an immigration pool scheduled to terminate on June 30, 1968.
4. No person could receive any preference as priority or be discriminated against in the issuance of an immigrant visa because of his or her race, sex, nationality, place of birth, or place of residence, except as provided by law.
5. Each independent country, self-governing dominion mandated territory, and United Nations trusteeship was to be treated as a separate foreign nation.

The 1965 act specified that visas were to be allotted as follows:

1. Visas were to be first made available in a number not to exceed 20 percent of the number specified to qualified immigrants who were the unmarried sons and daughters of citizens of the United States.
2. Visas were made available, in a number not to exceed 20 percent, to qualified immigrants who were the spouses or unmarried sons or daughters of an alien lawfully admitted for permanent residence.
3. Visas, not to exceed 10 percent, were to be given to professional individuals who, because of their exceptional ability in the sciences or the arts, would substantially benefit the United States.
4. Visas, not to exceed 10 percent, were to be issued to married sons or daughters of U.S. citizens.
5. Visas, not exceeding 24 percent of the total, were to be given to the brothers or sisters of U.S. citizens.
6. Visas, not to exceed 10 percent, were to be given to qualified immigrants who were capable of performing specified skilled or unskilled labor, not of a temporary or

seasonal nature, for which a shortage of employable and willing persons existed in the United States.

7. Additional entries were to be made available by the U.S. attorney general to persons who were facing persecution, were from communist areas, or were from the general area of the Middle East.

## Special Immigrants

The Immigration and Nationality Act of 1965 defined special immigrants as follows:

1. An immigrant who was born in any independent foreign country of the Western hemisphere or Canal Zone, including spouses and children.
2. An immigrant lawfully admitted for permanent residence who was returning from a temporary visit abroad.
3. An immigrant who was once a citizen of the United States.
4. An immigrant who wants to immigrate to the United States to carry on the vocation of minister of a religious denomination.
5. An immigrant who was an employee of the U.S. government.

## Admittance to the United States

The act refused admittance to the United States in the following cases (unless the attorney general decided otherwise):

1. No immigrant could be admitted to the United States if he or she did not have a valid unexpired immigrant visa or if he or she was born after such a visa was issued to the accompanying parent.
2. No immigrant could be admitted who could not present a valid unexpired passport or other suitable travel document.
3. For aliens seeking to enter the United States for the purpose of performing skilled or unskilled labor, the secretary of labor, secretary of state, and the attorney general had to certify that there are not enough workers already in the United States who were able or qualified workers and were available at the time of application for a visa and admission to the United States. In addition, these officials had to certify that the employment of aliens

would not affect the wages and working conditions of U.S. workers. (This restriction did not apply to special immigrants.)

### Select Commission on Western Hemisphere Immigration

The 1965 act established the Select Commission on Western Hemisphere Immigration to study the following matters:

1. Prevailing and projected demographic, technological, and economic trends, as they pertained to the Western hemisphere.
2. The interrelationship between immigration, present and future, and existing and contemplated national and international programs.
3. Effect of immigration on unemployment in the United States by occupation, industry, geographic area, and other factors in relation to immigrants from the Western hemisphere.
4. The operation of the immigration laws of the United States as they pertained to the Western-hemisphere nations, with an emphasis on Cuban refugees.
5. The implications of list items 1 through 4 with respect to the security and international relations of Western-hemisphere nations.
6. Any other matters that the commission regarded as important.

## Immigration Reform and Control Act of 1986

(November 6, 1986, Public Law 99-603, 100 Statute 3359)

The Immigration Reform and Control Act of 1986 amends the basic Immigration and Nationality Act of 1952 in order to improve control of aliens in the United States. It is developed under seven titles.

### Title I, Control of Illegal Immigration

#### Part A, Employment

According to Part A of Title I, employment of illegal aliens is unlawful when

1. An employer knows the person is an unauthorized alien.
2. An unauthorized person obtains employment through a contract, subcontract, or exchange.

Part A includes authorization of appropriations and an immigration emergency fund. The enforcement procedures include prohibiting unlawful transportation of aliens in the United States, specifications of the liability of owners and operators of transportation facilities to prevent unauthorized admittance of aliens, and restricting illegal entry in the case of outdoor agricultural operation.

Part A also specifies that it is an unfair immigration-related employment practice for a person to discriminate against an individual with respect to the hiring, recruitment, or employment referral for a fee of that individual because of

1. An individual's national origin.
2. An individual's citizenship.

### Part B, Improvement of Enforcement and Services

In Part B, Improvement of Enforcement and Services, Congress recognizes that the two major essential elements of the program of immigration control established in this act are

1. An increase in the border patrol and other inspection and enforcement activities of the Immigration and Naturalization Service and other appropriate federal agencies in order to prevent and deter the illegal entry of aliens into the United States.
2. An increase in examinations and other service activities of the Immigration and Naturalization Service in order to ensure prompt and efficient adjudication of petitions and applications.

Part B also specifies penalties for the unlawful transportation of aliens in the United States. The penalty may be a fine and/or imprisonment for not more than five years. Finally, Part B establishes an Immigration Emergency Fund to provide for an increase in the border patrol and for reimbursement of states and localities in providing assistance as requested by the attorney general to meet immigration emergencies.

### Title II, Legalization

Title II gave the attorney general the responsibility to change the status of an illegal alien to that of an alien lawfully admitted for temporary residence. This change was to occur in the following circumstances:

1. The alien established that he or she entered the United States before January 1, 1982, and had resided continuously in the United States in an unlawful status since then.
2. An alien entered the United States as a nonimmigrant before January 1, 1982. The alien had to establish that his or her permit as a nonimmigrant expired before that date through the passage of time or that the alien's unlawful status was known to the government as of that date.
3. If the alien was at any time a nonmigrant exchange alien, the alien had to establish that he or she was not subject to the two-year foreign residence requirement, had fulfilled that requirement, or had received a waiver of the requirement.

In order for the alien to be admissible to the United States, he or she has to be

1. Admissible to the United States as an immigrant who has not been convicted of any felony or of three or more misdemeanors committed in the United States.
2. Has not assisted in the persecution of any person on account of race, religion, nationality, membership in a particular social group, or political opinion.
3. Registered under the Military Selective Service Act.

Under Title II, for the purposes of applying the prohibitions against age discrimination under the Age Discrimination Act of 1970, the following regulation applies:

1. No person shall on the grounds of sex or religion be excluded from participation in, be denied the benefits, or be subjected to discrimination under any program or activity which is funded by the United States.

## Title III, Reform of Legal Immigration

Title III establishes regulations and control of immigrant agricultural workers by the Department of Labor and Department of Agriculture. The conditions under which such workers may be admitted to the United States include the following:

1. There are not sufficient workers who are able, willing, and qualified and will be available at the time and place needed to perform the labor and service required.

2. The employment of aliens in such labor and services will not adversely affect the wages and working conditions of U.S. workers similarly employed.

## *Title IV, Reports to Congress*

According to Title IV, the president must provide Congress with a comprehensive report every three years on the impact of immigration. This report must include

1. The number of foreign workers permitted to be employed under the program each year.
2. The compliance of employers and foreign workers with the terms and conditions of the programs.
3. The impact of the program on the labor needs of U.S. agricultural employers and on the wages and working conditions of U.S. agricultural workers.
4. Recommendations for modifying the program, including
   a. Improving the timeliness of decisions regarding admission of temporary foreign workers under the program.
   b. Removing any economic disincentives to hiring U.S. citizens or permanent resident aliens for jobs for which temporary foreign workers have been requested.
   c. Improving cooperation among government agencies, employers, employees, associations, workers, and other worker associations to end the dependence of any industry on a constant supply of temporary foreign workers
   d. The relative benefits to domestic workers and burdens upon employers of a policy that requires employers, as a condition for certification under the program, to continue to accept qualified U.S. workers.

The initial report to Congress had to describe the alien population in terms of

1. Geographical origins and manner of entry of aliens into the United States.
2. The demographic characteristics of those aliens.
3. A general profile and characteristics of the aliens.

Later reports are to discuss the following:

1. Impact of the program on the states and local government and on public health and medical needs of individuals in the different regions of the United States.
2. Patterns of employment of the legalized population.
3. Participation of legalized aliens in social service programs.

## Title V, State Assistance for Incarceration Costs of Illegal Aliens and Certain Cuban Nationals

Under Title V, the attorney general provides reimbursement to states for illegal aliens convicted of a felony who are in the United States unlawfully and either (1) whose recent entry into the United States was without inspection or (2) whose recent admission to the United States was as a nonimmigrant. States may also be granted assistance to pay for incarcerating a Cuban who was part of the Mariel boatlift and was convicted of a felony in the United States.

## Title VI, Commission for the Study of International Migration and Cooperative Economic Development

Title VI set up a commission to consult with the government of Mexico and other countries in the Western hemisphere who contributed to unauthorized immigration to the United States. The title called for the development of mutually beneficial, reciprocal trade and investment programs to alleviate these conditions. In accordance with Title VI, the commission was terminated after its initial report.

## Title VII, Federal Responsibility for Deportable and Excludable Aliens Convicted of Crimes

According to Title VII, the attorney general may deport any alien as quickly as possible when the alien is convicted of a crime.

# Immigration Technical Corrections Act of 1988

(October 24, 1988, Public Law 100-525, 102 Statute 2609)

Revised 1991.

The Immigration Technical Corrections Act of 1988 amends the Immigration and Nationality Act to make technical corrections in the immigration-related laws.

# Immigration Amendment of 1988
(November 15, 1988, Public Law 100-658, 102 Statute 3908)

The Immigration Amendment Act of 1988 extended for two years section 314 of the Immigration Reform and Control Act of 1986 to make additional visas available to immigrants from underrepresented countries, in order to enhance diversity of immigration. It also extended through December 31, 1989, nonimmigrant status for certain registered nurses. In both 1990 and 1991, the amendment made 10,000 visas available to qualified immigrants who were natives of underrepresented countries.

# Immigration Act of 1990
(November 29, 1990, Public Law 101-649, 104 Statute 4978)

Revised 1991.

The Immigration Act of 1990 amends the 1986 legislation and establishes present-day immigration regulations. It is the most comprehensive revision of the nation's immigration laws since the enactment of the Immigration and Nationality Act of 1952, which established the basic modern laws. The 1990 act makes significant changes to virtually every part of the 1952 statute and adds a number of new provisions. These changes include restructuring the immigrant selection system; revising a number of existing nonimmigrant categories and adding several new ones; revising and reorganizing the grounds for exclusion and deportation; tightening deportation procedures for all aliens and instituting tougher procedures for criminal aliens; replacing existing naturalization procedures; and creating new procedures for the protection of aliens fleeing civil unrest in their own countries. The act includes eight titles.

## Title I, Immigrants
Title I, defines aliens born in a foreign state or dependent areas who may be issued immigrant visas. These aliens include the following:

1. Family-sponsored immigrants. These persons include the unmarried sons and daughters of U.S. citizens and the spouses, unmarried sons, and unmarried daughters of an alien lawfully admitted to the United States for permanent residence. The number of visas is not to exceed 226,000; plus the qualified immigrants who are

the brothers and sisters of citizens of the United States, if such citizens are 21 years old.

2. Employed-based immigrants. Visas for employed-based immigrants, in order of preference, are allocated to: aliens with extraordinary ability, outstanding professors and researchers, certain multinational executives and managers, aliens of other exceptional abilities, skilled workers and other workers, and special immigrants with qualified specialties. The number of visas for this group is set at 120,000. There is also a group of special immigrants that includes those immigrants seeking entry to the United States for the purpose of engaging in a recent commercial enterprise.

3. Diversity immigrants. The attorney general shall determine the diversity of immigrants for the most recent five fiscal years for which data are available.

The attorney general determination is based on

a. Available estimates for each region and the total population of each region, not including the population of any high-admission state.

b. For each low-admission state, the ratio of the population of each region to the total population.

c. For each high-admission region, the ratio of the population of the region to the total population.

A commission was established in 1991 to review and evaluate the impact of the act and its amendments. Particular consideration is to be given to

1. Requirements of the citizens of the United States and of aliens lawfully admitted for permanent residence.

2. The impact of immigration on employment based on labor needs, type of employment, and other economic and domestic conditions in the United States.

3. The social, demographic, and natural resources impact of immigration.

4. The impact of immigration on foreign policy and national service interests of the United States.

5. The impact of the admission of nonimmigrants.

Under Title I, the immigrant selection system has been thoroughly revamped. Annual numerical ceilings have for the first time been placed on virtually all types of immigration. These ceilings insert an overall cap on family-sponsored immigrants, including immediate family members of U.S. citizens. The cap may rise in the future, however, but if the numbers of immediate family members increase, distant family-sponsored immigrants would be reduced.

### Title II, Nonimmigrants

Title II, provides information as to how nonimmigrants, including tourists and personnel from foreign vessels, can enter the United States. Personnel from vessels may secure temporary work in port cities. Penalties are imposed on illegal activities.

### Title III, Family Unity and Temporary Protected Status

The attorney general has the responsibility to see that a legal alien may not be deported or otherwise required to leave the United States. The legal alien may have temporary protected status for a specified period of time. During this period, the alien may be employed in the United States. He or she will need a local authorization with a specified time limitation.

The title provided special temporary protected status for Salvadoreans for 18 months beginning January 1, 1991.

### Title IV, Naturalization

Title IV, confers the sole authority to naturalize persons as citizens of the United States upon the attorney general and his or her representatives. An applicant may choose to have the oath of allegiance administered by the attorney general or by any district court of the United States located in any state or by any court of record in any state having a seal as clerk and jurisdiction in law or equity. A person whose application for naturalization is denied after a hearing before an immigration officer may seek a review before a U.S. district court and a decision will be determined.

### Title V, Enforcement

This title makes important changes to deportation procedures aimed at making certain that deportable aliens appear at hearings, permitting in absentia hearings if they fail to appear, penalizing attorneys for appeals deemed dilatory, and limiting the timing of instances in which forms of relief from deportation can be sought.

This title provides special regulations that are provided for the enforcement of the Immigration Act of 1990. These regulations specify

1. Criminal aliens.
2. Employer sanctions.
3. Types of illegal disrimination.

Beginning in 1991, the act authorized an appropriation for an increase of 1,000 persons in the border patrols of the Immigration and Naturalization Service.

In terms of substantive changes, the health-related and security-related grounds for exclusion are what were most drastically revised from the Immigration Act of 1906 to the Immigration Act of 1990. The latter act places an emphasis on narrowing the groups of aliens who can be excluded. The criminal-related grounds have been broadened, however, including the principal goals of restricting and removing from the United States aliens involved in criminal activity. The changes for deportation, enacted March 1, 1991, parallel in most respects the changes to controlling the grounds for exclusion.

## Title VI, Exclusion and Deportation

The law also provides a list of factors that are grounds for excluding aliens who wish to enter the United States. The following aliens may be excluded:

1. Persons who have a health-related disease of a physical or mental nature that may pose or has posed a threat to the personal safety or welfare of others.
2. Persons convicted of certain crimes, including violations of any laws or regulations of the United States or a state; persons who have a municipal criminal conviction; persons involved in moral turpitude, prostitution and commercialized vice, or terrorist activities; and members of a totalitarian party.
3. Laborers. Any alien laborer who seeks to enter the United States is excludable, unless the secretary of labor has determined and certified the following to the secretary of state and the attorney general:
   a. At the time of application for a visa and admission to the United States, there are not already sufficient workers at the appropriate place in the United

States who are able, willing, qualified, and available
to perform such skilled or unskilled labor.
b. The employment of such aliens will not adversely
affect the wages and working conditions of workers
similarly employed in the United States.
4. Previously deported aliens who
a. Had been arrested and deported.
b. Had fallen into distress and had been deported.
c. Had been removed as an alien enemy.
d. Had misrepresented a material fact.
e. Had been convicted of a crime.

### Title VII, Miscellaneous Provisions

Title VII specifies that the attorney general shall, by regulation,
establish measures to protect the confidentiality of information
concerning any abused alien spouse or child, including the location of the spouse or child.

### Title VIII, Education and Training

According to Title VIII, the secretary of labor is required to provide for grants to states to provide educational assistance and
training for legal aliens. Allocation of these funds takes into
account

1. The location of foreign workers admitted to the United
States.
2. The locations of individuals in the United States requiring and deserving educational assistance and training.
3. The locations of the employed and underemployed.

# Naturalization

## Naturalization Act of 1790

(March 26, 1790, Chapter 3, Statute 103)

Revised 1795, 1798, 1802, 1804, 1824, 1870, and 1906.

This law stated

Any alien, being a free white person, who shall have
resided within the limits and under the jurisdiction of
the United States for a time of two years, may be
admitted to become a citizen thereof, on application

to any common law court of record, in any one of the states whenever he shall have resided for a time of one year at least, and making proof to the satisfaction of the court, that he is a person of good character, and taking the oath of affirmation prescribed by law, to support the constitution of the United States, which oath or affirmation such court administers; and the clerk of such court shall record, each application and the proceedings thereon, and thereupon such person shall be considered as a citizen of the United States. And the children of such persons so naturalized, dwelling within the United States, being under the age of twenty one years at the time of such naturalization, shall also be considered as citizens of the United States. And the children of citizens of the United States may be beyond the sea, and out of the limits of the United States, shall be considered as natural born citizens: *Provided,* that the right of citizenship shall not descend to persons whose fathers who have never been residents of the United States. *Provided also,* that no person heretofore proscribed by any state, shall be admitted a citizen as aforesaid, except by an act of the legislation of the state in which such person was proscribed.

## Nationality Act of 1940

(October 14, 1940, Chapter 876, 54 Statute 1137)

Revised 1941, 1942, 1943, 1944, 1945, 1946, 1947, 1948, 1949, and 1950.

The Nationality Act of 1940 codifies the nationality laws of the United States into a comprehensive nationality code.

### Nationality at Birth

According to this law, the following are nationals and citizens of the United States at birth:

1. A person born in the United States.
2. A person born outside the United States who has at least one parent who is a U.S citizen.
3. A person born in an outlying possession of the United States who resides in the United States.
4. A child of unknown parentage found in the United States.

### Nationality through Naturalization
A person may currently petition for naturalization in any state court having naturalization jurisdiction.

No person can become a citizen

1. Who admits that he or she is a member of a political party that advocates opposition to all organized government.
2. Who writes, publishes, or causes to be written and distributes any material in opposition to the established government.
3. Who is a member of any organization that wants to overthrow the government.

This act gives general instructions concerning the nationalization process for former citizens, nationals who are not citizens, and persons misinformed of procedures.

### Loss of Nationality
According to this act, a person may lose his or her nationality by

1. Obtaining nationality in a foreign state.
2. Taking an oath of allegiance to a foreign state.
3. Serving in the armed forces of a foreign state.
4. Performing duties of a foreign government.
5. Voting in a political election of a foreign state.
6. Deserting the military of the United States.
7. Committing an act of treason.
8. Expatriating oneself (if one is a national).
9. Residing outside the United States.
10. Receiving money from a foreign government.

# Refugees

## Displaced Persons Act of 1948
(June 25, 1948, Chapter 647, 62 Statute 1009)

Revised 1950, 1951, and 1952.

The Displaced Persons Act defined an *eligible displaced person* as anyone who between September 1, 1938, and January 1, 1948, was (1) located in Germany, Austria, or Italy and had been a victim of persecution by the Nazi government and (2) was detained in or also was obliged to flee from persecution and was subsequently returned to one of these countries as a result of enemy action or of war circumstances.

These persons were

1. Qualified under the immigration laws of the United States for admission for permanent residence.
2. Given assistance by the Immigration Commission for Displaced Persons so that they could be employed without displacing some other person from employment or becoming a public charge.

The act also provided that any alien who had entered the United States prior to April 1, 1948, who was

1. A displaced person
2. Admissible under immigration laws

could become a citizen automatically.

### Quota System

This act extended the terms of the 1924 Immigration Act. The quota system set up by the 1924 act prevailed except with respect to contract laborers from Mexico, who were admitted to perform menial agricultural jobs, and new special preference provisions. These special preferences applied to the following eligible displaced persons:

1. Those who had been previously engaged in agricultural pursuits and who would be employed in the United States in agricultural pursuits. No less than 30 percent of the special preference visas were to be issued to these persons, including family members.
2. Those who were (a) household, construction, clothing, and garment workers and other workers needed in the locality of the United States in which such persons proposed to reside, or (b) eligible persons possessing special educational, scientific, technological, or professional qualifications.
3. Those who were the blood relatives of citizens or lawfully admitted aliens residing in the United States.
4. Those who during World War II bore arms against the enemies of the United States and could no longer return to the country to which they were nationals because of persecution or fear of persecution due to race, religion, or political opinion.

### Investigation

This act specified that "no eligible person will be granted a visa without a thorough investigation by U.S. agencies of his character, history, or eligibility. Further no visa will be granted to any person who has engaged in activities that are hostile to the U.S. or its form of government."

# Refugee Relief Act of 1953

(August 7, 1953, Chapter 336, 67 Statute 400)

Revised 1954.

The Refugee Relief Act of 1953 provided nonquota visas for persons who were refugees, escapees, and German expelees. *Refugee* was defined as follows:

> any person in a country or area which is neither Communist nor Communist dominated, who because of persecution, fear of persecution, natural calamity, or military operations is out of his usual place of abode and unable to return thereto, who has not been firmly resettled, and who is in urgent need of assistance for the essentials of life or for transportation

*Escapee* was defined as follows:

> any refugee who, because of persecution or fear of persecution on account of race, religion, or political opinion, fled from the Union of Soviet Socialist Republics or other Communist occupied areas of Europe including those parts of Germany under military occupation by the Union of Soviet Socialist Republics and who cannot return thereto because of fear of persecution on account of race, religion, or political opinion.

*German expelee* was defined as follows:

> any refugee of German ethnic origin residing in the area of the German Federal Republic, western sector of Berlin, or in Austria who was born in and was forcibly removed from or forced to flee from Albania, Bulgaria, Czechoslovakia, Estonia, Hungary, Latvia, Lithuania, Poland, Rumania, Union of Soviet Socialist Republics, Yugoslavia, or areas provisionally under the administration or control or domination of any

such countries, except the Soviet zone of military occupation of Germany. The total allocations of special visas were not to exceed

1. 55,000 visas to German expelees.
2. 35,000 visas to escapees residing in the area of the German Federal Republic, western section of Berlin, and Austria.
3. 10,000 visas for escapees residing within the European continental limits of the member nations of the North Atlantic Treaty Organization or in Turkey, Sweden, Iran, or the Free Territory of Trieste.
4. 2,000 visas to refugees who during World War II were members of the armed forces of Poland.
5. 45,000 visas to refugees of Italian ethnic origin residing in Italy or the Free Territory of Trieste.
6. 15,000 visas to other persons of Italian ethnic origin residing in Italy or the Free Territory of Trieste.
7. 15,000 visas to refugees of Greek ethnic origin residing in Greece.
8. 2,000 visas to other persons of Greek ethnic origin residing in Greece.
9. 15,000 visas to refugees of Dutch ethnic origin residing in continental Netherlands.
10. 2,000 visas to other persons of Dutch ethnic origin residing in continental Netherlands.
11. 2,000 visas to refugees residing within the district of a U.S. consular office in the Far East who were not indigenous to the area.
12. 3,000 visas to refugees residing within the district of a U.S. consular office in the Far East who were indigenous to the area.
13. 2,000 visas to refugees of Chinese ethnic origin whose passports for travel to the United States were endorsed by the Chinese National Government.
14. 2,000 visas to refugees who were eligible to receive assistance from the United Nations Relief and Works Agency for Palestine Refugees in the Near East.

## Orphans

This act allowed a total of 4,000 special visas to be granted to orphans who were under the age of 10. An eligible orphan was

1. A child whose parents were dead or who had been abandoned.
2. Lawfully adopted by a U.S. citizen.
3. A child who came from an area where the established quotas had been filled.

### Special Considerations

This act also specified a number of special considerations:

1. Adjustment in status. Any alien who entered the United States prior to July 1, 1953, was deemed a bonafide non-immigrant; if events occurred in this person's country to make him or her unable to return because of the risk of persecution, the person was allowed to apply for an American visa.
2. Assurance. No visa was to be issued until assessments could be given by an American citizen that such an alien would be suitably employed without displacing some other person from employment and that the alien and his family would not become public charges and would have housing without displacing some other person from such housing.
3. Intergovernmental arrangements. The Intergovernmental Committee for European Migration was established to oversee the transportation of persons issued visas.
4. Security. No alien could be issued a visa before a thorough investigation by agencies of the U.S. government, which were to investigate the alien's character, reputation, mental and physical health, and eligibility under the act.
5. Ineligible persons. No visa was to be granted to a person who advocated or assisted in the persecution of any person or group because of race, religion, or national origin.
6. Loans. The treasury was directed to make loans, not to exceed $5 million, to public or private agencies of the United States for the purpose of financing the transportation of immigrants to the United States.

## Migration and Refugee Assistance Act of 1962

(June 28, 1962, Public Law 87-510, 76 Statute 121)

Revised 1964, 1975, 1980, 1985, and 1990.

The purpose of the Migration and Refugee Assistance Act of 1962 was to assist in the movement of refugees and migrants by coordinating the number of immigrants.

The appropriations specified under this act are to

1. Contribute to the activities of the United Nations High Commission for Refugees.
2. Assist the refugees when the president determines that such assistance will contribute to the defense of the United States.
3. Assist refugees who have fled from nations out of fear of persecution concerning race, religion, political opinion, and other conditions.
4. Be used to transport refugees.
5. Establish projects for employment or refresh professional training of refugees.

## Refugee Education Assistance Act of 1980
(Public Law 96-422, Act. 100, 1980, 94 Statute 1999)

### Title I
The Refugee Education Assistance Act of 1980 deals with aliens who have fled from Cuba or Haiti on or after November 1, 1979, and Indochina after 1982 and have been admitted into the United States as aliens by the attorney general, or are applicants for asylum.

### Title II, General Assistance for Local Educational Agencies
Under Title II, the secretary of state was provided funds during 1981, 1982, and 1983 to aid state educational agencies for the purpose of providing basic education to these refugee children.

### Title III, Special Impact Assistance for Substantial Increase in Refugees
Title III provided funds to help ease the impact of increasing numbers of refugees entering the United States. The funds were used to provide the following:

1. English language instruction.
2. Other bilingual educational services.
3. Special materials and supplies.
4. Additional basic instructional services.
5. Special in-service training such as short courses.

In order to obtain funds, each state had to submit an application that

1. Outlined the educational programs, services, and activities for which the funds would be used.
2. Guaranteed that payment would be used specifically for refugee children's training.
3. Indicated how local agencies would use the funds.
4. Provided reports of results.

### Title IV, Adult Education Programs
This title specified funding for adult education programs for refugees. Specifically, the funds were to be used for

1. Programs for instructing adult refugees in basic reading and mathematics, to develop and enhance their necessary skills and to promote literacy.
2. Administration costs.
3. Educational support services.
4. Special projects to develop occupational and related skills for individuals.

## Refugee Act of 1980
(March 17, 1980, Public Law 96-212, 94 Statute 102)
Amended by Refugee Assistance Amendments of 1982 and Refugee Assistance Exclusion Act of 1986.

The Refugee Act of 1980 amends the Immigration and Nationality Act of 1952 and the Migration and Refugee Assistance Act of 1962 in order to establish a more uniform basis for providing assistance to refugees.

### Title I, Purpose
Title I declares that historically it has been policy of the United States to respond to the urgent needs of persons subject to persecution in their homelands, including humanitarian assistance for the care and maintenance of those persons in asylum areas; efforts to provide opportunities for resettlement or voluntary repatriation, as well as necessary transportation and processing; admission of refugees of special humanitarian concern to the United States; and transitional assistance to refugees in the United States. This title further declares that it is the policy of the United States to encourage all nations to provide assistance and resettlement opportunities to refugees to the fullest extent possible.

This title declares that the objectives of this act are to provide permanent and systematic procedures for the admission to the United States of refugees of special humanitarian concern to the United States and to provide comprehensive and uniform provisions for the effective resettlement and absorption of these refugees in the United States.

## Title II, Admission of Refugees

Title II provides general regulations on admission, including numerical limitations, emergency conditions, spouse or child admission, reports to congressional committees, asylum procedures, and deportation.

## Title III, United States Coordinator for Refugee Affairs and Assistance for Effective Resettlement of Refugees in the United States

Title III requires the president to appoint a coordinator for refugee affairs whose responsibilities are as follows:

1. To develop an overall U.S. refugee admission and resettlement policy.
2. To coordinate all U.S. domestic and international refugee admission and resettlement programs in a manner to ensure that the policy is timely.
3. To design an overall budget strategy.
4. To present to Congress the administration's overall refugee policy and the relationship of individual agency refugee budgets to the overall policy.
5. To advise the president and other governmental officials.
6. To advise foreign governments of U.S. refugee policy under the direction of the secretary of state.
7. To develop an effective liaison between the federal government and voluntary organizations.
8. To make recommendations to the president on policy decisions.
9. To review regulations, guidelines, and requirements.
10. To consult regularly with states, localities, and private institutions.

## Title IV, Miscellaneous and Refugee Assistance

Under Title IV, the Office of Refugee Assistance is established in the Department of Health and Human Services. This title considers authorization for programs for domestic resettlement and assistance, education, medical assistance, temporary care, legal and financial responsibilities, child welfare services, English training, congressional reports, and social services.

## Special Legislation

### Migrant Health Act of 1962
(September 25, 1962, Public Law 87-692, 76 Statute 592)

Revised 1965, 1968, 1970, 1973, 1974, and 1975.

The Migrant Health Act of 1962 amends Title III of the Public Health Service Act to authorize grants for family clinics for domestic agricultural migratory workers. The funds are to be used

1. To pay the costs of providing classes.
2. For special projects to improve health services and the health conditions of domestic agricultural migratory workers and their families.

### Migrant and Community Health Centers Amendment of 1978
(November 10, 1978, Public Law 95-626 Title 1, pt. A 101 to 107, 92 Statutes 3551 to 3562)

The Migrant and Community Health Centers Amendment of 1978 amends the Public Health Service Act and related health laws to service and extend the programs of financial assistance for the delivery of health services, the provision of preventive health services, and other purposes.

The major changes include the following:

1. The amount of a grant to a health center may be increased when expenses are greater than expected.
2. A grant may be used for improvements to private property in order to eliminate health hazards on the property.
3. A grant may be given to health agencies to plan and develop health service.
4. A center may charge fees, premiums, and third-party reimbursement for its operation.
5. Grants may be made to provide technical assistance such as medical equipment.

# Migrant and Seasonal Agricultural Workers Protection Act

(January 14, 1983, Public Law 97-470, 96 Statute 2583)

Revised 1985 and 1992.

The purposes of the Migrant and Seasonal Agricultural Workers Protection Act are

1. To remove the restraints on commerce caused by activities detrimental to migrant and seasonal agricultural workers.
2. To require farm labor contractors to register under the act's terms.
3. To ensure necessary protections for migrant and seasonal agricultural workers, agricultural associates, and agricultural employees.

## Title I, Farm Labor Contractors

According to Title I, a farm labor contractor shall not hire, employ, or use any individual to perform farm labor unless that individual has a certificate of registration. The farm labor contractor is held responsible for violations of this provision. This certificate provides information on the laborer's place of residence, the facilities and property used to house migrants, the laborer's fingerprints, and a declaration sworn to by the applicant. A certificate of registration may be revoked if the applicant

1. Has misrepresented facts on the certificate.
2. Is not the real party in the application for a certificate.
3. Has failed to pay court costs.
4. Has committed a crime or felony.

A certificate cannot be transferred.

In addition, no farm labor contractors may knowingly recruit, hire, employ, or use the services of any individual who is an illegal alien.

## Title II, Migrant Agricultural Workers Protection

In accordance with Title II, each farm contractor must maintain the following records of the workers recruited:

1. Place of employment.
2. Wage rates to be paid.

3. The crops and kinds of activities for which the worker is to be employed.
4. Period of employment.
5. Transportation, housing, and other employee benefits.
6. Existence of any strikes or work stoppages.
7. Existence of any other agreements between contractor and worker.

### Title III, Seasonal Agricultural Worker Protection

Title III dictates that the same type of reporting for migrant agricultural workers is required for seasonal workers.

### Title IV, Further Protection for Migrants and Seasonal Agricultural Workers

Title IV applies specifically to transportation of any migrant or seasonal agricultural worker. Farm labor contractors must register the following information concerning vehicles used to transport agricultural workers:

1. Type of vehicle.
2. Passenger capacity.
3. Distances workers will be transported.
4. Types of roads and highways.
5. What conditions would cause a hardship for the workers.

## Immigration Nursing Relief Act of 1989

(December 18, 1989, Public Law 101-238, 103 Statute 2099)

Revised 1990 and 1991.

The Immigration Nursing Relief Act of 1989 amends the Immigration and Nationality Act to provide for adjustments to regulations, with no numerical limitations, for certain nonimmigrant nurses. It also establishes conditions for the admission of such nurses during a five-year period as temporary workers.

Nurses seeking entry into the United States as nonimmigrants under this act must meet the following qualifications:

1. They must have obtained a full unrestricted license to provide professional nursing for a program in a facility in the United States.
2. They must have passed appropriate examinations.
3. They must be fully qualified under a U.S. license to engage in professional nursing.

# Immigration Marriage Fraud Amendment of 1986

(November 10, 1986, Public Law 99-639, 100 Statute 3537)

Revised 1988.

The purpose of the Immigration Marriage Fraud Amendment of 1986 is to deter immigration-related marriage fraud and other immigration fraud.

## Title I, Regulations

The regulations specify how aliens can obtain permanent residence status by marriage. The requirements specify the following:

1. That the attorney general shall provide to a spouse, son, or daughter the provisions of residence in the United States.
2. That a proper marriage is one that
   a. Was entered into in accordance with the laws of the place where this marriage took place.
   b. Has not been judicially annulled or terminated, other than through the death of the spouse.
   c. Was not entered into for the purpose of procuring an alien's entry as an immigrant.

Two essential elements in enforcement are

1. An increase in the border patrol and other inspection and enforcement activities of the Immigration and Naturalization Service.
2. An increase in examination and other service activities of the Immigration and Naturalization Service in order to ensure prompt and efficient adjudication of petitions and applications provided for under the Immigration and Nationality Act.

## Title II, Legalization

Title II provides the legal interpretation of the enforcement of this law. Particularly important are the sections on temporary resident status, termination of temporary residence, description of aliens qualified to receive an application to marry, reasons for grounds for exclusion, and temporary disqualification of newly legalized aliens from receiving certain public welfare assistance or state legalization impact assistance grants.

### Title III, Reform of Legal Immigration

Title III elaborates on the immigration of temporary agricultural workers. The attorney general and secretary of labor can admit agricultural workers if

1. There are not sufficient workers who are able, willing, and qualified and can be available at the time and place when needed to perform necessary agricultural services.
2. The employment of the alien in such labor or services will not adversely affect the wages or working conditions of workers.

A labor certificate may be denied if

1. There is a strike or lockout in the course of a labor dispute that precludes such certification.
2. An employer during the past two years has violated a request for certification.
3. An employer has not supplied the secretary of labor with satisfactory assurance that employment is not covered by the State Workers Compensation Law.
4. The secretary of labor determines that the employer has not made positive recruitment efforts for domestic workers.

Other legislation includes special rules for consideration of applications, lawful residence for certain special agricultural workers, and changes in the quotas and visas available to immigrants.

# Directory of Organizations 4

The organizations discussed in this chapter are topically placed into four categories. The first category considers the basic topic of general immigration. The second and third categories cover migration and migrant workers. The fourth category covers refugees. Many private organizations have been organized to aid a particular movement of people. Many organizations are established to treat a specific problem and are then terminated.

## Immigration

### Governmental Organizations*

**Executive Office for Immigration Review**
Department of Justice
Falls Church, VA 22041

*Description:* The attorney general is responsible for the administration and enforcement of the Immigration and Nationality Act of 1952 and all laws pertaining to the immigration and naturalization of aliens.

* All coded references in this and the following sections refer to: United States Code Service. *Aliens and Nationality*, Title 8, Sections 1–1557. Published by Lawyers Co-operative Publishing Co., 1995.

The attorney general has delegated some of his of her power and duties to the Executive Office for Immigration Review, which is independent of the Immigration and Naturalization Service. The Executive Office for Immigration Review includes the Board of Immigration Appeals, the Office of the Chief Immigration Judge, and the Office of the Chief Administrative Hearing Officer. It operates under the supervision of the associate attorney general and is headed by a director who acts as a supervisor.

*Purpose:* To work toward solving immigration problems.

### Board of Immigration Appeals

The Board of Immigration Appeals is a quasi-judicial body, including a chair, four members, and a chief attorney examiner who is an alternate board member. The board hears oral argument in Falls Church, Virginia. The board has a staff of attorney-advisors who help make decisions. The board hears appeals of decisions made by district and center directors of the Immigration and Naturalization Service and by immigration judges. The board is also responsible for hearing appeals regarding the barring from practice of attorneys and representatives before the Immigration and Naturalization Service and the Board of Immigration Appeals. All decisions of the board are binding unless overruled by the attorney general and are then subject to judicial review in federal court. Most appeals deal with deportation and request for relief from deportation. Other cases before the board include exclusion of aliens who want to be admitted to the United States, clarification of status of alien relatives for granting immigrant visas, fines imposed on carriers for violating immigration laws, and motions to reopen and reconsider decisions made previously.

When an appeal is made by the immigration judge, a record of the proceedings is given to the board, which reviews the questions raised, and the attorney-adviser drafts a proposed order for the board members to consider. Attorney-advisers also assist in administrative functions and analyze questions of constitutional, state, federal, and foreign civil and criminal law.

### Office of the Chief Immigration Judge

The Office of the Chief Immigration Judge supervises and directs immigration judges in performing their duties. It establishes policies for the offices of the immigration judges and evaluates the performance of those offices. This office is located in Falls Church, Virginia, and has a headquarters staff of management and legal personnel.

The immigration judges preside at formal quasi-judicial deportation and exclusion proceedings. The immigration judges work independently and their decisions are final unless appealed or certified to the Board of Immigration Appeals. In deportation cases, the judge decides if the person who has already entered the United States is deportable. In these cases, the judge considers applications for relief under the immigration laws. These include applications for change in status, suspension, or deportation; leaving voluntarily; relief under Section 212(c) of the Immigration and Nationality Act of 1952 (8 U.S.C. 1182); and applications for asylum and not being deported.

In exclusion proceedings the immigration judge decides whether a person arriving from a foreign country should be either allowed to enter the United States or deported. Immigration judges are located throughout the United States and consider various forms of relief available in exclusion proceedings, such as application for asylum and relief under section 243(h) of the Immigration and Nationality Act of 1952 (8 U.S.C. 1158, 1253).

### Office of the Chief Administrative Hearing Officer

The Office of the Chief Administrative Hearing Officer supervises the administrative law judges in performing their duties under 8 U.S.C. 1324a–1324c. Administrative law judge proceedings are required by the Immigration and Nationality Act concerning unlawful employment of aliens, immigration document fraud, and unfair immigration employment discrimination.

### Immigration and Naturalization Service
425 I Street, NW
Washington, DC 20536

*Description:* Founded by Congress on March 3, 1891 (8 U.S.C. 1551 note). Its responsibilities were also specified by the Immigration and Nationality Act, as amended (8 U.S.C. 1101 note), which makes the attorney general responsible for the administration and enforcement of its provisions. The attorney general in turn gives authority to the commissioner of the Immigration and Naturalization Service to see the provisions of the immigration law are enforced. Executive direction comes from Washington, D.C. There are 3 regional offices, 33 district offices, and 21 border control posts in the United States. Three district offices are maintained in Bangkok, Thailand; Mexico City, Mexico; and Rome, Italy.

*Purpose:* To see that immigration and naturalization provisions are carried out.

*Activities:* Facilitates entry of people who are legal immigrants or visitors to the United States. Prevents unlawful entry or employment. Provides assistance to those seeking asylum, naturalization, or temporary or permanent residence in the United States as stipulated in the Immigration and Naturalization Act. Apprehends and removes aliens who enter or remain illegally in the United States. It also is committed to strengthening criminal investigations and seeking effective deterrents to illegal immigration.

**Immigration and Naturalization Service User Fee Advisory Committee**
Office of the Assistant Commissioner, Inspections
Immigration and Naturalization Service
Chester Arthur Building
Room 7123
425 I Street, NW
Washington, DC 20536

*Description:* This is a public advisory committee of the Immigration and Naturalization Service, Department of Justice. The Program Analyst, Office of the Assistant Commissioner, Inspection serves as staff contact.

**Immigration Nursing Relief Advisory Committee (INRAC)**
Office of the Assistant Secretary for Policy
Department of Labor
Room S-2114
200 Constitution Avenue, NW
Washington, DC 20210

*Description:* Committee was established January 30, 1991, under the authority of Public Law 101-238, Immigration Nursing Relief Act of 1989. It is a public advisory committee of the Office of Assistant Secretary, Department of Labor. There are 18 members selected by the secretary of labor; they serve for two years. Members represent the Department of Health and Human

Services, the Office of the Attorney General, hospitals, labor organizations representing registered nurses, and other organizations. The committee meets twice a year and the chair can call a special meeting. Support staff is provided by the Office of the Assistant Secretary for Policy.

*Purpose:* To advise on the need for foreign nurses in the United States.

*Activities:* Advises secretary of labor on how effective the Immigration Nursing Relief Act of 1989 is and changes that are needed. Examines impact of new legislation on nursing shortage in the United States. Studies effects of legislation on demand for foreign nurses. Gives advice on the nursing shortage. Has programs that medical institutions hold to recruit and retain nurses, both U.S. citizens and immigrants, who are qualified to perform nursing services. Advises on extension of provisions of the Immigration Relief Act beyond its mandated five-year period.

**International Development Association (IDA)**
1818 H Street, NW
Washington, DC 20433

*Description:* The International Development Association started September 24, 1960, as an affiliate of the International Bank for Reconstruction and Development (IBRD).

*Purpose:* To promote economic development in underdeveloped areas.

*Activities:* The International Development Association operates through subscriptions and funds from more industrialized and developed members. Rich members make contributions. Repayments on earlier credits and transfers from its net earnings are also ways IDA is funded.

The IDA finances developmental requirements on concessionary terms that bear less heavily on the balance of payments than regular loans. In this way, IDA promotes economic development and raises the standard of living in less developed areas and at the same time furthers the objectives of IBRD. In 1993 IDA made new commitments of $6,751 million in the poorest countries in sub-Saharan Africa and Asia.

**International Organization for Migration (IOM)**
P.O. Box 71
CH 1211, Geneva, 19 Switzerland

1750 K Street, NW
Suite 1110
Washington, DC 20006

1123 Broadway
Room 717
New York, NY 10010

*Description:* This nonpolitical and technical organization has three addresses. The International Organization for Migration, formerly the Intergovernmental Committee for Migration (ICM), was created in 1951 at a conference in Brussels sponsored by Belgium and the United States. The organization has a membership of 42 countries, and 40 countries act as observers. Sixty countries, including some nonmember countries, have operational offices.

*Purpose:* To plan and operate refugee resettlement, relief programs, and national immigration.

*Activities:* Processes the movement of refugees to countries, giving them resettlement opportunities. Promotes immigration to satisfy the needs of the countries of departure and destination. Transfers technology through immigration to promote economic, educational, and social advancement, especially in Latin America and Africa. Holds forums to discuss views and experiences to promote cooperation and coordination on immigration issues.

**Office of Immigration Litigation**
Department of Justice
Tenth Street and Pennsylvania Avenue, NW
Washington, DC 20530

*Activities:* This office is in the Department of Justice and conducts civil litigation against employees of the Immigration and Naturalization Service under the Immigration and Nationality Act (8 U.S.C. 1101). It also represents the United States in civil litigation. It takes care of district court litigation, deportation, and habeas corpus review proceedings, as well as immigration appellate matters. The office is responsible for cases related to issuing visas and passports. It is also responsible for litigation arising under the amnesty and employer sanctions provisions of the Immigration Reform and Control Act of 1986 (8 U.S.C. 1255a, 1324a) and 1990 immigration reforms.

## Office of Refugee Settlement
Administration for Children and Families
Department of Health and Human Services
370 L'Enfant Promenade, SW
Washington, DC 20447

*Description:* This office is a part of the Department of Health and Human Services.

*Purpose:* To help refugees resettle.

*Activities:* Through the assistant secretary for children and families it keeps the secretary of the Department of Health and Human Services informed regarding refugee resettlement, legalized aliens, and repatriation matters. The office plans, develops, and directs a comprehensive program for domestic refugee and entrant resettlement issues. It provides direction and technical guidance to the nation's administration of programs such as Refugee and Entrant Resettlement, State Legislation Impact Assistance Grants, and the U.S. Repatriate Program.

## Office of Special Counsel for Immigration Related Unfair Employment Practices
P.O. Box 27728
Washington, DC 20038

*Description:* The Office of Special Counsel for Immigration Related Unfair Employment Practices was established pursuant to section 102 of the Immigration Reform and Control Act of 1986 (8 U.S.C. 1324b).

*Purpose:* To investigate and prosecute charges of discrimination based on national origin and citizenship status in hiring, recruiting, or firing.

*Activities:* Files complaints before an administrative law judge based on charges filed with the special counsel. Appeals of administrative decisions are made to the U.S. Court of Appeals. Has jurisdiction over national charges not covered by the Equal Employment Opportunity Commission. The Special Counsel coordinates with the Immigration and Naturalization Service, the Equal Employment Opportunity Commission, and other federal agencies to promote public awareness of the antidiscrimination provisions of the act through public and employer conferences, public service announcements, and distribution of enforcement information nationally.

## Private Organizations

**American Civic Association (ACA)**
131 Front Street
Binghamton, NY 13905

*Description:* Founded 1939. Has 2,000 members and 6 staff. Holds annual meeting—always in Binghamton, New York.

*Purpose:* To help foreign-born persons.

*Activities:* Established by naturalized citizens and helps foreign-born people faced with problems because of foreign birth. Encourages these persons to become U.S. citizens and use schools to learn the language. Provides a common ground for new Americans to enter into life of the community. Helps foreign-born people make contributions to benefit their new country.

*Publications: American Civic Association Newsletter,* monthly.

**American Council on International Personnel (ACIP)**
510 Madison Avenue
New York, NY 10022

*Description:* Founded 1971. Has 250 members. Holds annual meeting.

*Purpose:* To work on immigration issues.

*Activities:* Corporations and organizations work together to serve the business community regarding matters involving immigration. Disseminates information on immigration practices and laws. Sponsors symposia and conferences to help keep personnel managers and counsel of international companies aware of immigration policies.

*Publications: ACIP Newsletter,* bimonthly. Publishes *Immigration Handbook: Employment of Foreign Nationals.*

**American Immigration Control Foundation (AICF)**
Box 525
Main Street
Monterey, VA 24465

*Description:* Founded 1983. Has 150,000 members and 6 staff. Has $2 million budget. Holds a periodic conference.

*Purpose:* To educate Americans and leaders about the need for control over immigration and problems caused by illegal immigration.

*Activities:* Seeks to control immigration and resolve the crisis caused by illegal immigration practices. Conducts research projects on immigration policies and issues. Maintains 2,000-volume library. Conducts seminars.

*Publications: Border Watch,* monthly; *Newsletter;* books, research findings, and monographs; issues videotapes.

**American Immigration Lawyers Association (AILA)**
1400 Eye Street, NW
Suite 1200
Washington, DC 20005

*Description:* Founded 1946. Has 3,700 members and 34 local groups. Holds annual conference (with exhibits—usually June). Also holds regional meeting and conference 6–10 times per year. Members are lawyers specializing in immigration and nationality law.

*Purpose:* To see that immigration laws are upheld.

*Activities:* Fosters and promotes overseeing of justice with respect to the immigration and nationality laws of the United States. Sponsors immigration litigation workshops. Bestows awards. Holds seminars.

*Publications: AILA Membership Directory,* annual; *AILA Monthly Mailing, Immigration and Nationality Law Handbook,* annual.

**Americans for Immigration Control (AIC)**
717 2nd Street, NE
Suite 307
Washington, DC 20002

*Description:* Founded 1982. Has $8,000 budget.

*Purpose:* To improve effectiveness of border controls.

*Activities:* Lobbies for increase in the budget of the U.S. Immigration and Naturalization Service. Advocates making border patrols more effective and using military force if necessary to help border patrols. Favors no amnesty for illegal immigrants in the United States. Favors sanctions against those who knowingly hire illegal immigrants.

**Association of Immigration Attorneys (AIA)**
291 Broadway
Suite 1000
New York, NY 10007

*Description:* Founded 1983. Has 50 members. Holds monthly dinner meeting. Members are lawyers.

*Purpose:* To help aliens with their legal rights.

*Activities:* Its 50 lawyers specialize in immigration law to provide legal aid to aliens in the United States. Lobbies Congress on behalf of aliens. Initiates legislation to strengthen and clarify the legal position of aliens in the United States.

**Caribbean Action Lobby (CAL)**
c/o Dr. Waldaba Stewart
391 Eastern Parkway
Brooklyn, NY 11216

*Description:* Founded 1980. Has 4,000 members. Holds semi-annual conference with exhibits. Includes Caribbeans, Caribbean Americans, and anyone interested in Caribbean issues.

*Purpose:* To assist Caribbean immigrants as problems arise.

*Activities:* Educates Caribbean immigrants on U.S. immigration laws, U.S. government, and voting. Tries to make elected officials aware of the needs and problems affecting the Caribbean immigrant. Lobbies. Holds workshops and seminars.

*Publications: Newsletter,* monthly.

**Center for Immigrants Rights (CIR)**
48 St. Marks Place
4th Floor
New York, NY 10003

*Description:* Founded 1981. Has 1,100 members and 7 staff. Has $330,000 budget. Holds periodic meetings.

*Purpose:* To help immigrants know their rights.

*Activities:* Provides paralegal training and educational programs concerning immigration law for church, community, and labor organizations. Tries to influence public policy. Works in employer discrimination against immigrants. Offers training programs, clinics, workshops, and seminars on labor rights concerning immigrants. Conducts community outreach. Maintains speakers' bureau. Has several committees, divisions, and special programs.

**Emerald Isle Immigration Center (EIIC)**
5926 Woodside Avenue
Woodside, NY 11377

*Description:* Founded 1987. Has 25 state groups and 6 local groups. Includes Irish immigrants and U.S. citizens of Irish descent. Holds a meeting every 2 or 3 months; also holds monthly council meeting—always New York City.

*Purpose:* To improve conditions for Irish immigrants.

*Activities:* Secures amnesty for illegal Irish immigrants in United States. Obtains quota of nonpreference visas from U.S. government for Irish immigrants and also immigrants from other European countries. Lobbies Congress for favorable legislation. Maintains speakers' bureau. Compiles statistics.

*Publications: News Bulletin,* monthly.

**Emergency Committee to Suspend Immigration (ECSI)**
P.O. Box 1211
Marietta, GA 30061

*Description:* Founded 1989. Has 1,300 members and 2 staff.

*Purpose:* To work to stop problem immigrants from coming to the United States.

*Activities:* Publicizes problems created by non-European immigrants (legal and illegal). Feels that drug problems are caused primarily by non-European immigrants. Hopes to have all non-European immigration outlawed until United States has better control of its borders. ECSI favors increased European immigration to the United States.

**Ethiopian Community Mutual Assistance Association (ECMAA)**
c/o Fetone Hailu
554 West 114th Street
Suite 2R
New York, NY 10025

*Description:* Founded 1981. Has 500 members. Holds annual meeting—always summers in New York City. Members live primarily in New York City area.

*Purpose:* To assist new Ethiopian immigrants and those already living in New York City.

*Activities:* Helps Ethiopians already here and looks out for their economic well-being. Hopes to preserve Ethiopian culture. Promotes understanding between Ethiopians and non-Ethiopians. Operates refugee assistance project for refugees and migrants regarding education, health, job placement, and guidance in general. Conducts a community-wide education and information program to hasten Ethiopians' social adjustment in the United States. Maintains museum. Hopes to establish emergency aid funds, cultural center, job bank data, and referral system. Has several committees.

**Federation for American Immigration Reform (FAIR)**
1666 Connecticut Avenue, NW
Suite 400
Washington, DC 20009

*Description:* Founded 1979. Has 45,000 members and 15 staff. Has one state group. Holds annual meeting; also holds seminars and regional meetings.

*Purpose:* To seek to improve present immigration policies.

*Activities:* Works to reform present immigration policies to conform with present-day environmental, demographic, and labor-force policies. Promotes laws against illegal immigration. Advocates establishing a stable ceiling for all legal immigration, including refugees. Favors prohibiting employment of illegal immigrants and enforcing U.S. border controls. Promotes recording visitors and guests in the United States to prevent visa abuses and excluding illegal residents from census figures used for reapportionment of Congress. Encourages diplomatic and economic efforts to help leaders in other countries deal with overpopulation and underdevelopment that leads to immigration pressure. Hopes to develop better information on immigration for public and government use. Maintains book and videocassette library dealing with immigration, labor economics, population, and government.

*Publications: FAIR Immigration Report,* periodic; *Newsletter; FAIR Information Exchange,* bimonthly; *FAIR Papers* (monograph series) and brochures.

**Hebrew Immigrant Aid Society (HIAS)**
333 7th Avenue
New York, NY 10001-5004

*Description:* Founded 1880. Has 8,000 members and 150 staff. Holds annual meeting, usually during spring in New York City. Also holds quarterly board meeting and annual dinner.

*Purpose:* To be of assistance to Jewish refugees and migrants.

*Activities:* Helps Jewish migrants and refugees from Europe, North Africa, the Middle East, and other areas to resettle in United States, Canada, Latin America, and Australia. Has offices and committees around the world to help locate friends and relatives. Prepares documents. Arranges for transportation. Provides resettlement and reception services. Assists Indo-Chinese, Afghan, and Ethiopian refugees as requested by the U.S. government. Bestows awards. Presents scholarships. Maintains speakers' bureau and biographical and photo archives. Compiles statistics. Has many committees, departments, and divisions.

*Publications: Annual Report; Headlines and Highlights,* monthly.

**Immigrant Genealogical Society (Genealogy) (IGS)**
P.O. Box 7369
Burbank, CA 91510-7369

*Description:* Founded 1982. Has 575 members. Holds monthly meeting. Also holds annual seminar, usually in October.

*Purpose:* To help people trace their foreign ancestry.

*Activities:* Provides research services. Includes people who wish to trace their foreign ancestors, especially from German-speaking areas of Europe. Does searches of German genealogical bibliographies, telephone directories, and *FamilienKundliche Nachrichten,* a German genealogical publication. Answers mail-order inquiries from individuals who are tracing their ancestral origins. Conducts classes, workshops, and seminars. Maintains library of German immigrant sources, including passenger lists.

*Publications: German American Genealogy,* semiannual; *Immigrant Genealogical Society Newsletter,* monthly; *1993 Updated Postal Codes to German Repositories.*

**Immigration History Society (IHS)**
c/o Roger Daniels
Department of History
University of Cincinnati
Cincinnati, OH 45221

*Description:* Founded 1965. Has 830 members. Budget is less than $25,000. Holds monthly meetings. Members are interested in immigration to the United States and Canada.

*Purpose:* To study immigration-related problems.

*Activities:* Serves a means of communication for economists, sociologists, historians, and others doing research on immigration. Disseminates information on current research projects and publications. Bestows the Theodore Saloutos Memorial Book Award in Immigration History.

*Publications: Immigration History Newsletter,* semiannual; *Journal of American Ethnic History,* semiannual.

**National Immigration Forum (NIF)**
220 Eye Street, N.E.
Suite 220
Washington, DC 20002

*Description:* Founded 1982. Has 200 members and 8 staff. Holds periodic regional meeting.

*Purpose:* To defend the rights of U.S. newcomers.

*Activities:* Coalition helps immigrants get settled in communities. Serves as a link between local and national organizations. Investigates policies on immigration, refugee, and citizenship issues. Conducts research and policy analysis on related topics. Has a reference library.

*Publications: Action Alerts,* 12–15 times a year; *Advocacy Matters,* monthly; *Conference Proceedings,* 1–2 times a year; *EPIC Events,* bimonthly.

**National Immigration Law Center (NILC)**
1636 West 8th Street
Suite 215
Los Angeles, CA 90017

*Description:* Founded 1977. Has 11 staff. Holds periodic conference.

*Purpose:* To improve the rights of immigrants.

*Activities:* Serves as a clearinghouse on immigration and refugee issues for community, church, and other nonprofit organizations. Conducts training and research programs. Seeks federal litigation in the area of immigrants' rights. Acts as advocate for legal rights of immigrants in the United States. Distributes information to advocates concerning immigrants and refugees.

*Publications: Directory of Nonprofit Agencies That Assist Persons in Immigration Matters,* annual; *Legalization Update,* monthly; *Immigrants' Rights Manual;* and *INS Misconduct Manual.*

## National Immigration Project of the National Lawyers Guild (NIP/NLG)
14 Beacon Street
Suite 506
Boston, MA 02108

*Description:* Founded 1973. Has 400 members and 3 staff. There are 6 state groups. Holds annual conference. Members are lawyers, law students, and legal workers.

*Purpose:* To work for improvement in immigration law.

*Activities:* Remains informed of changes in immigration laws. Defends civil liberties of foreign born. Holds immigration law seminars. Collects texts, pamphlets, and manuals on immigration law and problems of foreign-born persons in the United States. Maintains Brief Bank, a library of briefs, memoranda, and immigration law decisions.

*Publications: National Immigration Project Newsletter,* quarterly. Also publishes *Immigration Law and Crime, Immigration Law and Defense,* and *Immigration Act of 1990 Handbook.*

## National Network for Immigrant and Refugee Rights (NNIRR)
310 8th Street
No. 307
Oakland, CA 94607

*Description:* Founded 1986. Members are advocates, supporters, and organizers of immigrant and refugee rights. Holds biannual conference.

*Activities:* Promotes fair immigration policy. Defends immigrant and refugee rights. Coordinates campaigns. Maintains speakers' bureau. Has reference library. Compiles statistics. Has several departments.

*Publications: Network News,* bimonthly.

## Polish American Immigration and Relief Committee (PAIRC)
140 West 22nd Street
New York, NY 10011

*Description:* Founded 1947. Holds annual conference.

*Purpose:* To assist Polish immigrants and refugees.

*Activities:* Counsels Polish immigrants, political refugees, and recent escapees. Helps with resettlement and integration. Provides financial assistance. Serves as liaison between relatives and refugees.

**United States Naturalized Citizen Association (USNCA)**
P.O. Box 19822
Alexandria, VA 22320

*Description:* Founded 1925. Has 450,000 members. Has $250,000 budget. Holds annual meeting.

*Purpose:* To work for welfare of people from Europe, Asia, Africa, and Latin America who become U.S. citizens.

*Activities:* Helps newly naturalized citizens find employment. Promotes their general welfare. Supports homes for aged, hospitals, and schools for handicapped children. Works for adoptions, relief for refugees, and work for minorities. Operates Chinese Acupuncture Advance Research Institute and Employment Training Center. Maintains speakers' bureau and library. Plans to establish a museum and bestow awards. Has many committees and councils.

*Publications: Interdependent Voice,* periodic.

# Migration

## Private Organizations

**American Committee on Italian Migration (ACIM)**
352 West 44th Street
New York, NY 10036

*Description:* Founded 1952. Has 10,000 members. Holds an annual conference.

*Purpose:* To assist Italian immigrants.

*Activities:* Helps Italians coming to the United States deal with immigration laws. Offers them assistance to get resettled and become familiar with ways of living in the United States.

*Publications: ACIM Newsletter* (in English) bimonthly; *La Nuova Via* (in Italian), bimonthly.

**Center for Migration Studies of New York (CMS)**
209 Flagg Place
Staten Island, NY 10304

*Description:* Founded 1964. Budget is $550,000. Holds an annual

Legal Conference on Immigration and Refugee Policy (with exhibits).

*Purpose:* To assist various ethnic groups.

*Activities:* Encourages study of sociological, economic, demographic, historical, etc., aspects of human migration and ethnic groups. Maintains 21,000-volume library and archives on migration, ethnicity, and refugees. Conducts seminars and does research on immigration problems.

*Publications: CMS Newsletter,* semiannual; *International Migration Review,* quarterly; *Migration World Magazine,* bimonthly; *Proceedings of the CMS Annual National Legal Conference on Immigration and Refugee Policy.* Also publishes monographs, bibliographies, occasional papers, and related books.

**International Organization for Migration (IOM)**
1750 K Street, NW
Suite 1110
Washington, DC 20006

*Description:* Founded 1951. Budget is $270,000. Holds annual meeting.

*Purpose:* To help migrants immigrate.

*Activities:* Helps with transportation of migrants who have difficulties resettling. Provides service in processing, language, vocational training, and integration of migrants and refugees. Works with volunteer agencies to help those not eligible under government criteria for migration. Participates in development activities of Latin American and African countries to train skilled individuals so they can return to their countries and foster economic progress. Works toward land settlement programs in Latin America. Helps governments set up technical demonstration programs.

*Publications: International Migration,* quarterly; *IOM News.* Also publishes ad hoc material to inform governments and the public on IOM activities.

**International Social Service, American Branch (ISS/AB)**
95 Madison Avenue
3rd Floor
New York, NY 10016

*Description:* Founded 1924. Has 13 international branches. Budget is $230,000. Holds an annual meeting.

*Purpose:* To help those families that have become separated because of migration.

*Activities:* This is an international social work organization to help families, children, and individuals needing help because their families have been separated because of migration. Gives help in custody and care of children, inter-country adoption and migration. Helps if needed in cases concerning health problems, pensions, and sociolegal problems. Plays advocate role on behalf of children in migration across national boundaries.

**Research Foundation for Jewish Immigration (RFJI)**
570 7th Avenue
3rd Floor
New York, NY 10018

*Description:* Founded 1971. Does not hold a meeting.

*Purpose:* To assist German-speaking immigrants.

*Activities:* Educational foundation helps immigrants with research, writing, and editing the history of immigrants of the Nazi period. Works with the Institut fur Zeitgeschichte in Munich, where there is an archives of 25,000 biographies of important emigres of the Nazi period. Maintains oral history collection on German-Jewish immigrants coming to the United States since 1933. Maintains master file.

*Publications: Jewish Immigrants of the Nazi Period in the U.S.A. (Series); International Biographical Dictionary of Central European Emigres, 1933–1945.*

# Migrant Workers

## Governmental Organizations

National Advisory Council on Migrant Health
Department of Health and Human Services
5600 Fishers Lane
Parklawn Building
Room 7A-55
Rockville, MD 20857

*Description:* Council was established November 28, 1975, by the secretary of health, education, and welfare under the authority of the Special Health Revenue Sharing Act of 1975, Public Law

94-63, which amends the Public Health Service Act. It is a public advisory council of the Health Services Administration, Department of Health and Human Services. The council has 15 members. At least 12 are members of the governing boards of migrant health centers or other entities assisted under Section 329 of the Public Health Service Act. Nine of the 12 are chosen from governing boards familiar with health care or migratory and seasonal agricultural workers. The remaining three are qualified individuals in medical sciences and administration of health programs. Members serve four-year terms. Staff support is provided by the Migrant Health Branch, Bureau of Primary Health Care, Health Services Administration. The council meets at least twice a year, at the request of the chairperson.

*Purpose:* To provide for health welfare of migratory and seasonal agricultural workers.

*Activities:* The secretary of health and human services is authorized under Section 329 of the Public Health Service Act to improve health services for agricultural migrant and seasonal workers and their families. Council provides technical and financial assistance to public and nonprofit organizations in establishing and operating family health service clinics, inpatient care, and other health projects. Council advises and makes recommendations to the secretary of health and human services on matters concerning the organization, selection, operation, and funding of migrant health centers.

*Publications: Annual Report; Minutes of Meetings; Annual Recommendations.*

## Private Organizations

**Association of Farmworkers Opportunity Programs (AFOP)**
1925 North Lynn Street
Suite 701
Arlington, VA 22209

*Description:* Founded 1971. Has 37 members. Budget is $400,000. Holds quarterly conference (with exhibits). Also has periodic worker safety protection workshops and periodic pesticide training workshops.

*Purpose:* To support migrant and seasonal farmworkers.

*Activities:* Represents 48 state organizations that have employment, training, and legislative programs for the workers.

Conducts research. Analyzes federal legislation affecting farm-workers. Provides legal assistance for undocumented individuals under the Immigration Reform and Control Act of 1986. Has speakers' bureau. Compiles statistics. Has consulting service. Bestows awards. Maintains hall of fame.

*Publications: AFOP News,* bimonthly; *Association of Farmworker Opportunity Programs,* annual; *Farmworker Nutrition Education Resource Guide.*

**East Coast Migrant Health Project (ECMHP)**
1234 Massachusetts Avenue, NW
Suite 623
Washington, DC 20005

*Description:* Founded 1970. Holds semiannual board meeting.

*Purpose:* To see that migrant workers have health and social care.

*Activities:* Provides health and social care for migrants and their families. Parahealth professionals in several states provide the services. Helps strengthen migrant workers and their families through health and social education. Provides orientation for staff. Has in-service education, health education, and cultural awareness. Maintains placement service.

**Farm Labor Organizing Committee (FLOC)**
507 South St. Clair Street
Toledo, OH 43602

*Description:* Founded 1967. Has 7,500 members and 13 staff. Budget is $250,000. Holds triennial meeting—held one in 1994. Members are Hispanic migrant farmworkers from Texas or Florida and work in Ohio, Michigan, and Indiana.

*Purpose:* To help Hispanic farmworkers organize unions.

*Activities:* Helps Hispanic farmworkers organize into labor unions. Concentrates efforts in the Hispanic community of northwest Ohio. Organized farmworker boycott of Campbell Soup Company, Camden, New Jersey, because canners refused to negotiate with farmworkers. Has contracts with Campbell and Vlasic Food Company, Camden, New Jersey, covering 1,800 cucumber and tomato harvesters in Ohio and Michigan. Recent contract eliminates independent contractors and considers farm-workers as employees.

*Publications: Dignidad,* periodic.

**Farmworker Justice Fund (FJF)**
2001 S Street, NW
Suite 210
Washington, DC 20009

*Description:* Founded 1981. Has four staff. Holds quarterly board meeting. Attorneys and others taking part in federal and state legislation and judicial advocacy on behalf of the migrant and seasonal farmworkers and their families make up the group.

*Purpose:* To help migrant farmworkers with legal problems.

*Activities:* Aims to improve health, sanitary, and working conditions. Works for improved wages, occupational safety, and housing. Wants better education for farmworkers' children and encourages them to finish high school. Cooperates with farm labor unions and other organizations to help migrant farmworkers. Conducts research.

*Publications: Newsletter,* quarterly. Also publishes books, monographs, and materials on the problems of the agricultural workers.

**Interstate Migrant Education Council (IMEC)**
707 17th Street
Suite 2700
Denver, CO 80202-3427

*Description:* Founded 1976. Has 55 members and 3 staff. Has 17 state groups. Holds periodic forum.

*Purpose:* To meet educational needs of migrant workers.

*Activities:* Education commission of various states works toward education needs of migrant students by coordinating with U.S. government, business, and educational leaders. Discusses problems faced by migrant youth. Recognizes problems and helps solve them. Serves as liaison among education, health, agriculture and labor organizations. Provides U.S. Congress with data and recommendations. Conducts research. Maintains library. Holds workshops and seminars. Disseminates information obtained from research.

*Publications: Annual Report; Directory,* periodic; *Issugram,* periodic; *News Report,* quarterly; *Proceedings,* three times a year; *Migrant Education;* and *Consolidated View.*

**Migrant Dropout Reconnection Program (MDRP)**
c/o Robert Lynch
BOCES Geneseo Migrant Center
Holcomb Building, Room 210
Geneseo, NY 14454

*Description:* Founded 1983. Has 10,000 members and 3 staff. Has 33 state groups. Has no meeting.

*Purpose:* To help educate migrant farmworkers.

*Activities:* Works to have migrant farmworker youth enroll in educational and vocational programs. Disseminates information on health, financial aid, education, and career services to youth. Offers scholarships through the Gloria and Joseph Mattera National Scholarship Fund for migrant children. Provides placement services. Maintains 5,000-volume library. Compiles statistics. This is a program for the BOCES Geneseo Migrant Center.

**Migrant Legal Action Program (MILAP)**
2001 S. Street, NW
Suite 310
Washington, DC 20009

*Description:* Founded 1970. Has 12 staff. Not a membership organization. Budget is $737,085. Holds board meetings four times a year.

*Purpose:* To help migrant workers as needed.

*Activities:* Provides legal assistance to migrant workers. Assists them on such issues as working conditions, education, minimum wage, health hazards, and occupational safety. Provides administrative and legislative monitoring. Assists local lawyers on representation. Maintains 5,000-volume library.

*Publications: Field Memo,* biweekly.

**National Association of State Directors of Migrant Education (NASDME)**
c/o Dr. Richard Bove
Migrant Unit
State Education Department
883 Education Department Annex
Albany, NY 12234

*Description:* Founded 1975. Has 50 members. Budget is less than $25,000. Holds annual conference (with exhibits). State directors of migrant education programs are members. Funded under Chapter 1 of the Education Consolidation and Improvement Act.

*Purpose:* To keep people informed regarding migrant education.

*Activities:* Keeps members informed and establishes policy. Fosters interstate cooperation. Sponsors regional workshops.

*Publications: Chapter I Migrant Education Program State Directors,* annual.

**National Committee on the Education of Migrant Children (of the National Child Labor Committee) (NCEMC)**
1501 Broadway
Room 1111
New York, NY 10036

*Description:* Founded 1963. Holds no meeting. Affiliated with National Child Labor Committee.

*Purpose:* To work toward educating migrants' children.

*Activities:* Has special projects and programs to help educate children of migrant workers.

**National Farm Worker Ministry (NFWM)**
1337 West Ohio Street
Chicago, IL 60622

*Description:* Founded 1971. Holds semiannual meeting.

*Purpose:* To support overall improvement for farmworkers.

*Activities:* Brings together people who work to help farmworkers survive with dignity. Works with and supports United Farm Workers of America and Farm Labor Organizing Committee.

*Publications: NFWM Newsletter,* quarterly.

**National Migrant Resource Program (NMRP)**
1515 Capital of Texas Highway
Suite 220
Austin, TX 78476

*Description:* Founded 1975. Has 12 staff. Holds annual Migrant Health Conference.

*Purpose:* To help protect health of migrant workers.

*Activities:* Aims to provide primary health care to migrant and seasonal farmworkers. Sponsors establishment of a national network of migrant health centers. Provides technical assistance for health development and research. Develops working relationship between agencies serving migrant farmworkers. Disseminates health referral cards (in English and Spanish) to help migrants. Maintains job/resume bank, biographical archives, and library. Has speakers' bureau. Operates placement service. Compiles statistics. Bestows awards.

*Publications: Migrant Health Newsline,* bimonthly; *Migrant Health Referral Directory,* annual. Also publishes *Chronic Care Guidelines, Uniform Formulary on Chronic Medication,* resource books, catalogs, and medical referral directories. Also makes available health care video programs.

**National Migrant Workers Council (NMWC)**
Lourdes Building
4th Floor
6131 Outer Drive
Detroit, MI 48235

*Description:* Founded 1969. Has 280 members and 1 staff. Budget is $40,000. Holds annual meeting.

*Purpose:* To help migrant worker families in various ways.

*Activities:* Provides and oversees provision of health education and social services for migratory families. Sponsors East Coast Migrant Health Project and Midwest Migrant Health Information Office. Maintains small library.

*Publications: Catalyst,* two times a year; *Directory for Migrant Health Services—Midwest Region,* annual; *Membership List,* annual. Also publishes *Health for the Nation's Harvesters: A History of the Migrant Health Program in Its Economic and Social Setting* and brochures and pamphlets on migrant health needs.

**United Farm Workers of America (UFW)**
P.O. Box 62—La Paz
Keene, CA 93531

*Description:* Founded 1962. Has 100,000 members. Budget is $5 million. Holds triennial meeting—met in 1994.

*Purpose:* To work for rights of farmworkers.

*Activities:* Seeks collective bargaining rights for U.S. farmworkers. Helps them have pride and dignity in their work by improving working and safety conditions and wages. Trains workers in skills needed in the field. Promotes nonviolence. Archives of the union are kept at Wayne State University Labor Archives.

# Refugees

## Governmental Organizations

**Bureau of Refugee Programs**
2201 C Street, NW
Washington, DC 20005

*Description:* This bureau operates as one of the functional areas of the Department of State. In cooperation with other governments, private and international organizations, the Agency for International Development, the Immigration and Naturalization Service, and the Office of Refugee Resettlement, it is responsible for carrying out refugee programs overseas.

*Purpose:* To work with refugee programs overseas.

*Activities:* Programs include relief and repatriation of refugees. The bureau selects, trains, and processes refugees to be admitted to the United States after consulting with Congress and state and local governments. Programs are carried out through grants to private voluntary agencies and international organizations such as the International Organization for Migration, the United Nations High Commissioner for Refugees, and United Nations Relief.

## Private Organizations

**Afghan Community in America (ACA)**
P.O. Box 311
Flushing, NY 11352

*Description:* Founded 1980. Budget is less than $25,000. No meeting scheduled. Members are people interested in ACA's goals.

*Purpose:* To keep people aware of circumstances in Afghanistan.

*Activities:* Increases awareness of conditions in Afghanistan through press releases and radio and television messages. Provides assistance in employment, housing, and immigration matters. Sponsors weekly radio programs in Pashto and Dari, Afghanistan.

**Afghan Refugee Fund (ARF)**
P.O. Box 176
Los Altos, CA 94023

*Description:* Founded 1983. No meetings scheduled.

*Purpose:* To help refugees from Afghanistan.

*Activities:* Provides medical, vocational, and educational help to refugees. Keeps them informed regarding refugees and conditions in Afghanistan. Raises funds for refugee relief.

*Publications: Brochure,* annual.

**Afghanistan Relief Committee (ARC)**
667 Madison Avenue
18th Floor
New York, NY 10021

*Description:* Founded 1980. Has two staff. Not a membership organization. Holds an annual meeting.

*Purpose:* To assist people from Afghanistan.

*Activities:* Provides charitable, educational, and humanitarian assistance to Afghanistan people. Raises funds and donations for Afghanistan refugees. Keeps public aware of refugee problems.

**Amer Medical Division, American Near East Refugee Aid (ANER)**
1522 K Street, NW
Suite 202
Washington, DC 20005

*Description:* Founded 1948. Has staff of one. Budget is $200,000. Not a membership organization. Holds annual meeting—always September in Washington, D.C.

*Purpose:* To provide medical aid to refugees in the Middle East.

*Activities:* Serves as division of American Near East Refugee Aid. Ships medical aid to Middle East countries.

**American Fund for Czechoslovak Refugees (AFCR)**
1776 Broadway
Suite 2105
New York, NY 10019

*Description:* Founded 1948. Has 19 staff. Has 6 regional groups. Budget is $975,000. No meetings scheduled.

*Purpose:* To help Czechoslovak and communist countries' refugees.

*Activities:* Helps refugees with housing, counseling, and processing for immigration to the United States. Helps refugees from Communist countries such as Uganda and Indochina to get settled. Meets refugees coming to United States and helps them with housing and employment.

**American Near East Refugee Aid (ANERA)**
1522 K Street, NW
Suite 202
Washington, DC 20005

*Description:* Founded 1968. Has 30,000 members and 25 staff. Budget is $4.5 million. No meetings scheduled. Members are people and organizations interested in refugee relief.

*Purpose:* To provide relief to Arab refugees.

*Activities:* Gives help to Palestinian, Lebanese, and other ·refugees from the Arab world. Keeps public aware of the problems faced by Arabs. Sponsors programs to get electricity into rural areas. Sponsors agricultural cooperatives. Sponsors nursing school for young Palestinians. Offers scholarship programs. Provides education for children. Has job-training programs for adults. Provides humanitarian relief for people in Lebanon. Has fund-raising events for refugee relief. Prepares and distributes information regarding the Middle East crisis.

*Publications: ANERA Newsletter,* quarterly; *Annual Report.*

**American Refugee Committee (ARC)**
2344 Nicollet Avenue
Suite 350
Minneapolis, MN 55404

*Description:* Founded 1979. Has 19 staff. Has two state groups and one local group. Budget is $2,895,548. No meetings scheduled.

*Purpose:* To give assistance to refugees.

*Activities:* Provides medical care and training to refugees who fled their homeland because of war, natural disaster, or health crises. Gives medical aid and training to Southeastern Asian refugees seeking asylum in Thailand and to Mozambican refugees in Malawi. Has child survival program and public health project in Pursat Province of Cambodia. Helps refugees adjust to American life. Trains refugees so they will be self-sufficient. Educates refugees in the Western way of life. Offers cross-cultural programs to hospitals and health care institutions so they will be aware of refugee problems. Maintains speakers' bureau.

*Publications: Annual Report; ARC Updates,* three times a year; *Bridges Newsletter,* two times a year.

**Association of Cambodian Survivors of America (ACSA)**
6616 Kerns Road
Falls Church, VA 22042

*Description:* Founded 1981. Has 100 members. No meetings scheduled.

*Purpose:* To provide relief to Cambodian refugees.

*Activities:* Volunteer relief groups help Cambodian refugees in the United States and at the Kampuchean-Thai border. Offers counseling and information referrals.

**Buddhist Council for Refugee Rescue and Resettlement (BCRRR)**
1777 Murchison Drive
Burlingame, CA 94010

*Description:* Founded 1979. Has 27 members and 18 staff. No meetings scheduled. Members are from Buddhist congregations and mutual aid associations.

*Purpose:* To help Indochinese refugees in the United States.

*Activities:* Helps Indochinese refugees resettle in the United States. Has training center for them to learn the English language. Offers employment training and placement service. Has child care when refugees receive training. Also offers medical aid.

*Publications: Buddhist Council Newsletter,* periodic.

**Catholic Relief Services (U.S. Catholic Conference) (CRS-USCC)**
209 W. Fayette Street
Baltimore, MD 21201

*Description:* Founded 1943. Has 1,500 staff. Budget is $246 million. No meetings scheduled.

*Purpose:* To provide overseas relief.

*Activities:* This is a nonpolitical, nonevangelical overseas relief and self-help development agency of the American Catholic Community. Conducts programs in disasters, refugee relief, rehabilitation, social welfare, etc., in 67 countries. Distributes food, clothing, and medicine.

*Publications: Catholic Relief Services (U.S. Catholic Conference) Annual Report; The Wooden Bell,* quarterly.

**Central American Refugee Center (CARECEN)**
3112 Mt. Pleasant Street, NW
Washington, DC 20010

*Description:* Founded 1981. Has 13 members. Budget is $300,000. No meetings scheduled.

*Purpose:* To primarily help undocumented refugees from Central America.

*Activities:* Provides refugees legal assistance concerning immigration and applying for political asylum. Holds seminars on immigration law and international law regarding refugees. Sponsors legal training on emergency immigration, housing, and labor matters for refugee organizers. Operates social service referral program. Sponsors Clinica del Pueblo, a free outpatient clinic for refugees. Offers training program on health. Researches human rights violations in El Salvador. Serves on community committees regarding Hispanic and refugee rights. Presents programs in local schools where refugees are present.

*Publications: CARECEN Speaks* (in English and Spanish), bimonthly. Also publishes short documents and pamphlets on refugees and legal matters.

**Church World Service, Immigration and Refugee Program (Refugees) (CWSIRP)**
475 Riverside Drive
Room 656
New York, NY 10115

*Description:* Founded 1946. No meetings scheduled.

*Purpose:* To help refugees get settled.

*Activities:* Helps refugees from around the world to get established through congregations and offices of participating denominations. Affiliated with the National Council of the

Churches of Christ in the United States. Works to protect refugees seeking to live safely in the United States.

*Publications: Refugee Resettlement Appeal,* periodic.

**El Rescate (ER) ("The Rescue")**
1340 South Bonnie Brae
Los Angeles, CA 90006

*Description:* Founded 1981. Has 22 staff. Budget is $800,000. No meetings scheduled.

*Purpose:* To assist Central American refugees in California.

*Activities:* Provides food, shelter, clothing, and social and legal assistance to refugees from Central America. Investigates problems of human rights and responds to violations. Maintains speakers' bureau.

*Publications: Chronology of Human Rights Violations,* semiannual; *El Rescate Newsletter,* quarterly; *El Salvador-Human Rights Chronology,* monthly. Has also published *Labor under Siege and Counterterrorism in Action; The Jesuit Assassinations;* and *The Writings of Ellacuria Bario and Montes.*

**Ethiopian Community Development Council (ECDC)**
1036 S. Highland Street
Arlington, VA 22204

*Description:* Founded 1983. Not a membership organization. No meetings scheduled.

*Purpose:* To promote personal development of Ethiopians in United States.

*Activities:* Develops cultural, educational, and economic development of the Ethiopian community. Works and encourages friendship between Ethiopian and American communities. Helps Ethiopians become self-sufficient. Encourages them to establish small businesses. Has discussions on Ethiopian problems. Operates Center for Ethiopian Studies. Provides vocational and cultural training and immigration counseling. Offers workshops and seminars. Does research.

*Publications: Assessing the Development Needs of Ethiopian Refugees in the United States.* Also publishes brochures, educational materials, monographs, and proceedings.

**Guatemala Partners**
945 G Street, NW
Washington, DC 20001

*Description:* Founded 1993. Has two staff. Budget is $168,000. Not a membership organization. No meetings scheduled.

*Purpose:* To assist Guatemalans in their country.

*Activities:* Provides funds and personnel to help train people in Guatemala to aid those villagers who need help. Provides farming supplies. Works to keep the United States aware of circumstances in Guatemala. Funds education and leadership training. Maintains library. Formed by merger of PEACE for Guatemala and Guatemala Health Rights Support Project.

*Publications: Annual Report.*

**Haitian Refugee Center (HRC)**
119 N.E. 54th Street
Miami, FL 33137

*Description:* Founded 1974. Has 31 directors. No meetings scheduled.

*Purpose:* To provide services to Haitian aliens.

*Activities:* Gives free legal assistance to indigent Haitian aliens so they know the legal rights of asylum seekers. Tries to keep them from being deported. Publicizes plight of Haitian refugees. Documents U.S. Immigration and Naturalization Service abuses. Represents Haitian refugees in lawsuits because of violations involving political asylum.

*Publications:* Press releases, legal documents, and briefs.

**International Rescue Committee (IRC)**
386 Park Avenue South
10th Floor
New York, NY 10016

*Description:* Founded 1933 by Albert Einstein. Has 500 staff. Not a membership organization. Budget is $44 million. Has a semi-annual board-of-directors meeting, always in New York City. Members are volunteers.

*Purpose:* To assist refugees who need help.

*Activities:* This is a volunteer agency—nonpartisan and nonsectarian—supported by individuals, organizations, foundations, corporations, educational groups, etc. Assists refugees who are victims of famine, war, and persecution based on religion, race, or politics. Has programs in Africa, Asia, Central America, Europe, North America, and the Middle East.

*Publications: International Rescue Committee—Annual Report; Newsletter,* three times a year. Also publishes *Children in Flight* and fact sheet.

**Jesuit Refugee Service/U.S.A. (JRS/USA)**
1424 16th Street, NW
Suite 300
Washington, DC 20036

*Description:* Founded 1983. Not a membership organization. Budget is $65,000. No meetings scheduled.

*Purpose:* To provide worldwide refugee services.

*Activities:* Members of the Jesuit Society or lay members provide direct service to refugees around the world. Sponsors refugees seeking admission to the United States. Works to make known the problems faced by refugees. Disseminates information about refugee-related subjects. Reports on issues affecting refugees including legal and regional activity in the United States and abroad.

*Publications: The Mustard Seed,* quarterly.

**Lutheran Immigration and Refugee Service (Refugees) (LIRS)**
390 Park Avenue, South
New York, NY 10016-8803

*Description:* Founded 1939. Budget is $5,572,200. Has 26 regional groups. Holds an annual conference.

*Purpose:* To work with Lutheran immigrants and refugees.

*Activities:* Trains Lutheran groups in advocacy processes. Recruits and trains Lutheran congregations and community groups to sponsor refugees. Finds foster homes for children. Offers counseling on immigration. Helps Lutherans to form church and community groups.

*Publications: LIRS Bulletin,* periodic. Also publishes *Face to Face: The Ministry of Refugee Resettlement; Seeking Safe Haven: A Congregational Guide to Helping Central American Refugees in the United States;* and papers.

**Mutual Aid Association of the New Polish Immigration (MAANPI)**
4841 Rutherford Street
Chicago, IL 60656

*Description:* Founded 1949. Has 800 members. Members are post–World War II Polish immigrants mainly in the Chicago area. Holds annual meeting—always in February in Chicago.

*Purpose:* To assist Polish immigrants.

*Activities:* Helps with immigration problems. Conducts cultural programs. Has Polish language school for children. Gives charitable aid to members in need. Sponsors classes in English, computer programming, etc. Offers placement service. Maintains 7,000-volume library pertaining to Polish literature.

**National Coalition for Haitian Refugees (NCHR)**
16 E. 42nd Street
3rd Floor
New York, NY 10017

*Description:* Founded 1982. Has 47 members. Budget is $150,000. Members are from several organizations united to provide humane treatment and legal help for Haitians seeking asylum in the United States. No meetings scheduled.

*Purpose:* To help Haitians seeking asylum in the United States.

*Activities:* Seeks to end U.S. Coast Guard interdiction of Haitian boats on the high seas. Educates the public so they understand the social, economic, and political reasons for the Haitians' flight from their country.

*Publications: Haiti Insight,* monthly; *Haiti Insight Dossiers,* five times a year. Also publishes human rights reports and articles.

**Polish American Immigration and Relief Committee (PAIRC)**
140 W. 22nd Street
New York, NY 10011

*Description:* Founded 1947. Holds annual conference.

*Purpose:* To help Polish immigrants.

*Activities:* Cousels Polish immigrants, refugees, and escapees. Assists them with financial aid. Helps them to resettle. Acts as liaison between relatives and refugees.

**Pontifical Mission for Palestine (PMP)**
1011 1st Avenue
New York, NY 10022

*Description:* Founded 1949. Has 40 staff. No meetings scheduled.

*Purpose:* To help people of the Middle East.

*Activities:* Papal agency for humanitarianism assistance. Gives assistance to those facing conflicts in the Middle East regardless of their religious affiliation. Sponsors programs to help provide relief, rehabilitation, and development.

*Publications: Catholic Near East Magazine,* bimonthly. Also publishes *Resource Guide.*

**Rav Tov International Jewish Rescue Organization (Refugees) (RTIJRO)**
500 Bedford Avenue
Brooklyn, NY 11211

*Description:* Founded 1973. Has 40 staff. Holds annual meeting.

*Purpose:* To help refugees who want to come to the United States.

*Activities:* Has international network of offices to help refugees who wish to immigrate to the United States or any Western country. Provides financial assistance until the refugees become self-supporting. Holds domestic assistance programs. Assists with visa applications and housing. Provides moral and religious support. Maintains employment service with job placement and on-the-job training. Offers preschool, kindergarten, elementary school, and adult religious instruction. Conducts training program using English as a second language.

*Publications: Achievement Bulletin,* quarterly.

**Refugee Policy Group (RPG)**
1424 16th Street, NW
Suite 401
Washington, DC 20036

*Description:* Founded 1982. Has ten staff. Budget is $868,000. Holds a periodic meeting and symposium.

*Purpose:* To work to improve refugee programs overall.

*Activities:* Gives more power to those involved in refugee programs to study issues. Helps those people become more aware of refugee issues and their relationship to immigration, human rights, security, etc. Collects, catalogs, and retrieves refugee information. Improves communication between those involved in refugee programs and the public and private sectors. Shares, discusses, and analyzes information in a neutral environment. Holds symposia. Conducts research. Maintains resource center for researchers involved with refugees.

*Publications: RPG Review,* periodic. Also publishes books, research papers, reviews, reports, and other materials.

**Refugee Relief International (RRI)**
P.O. Box 693
Boulder, CO 80306

*Description:* Founded 1982. Has eight members. Budget is less than $25,000. Physicians, nurses, and paramedics who had military experience are members. Holds annual meeting in January in Boulder, Colorado.

*Purpose:* To assist war-torn areas of the world.

*Activities:* Provides medical teams and equipment to war-torn areas.

**Refugee Voices, a Ministry with Uprooted Peoples**
c/o Fr. Frank Moan, S.J.
3041 4th Street, NE
Washington, DC 20017-1102

*Description:* Founded 1987. Has 15,500 members and 5 staff. Budget is $100,000. Holds annual Mickey Leland Award Dinner meeting.

*Purpose:* To give help as needed to refugees.

*Activities:* Campaigns to educate Americans about the troubles of refugees, displaced persons, aliens, etc., so they can be helped. Recognizes contributions of refugees to society. Acts as clearinghouse for groups aiding refugees. Sponsors educational programs. Bestows awards. Has radio program—Refugee Voices.

*Publications: Refugee Voices,* quarterly. Also publishes brochures.

**Refugee Women in Development (Ref WID)**
810 1st Street, NE
Suite 300
Washington, DC 20002

*Description:* Founded 1981. Has 1,200 members and 2 staff. Budget is $200,000. Members are refugee women in the United States. No meetings scheduled.

*Purpose:* To give assistance to refugee women.

*Activities:* Helps refugee women attain social and economic independence and security by helping them with their education. Holds education and research programs and training programs to help them adjust to their environment. Develops leadership programs.

*Publications: Understanding Family Violence Within U.S. Refugee Communities: A Training Manual; The Production and Marketing of Ethnic Handcrafts in the U.S.; Leadership Development Model for Refugee Women: A Replication Guide.*

**Refugees International (RI)**
21 Dupont Creek, NW
Washington, DC 20036

*Description:* Founded 1979. Has 3,000 members and 5 staff. Budget is $275,000. Holds annual briefing meeting.

*Purpose:* To give worldwide assistance to refugees and displaced persons.

*Activities:* Gives worldwide support to displaced persons and refugees. Helps them in their resettlement problems. Operates emergency need program. Assists and supports existing refugee relief programs. Monitors and reports on events regarding refugees. Provides funds, supports refugee families, gives medical service, and requests government support to help refugees around the world. Maintains 500-volume library.

*Publications: RI Action Alert,* monthly; *RI Bulletin,* periodic; *RI Newsletter,* quarterly. Also publishes crisis press releases.

**Southeast Asia Center (SEAC)**
1124-1128 W. Ainslie
Chicago, IL 60640

*Description:* Founded 1979. Has 2,500 members and 20 staff. Budget is $450,000. No meetings scheduled.

*Purpose:* To assist refugees from Indochina.

*Activities:* Works for independence of Indochinese refugees and immigrants and encourages cooperation among all minorities.

Tries to make people realize the difficulties faced by those who do not speak English. Has interpreters to assist refugees in hospitals and government agencies and when needed. Promotes allocating public and private funding. Supports minorities through national and international media. Organizes lobbying and legal action. Offers social services and English classes.

*Publications: New Life News,* quarterly; *Building Bridges,* quarterly.

**Southeast Asia Rescue Foundation (SARF)**
2616 Byron Circle
Tallahassee, FL 32308

*Description:* Founded 1982. Budget is $50,000. Holds a quarterly conference.

*Purpose:* To assist and protect refugees from Southeast Asian countries.

*Activities:* Develops programs in medicine, economics, agriculture, and education for those who would have left Southeast Asia. Performs charitable and humanitarian work. Encourages respect for human rights and freedom of all refugees. Sponsors lectures on Southeast Asian refugee situation. Has audiovisual and educational activities. Maintains 1,000-volume library of books, slides, tapes, and other material. Compiles statistics. Has biographical archives. Bestows awards. Provides children's services.

**Southeast Asia Resource Action Center (SEARAC)**
1628 16th Street, NW
3rd Floor
Washington, DC 20009

*Description:* Founded 1979. Has seven staff. Budget is $500,000. Has 150 local groups. Holds a semiannual conference. A merger of the former Indochina Refugee Action Center and Indochina Resource Action Center.

*Purpose:* To help refugee organizations dealing with Southeast Asian refugees.

*Activities:* Advocates refugee protection and human rights. Acts as clearinghouse for Indochinese refugees. Maintains library of international and domestic refugee documents. Conducts research on their needs. Writes reports on refugee issues such as health, training, and employment. Holds workshops. Offers technical assistance to refugee organizations.

*Publications: The Bridge,* quarterly; *Indochinese Business Directory in the Washington, DC Metropolitan Area,* annual; *Resource Bulletin,* quarterly. Also publishes *A Bibliography of Overseas Vietnamese Periodicals and Newspapers: 1975–1985.*

**Spanish Refugee Aid (SRA)**
122 East 43rd Street
New York, NY 10007

*Description:* Founded 1953. Has 34 members and 3 staff. Budget is $200,000. No meetings scheduled.

*Purpose:* To help Spanish refugees.

*Activities:* This is a part of the International Rescue Committee. Collects and provides funds for old, sick, and needy refugees of the Spanish Civil War. Helps refugees with problems. Sponsors programs for refugees. Helps those hospitalized.

*Publications: Annual Report; Newsletter,* semiannual.

**Tibetan Aid Project (TAP)**
2425 Hillside Avenue
Berkeley, CA 94704

*Description:* Founded 1974. Holds annual prayer meeting for World Peace.

*Purpose:* To assist Tibetan refugees.

*Activities:* Gives help to Tibetan refugees in India, Nepal, Bhutan, and Sikkim. Sponsors Tibetan Pen Friend Program. Sponsors relief for religious and community activities. Holds prayer sessions for world peace. Supports college-level philosophy schools.

*Publications: Refugees of Tibet: From the Roof of the World.* Also plans to distribute a film of Bodh Gaya Styra history.

**U.S. Catholic Conference**
Migration and Refugee Services (Refugees) (MRS)
c/o U.S. Catholic Conference
3211 4th Street, NE
Washington, DC 20017-1194

*Description:* Founded 1920. Budget is $20 million. Holds a periodic conference.

*Purpose:* To help immigrants with their problems.

*Activities:* Program supports regional coordination for resettlement and immigration offices. Helps immigrants find employment. Holds orientation programs for sponsors and refugees. Meets refugees at airport and helps with social security and school registration. Provides housing and training courses. Operates Catholic Legal Immigration Network to help diocesan organizations involved in immigration and nationalism.

*Publications: Legislative Monitor,* periodic; *MRS Annual Review; MRS Resettlement and Immigration Directory,* annual; *Update,* monthly. Also publishes analysis papers.

**United States Committee for Refugees (USCR)**
1717 Massachusetts Avenue, NW
Suite 701
Washington, DC 20036

*Description:* Founded 1958. No meetings scheduled.

*Purpose:* To inform the American people of the plight of refugees with an aim to provide help.

*Activities:* Provides nongovernmental focal point for humanitarian concern to meet the needs of the world refugee situation. Consults with national and international leaders. Maintains liaison with voluntary organizations. Supports UN agencies helping to improve refugee problems. Monitors hearings and legislation of U.S. Congress and policies of U.S. government on refugee affairs. Compiles statistics. Conducts research.

*Publications: Issue Papers,* quarterly; *Refugee Reports,* monthly; *World Refugee Survey,* annual. Also publishes papers on special refugee situations.

**Vietnam Refugee Fund (VRF)**
6433 Nothana Drive
Springfield, VA 22150

*Description:* Founded 1971. No meetings scheduled.

*Purpose:* To help Vietnamese refugees who come to the United States.

*Activities:* Volunteers help Vietnamese refugees settle in the United States. Gives counseling, job information, and placement aid. Has programs to help refugees with language difficulties. Offers legal assistance. Organizes citizenship classes. Has Vietnamese radio programs in Washington, D.C., area. Maintains

3,000-volume library. Offers seminars in the literature, art, and language of Vietnam. Affiliated with National Association for the Education and Advancement of Cambodian, Laotian and Vietnamese Americans.

*Publications:* Pamphlets.

## Organization Sources

*Encyclopedia of Associations,* Vol. 1, *National Organizations of the United States,* Detroit, MI: Gale Research, 1995.

*Encyclopedia of Associations,* Vol. 2, *International Associations,* Detroit, MI: Gale Research, 1995.

*Encyclopedia of Governmental Advisory Organizations, 1996/97,* Detroit, MI: Gale Research, 1995.

*The United States Government Manual, 1995/96,* Washington, D.C.: Government Printing Office, 1995.

# Bibliography

As the immigration of people around the world has increased, the literature on the subject has grown dramatically. Immigration remains an international problem that reflects a number of adverse conditions in the world. Political unrest, wars, and economic uncertainty are among the reasons people leave their traditional homes. The literature on the subject of immigration presents a wide range of viewpoints. The sources in this selected bibliography provide diverse perspectives on one of the great human problems of the twentieth century, with particular emphasis on the United States.

## Reference Sources

Cardasco, Francesco, ed. *Dictionary of American Immigration History.* Metuchen, NJ: Scarecrow Press, 1990, 784 pp.

Casey, Verna. *Border Patrol During the Eighties: A Selected Bibliography.* Public Administration Series, Bibliography no. 2525. Monticello, IL: Vance Bibliographies, 1988, 11 pp.

Emerson, Robert D., and Anita L. Battiste. *U.S. Agriculture and Foreign Workers: An Annotated Bibliography.* Economic Research Service, U.S. Dept. of Agriculture. Springfield, VA: National Technical Information Service, 1988, 112 pp.

Fragomen, Austin T., Jr., and Steven C. Bell. *1990 Immigration Employment Compliance Handbook: The Guide to Employment Authorization, Verification Procedures, INS Investigations, and Fine Proceedings under IRCA.* New York: Clark Boardman Company, 1990, various paging. ISBN 0-87632-729-3.

Fragomen, Austin T., Jr., Alfred J. DelRey, and Steven C. Bell. *1990 Immigration Procedures Handbook (update supplement): A How To Guide for Legal and Business Professionals.* New York: Clark Boardman Company, 1990, various paging, ISBN 0-87632-679-3.

Garwood, Alfred N. *Hispanic Americans: A Statistical Sourcebook.* Boulder, CO: Numbers & Concepts, 1991, 239 pp. ISBN 0-929960-06-8.

Serow, William J., et al., eds. *Handbook on International Migration.* New York and Westport, CT: Greenwood Press, 1990, 385 pp.

Siegel, Martha S., and Laurence A. Canter. *U.S. Immigration Made Easy: An Action Guide.* Tucson, AZ: Chandler Co., 1989, various paging.

———. *U.S. Immigration Made Easy, 1993–1994; The Insiders' Guide.* Scottsdale, AZ: Sheridan Worldwide, Inc., 1993, various paging.

———. *U.S. Immigration Made Easy, 1991–1992: The Insiders' Guide.* Tucson, AZ: Sheridan Chandler Co., 1991, various paging.

———. *The Insiders' Guide to the New U.S. Immigration Act of 1990.* Tucson, AZ: Sheridan Chandler Co., 1990, 44 pp.

Thernstrom, Stephan, ed. *Harvard Encyclopedia of American Ethnic Groups.* Cambridge, MA: Belknap Press of Harvard University, 1980, 1076 pp.

Tysse, G. John. *The New Immigration Law: An Employer's Handbook.* Publication no. 7009. Washington, DC: Chamber of Commerce of the United States, 1987, 60 pp.

Zimmerman, Diana, et al. *A Directory of International Migration: Study Centers, Research Programs and Library Resources.* Bibliographies and Documentation Series. Staten Island, NY: Center for Migration Studies of New York, 1987, 299 pp.

# Books

## General

Alba, Richard D. *Ethnic Identity: The Transformation of White America.* New Haven, CT: Yale University Press, 1990, 374 pp. ISBN 0-300-04737-1.

Data for the book were obtained by surveys of residents of the counties of Albany, Rensselaer, Saratoga, and Schenectady, New York. This volume deals with the transformation of ethnicity among Americans with European backgrounds. The author calls this group European Americans based on ancestry. He discusses how non-European immigrants also try to retain their ethnic identity while at the same time being American. The book has many tables to illustrate statements. Chapters have bibliographical notes. There are several pages of bibliographic information.

Alonso, William, ed. *Population in an Interacting World.* Cambridge, MA: Harvard University Press, 1987, 286 pp. ISBN 0-674-69008-7.

This volume was written by several authors. The project was conceived by a group at the Harvard Center for Population Studies and was supported by a grant from the Dräeger Foundation of the German Federal Republic. The book is divided into two parts. Part one discusses the history and structure of population trends affected by immigration. Part two deals with economics, politics and communities. Immigration trends are discussed. One chapter focuses on refugees searching for a better life. Only a few tables and figures are given. Contributors are listed. Several pages of bibliography for additional reading are found.

Bach, Robert, et al. *Changing Relations: Newcomers and Established Residents in U.S. Communities.* New York: Ford Foundation, 1993, 72 pp. ISBN 0-916584-48-8.

This small volume by the National Board of the Changing Relations Project was written at the State University of New York and given as a report to the Ford Foundation, the board's founder. A national board of scholars organized the research and defined its scope. The study aimed to develop a portrait of the full range of relations between immigrants and native residents and then disseminate the information to a wide audience. The project has produced a 90-minute documentary called

*America Becoming*. The project also published a volume entitled *Structuring Diversity: Ethnographic Perspectives on the New Immigration*. A list of members of the research team is found at the beginning of the book.

Brubaker, William Rogers, ed. *Immigration and the Politics of Citizenship in Europe and North America*. Lantham, MD: University Press of America, 1989, 187 pp. ISBN 0-8191-7428-9.

Essays in this book are the results of an international conference hosted in 1987 by the German Marshall Fund of the United States and held at Coolfont, West Virginia. Six nations—Canada, France, Sweden, West Germany, the United Kingdom, and the United States—were represented by a select group of administrators and policymakers. The essays deal with immigration and citizenship. Each country at the conference had a different viewpoint. Essays in the first part make arguments about the nature and meaning of citizenship and membership, whereas those in the second part give a comparative overview of citizenship and membership policies. The book has a few tables and a list of contributors and conference participants. Bibliographical notes are given for each chapter or essay.

Cornelius, Wayne A., Philip L. Martin, and James F. Hollifield, eds. *Controlling Immigration: A Global Perspective*. San Diego, CA: Center for U.S.-Mexican Studies, University of California, San Diego, 1995, 442 pp. ISBN 0-8047-2498-9.

This volume provides a systematic, comparative study of immigration policy and policy outcomes in nine industrialized democracies. It reports the findings of a three-year multidisciplinary research project originating from the Center for U.S.-Mexican Studies, as well as the findings of 15 leading immigration experts. The book presents two central interrelated hypotheses. The first, the convergence hypothesis, provides data that there is a growing similarity among industrial democracies in terms of policy. The second theory, the gap hypothesis, argues that the gap between the goals of immigration policy (laws, regulations, executive actions) and the results of those policies is wide and growing wider. The book highlights the fundamental economic, social, demographic, and political features of industrial democracies that mitigate against the long-term success of many of the immigration control measures.

Gibson, Margaret A., and John U. Ogbu. *Minority Status and Schooling: A Comparative Study of Immigrant Involuntary Minorities.* Garland Reference Library of Social Science, vol. 618. Reference Books in International Education, vol. 7. New York: Garland, 1991, 407 pp. ISBN 0-8240-3534-8.

This volume discusses problems faced by migrants and minorities in schools. The book is divided into three sections. The first gives the framework for the book, the second presents case studies, and the third part provides a summary and policy to practice. The case studies deal with immigrant minorities. Notes and references are given for each chapter. Finally, there is a list of books for supplementary reading.

Hoskin, Marilyn. *New Immigrants and Democratic Society: Minority Integration in Western Democracies.* New York: Praeger, 1991, 164 pp. ISBN 0-275-94004-7.

This volume deals with the problems created by the surge of immigrants from third world countries to the United States. Even small towns now have cultural fairs and struggle to meet the linguistic and social needs of children of immigrant families. This book looks at how immigrants are accepted in their new surroundings. Chapters 4 and 6 discuss the economic, social, and political dimensions of immigrant acceptance and attitudes. The book has a few tables and several pages of bibliography.

Jacobson, Matthew Frye. *Special Sorrows: The Diasporic Imagination of Irish, Polish, and Jewish Immigrants in the United States.* Cambridge, MA: Harvard University Press, 1995, 321 pp. ISBN 0-674-83185-3.

This book was financed in part by grants from Brown University's Center for International Studies and the Social Sciences Division of the State University of New York at Stony Brook. This scholarly work is divided into two parts. Part one examines the nationalism in Irish, Polish, and Yiddish cultures and traces their daily ideologies in the nineteenth century, as well as the popular culture, religion, and literary life of immigrants. Part two delves into the immigrants' response to their adopted country's wars. The Cuban and Philippine situations are discussed. The book ends showing a link between the political and ethnic issues of immigrants and their offspring. The book has a glossary of names and bibliographical notes for each chapter.

Light, Ivan, and Parminder Bhachu, eds. *Immigration and Entrepreneurship: Culture, Capital, and Ethnic Networks*. New Brunswick, NJ: Transaction Publishers, 1993, 381 pp. ISBN 1-56000-070-8.

This book emerged from a conference held at the University of California, Los Angeles, in April 1990 titled "California Immigrants in World Perspective." The conference included 12 immigration researchers from the United States and 7 from foreign countries, representing anthropology, geography, history, political science, urban planning, and sociology. California receives more immigrants than any other state and finds it difficult to absorb them when they are of different ethnoracial stock than the settled population. There was never much trouble in California until the Los Angeles riot and arson of 1992, but California still needs to manage its immigrant-related responsibilities and challenges better. The book compares immigrant groups and immigration-related issues with the same groups in other parts of the world. Immigrant entrepreneurship is an important theme in the book. Several chapters are devoted to the entrepreneurship of American, Korean, and Asian Indian immigrants. The last chapter is devoted to California's Mexican migrants—the largest single group of migrants in the state. Each chapter has notes and references. There are many tables and figures to illustrate the book. A list of contributors is also given.

Serow, William J., et al., eds. *Handbook on International Migration*. New York and Westport, CT: Greenwood Press, 1990, 385 pp. ISBN 0-383-26117-2.

The expertise of several authors is reflected in this handbook. The chapters provide an overall view of the process of immigration in each individual country. Nineteen different countries are examined by a specialist from the country. For consistency, each author was given an outline to follow in preparing his or her chapter. The chapter dealing with the United States was written by Robert W. Gardner and Leon F. Bouvier; they indicate that the United States is by far the world's leading country of immigration. John F. Kennedy once stated that the United States is "a nation of immigrants." The authors mention the fact that some U.S. residents are leaving to live elsewhere, but the chapter is devoted to immigration into the country. Chapters have many tables and references, with a list of selected references at the end. Information is also given on the editors and contributors.

Wheeler, Thomas C., ed. *The Immigrant Experience: The Anguish of Becoming an American.* New York: Dial Press, 1971, 212 pp. No ISBN.

Many writers of various ethnic backgrounds cooperated to write this book. Writers were English, Irish, Norwegian, Jewish, Chinese, Polish, black, Italian, and Puerto Ricans. All the writers tell the story of their lives as immigrants. The chapters describe how some immigrants to the United States died as a result of being separated from family and customs and the many hardships they faced. The book is very easy reading but quite emotional. No references are given since each chapter presents personal experiences. A list of contributors is found in the back of the book.

## Policy Development

Gibney, Mark, ed. *Open Borders? Closed Societies? The Ethical and Political Issues.* Contributions in Political Science, no. 226. Westport, CT: Greenwood Press, 1988, 199 pp. ISBN 0-313-25578-4.

The United States has faced an immigration problem for many years, especially in terms of illegal aliens crossing the national borders. This book examines the basis for an ethical or moral alien admission policy for Western societies. It discusses the Simpson-Rodino Bill of 1986, which, had it passed, would have given the nation control over its borders and allowed only those aliens who would serve U.S. national interests to be admitted. The book is divided into two parts. Part one discusses immigration questions, and part two is devoted to the admission of refugees. Both the political and moral issues for alien admission policies are examined. Each chapter has notes and a bibliography. There is also a selected bibliography at the end. The last chapter has a few tables. Information about the contributors is included.

Harles, John C. *Politics in the Lifeboat: Immigrants and the American Democratic Order.* Boulder, CO: Westview Press, 1993, 245 pp. ISBN 0-8133-8368-4.

This book studies the ethnic diversity of the United States, providing an analysis of advantages and disadvantages. It presents the case that immigrants to the United States are politically acceptable when they arrive; they are thus Americans when they first set foot on U.S. soil. This book discusses such topics as immigrant enhancement and political stability, immigrants in the theory and practice of U.S. politics, the nature of the U.S. consensus, and immigrants and political participation. Appendix A gives a biographical schedule, and Appendix B explains the details of how the research project was conducted. Chapters have bibliographical notes. A few tables are found in the book. There are several pages of bibliography and a note about the book and author.

Hoskin, Marilyn B. *New Immigrants and Democratic Society: Minority Integration in Western Democracies.* New York: Praeger, 1991, 164 pp. ISBN 0-275-94004-7.

This volume examines how public societies receive foreign immigrants. It examines both positive and negative elements in the economic, political, and social factors involved. Such topics as the challenge of new minorities, politics of immigration, and public opinion toward immigrants are explored. There are a few tables and a lengthy bibliography in the book.

Le May, Michael C., ed. *The Gatekeepers: Comparative Immigration Policy.* New York: Praeger, 1989, 208 pp. ISBN 0-275-93079-3.

This book is a compilation of chapters written by several authors on various aspects of immigration policy. It examines the immigration policies and politics of the United States, Australia, Great Britain, Germany, Israel, and Venezuela. The individual authors are well versed in the immigration policies of the countries about which they write. Most of these countries represent a unique situation. Australia is unique because of its geographic location far from the rest of the world. Israel poses a unique case because of its religious considerations. The United States is a major country that receives aliens from a bordering Third World country. Great Britain receives refugees because of its commonwealth political structure. Venezuela faces the immigration policy problems of the Third World. Germany has a "non-immigration policy." The book has many tables and figures and several pages of bibliography.

Mitchell, Christopher, ed. *Western Hemisphere Immigration and United States Foreign Policy.* University Park, PA: The Pennsylvania State University Press, 1992, 314 pp. ISBN 0-271-00789-3.

This volume, an analytic-historical study of immigration policy, was compiled by several authors who had each done research in a specific area. The five case studies discussed cover Central America, Mexico, Cuba, Dominican Republic, and Haiti. Each study deals with how the United States' foreign policy affects how it deals with immigrants. The book has a few tables and bibliographical notes.

Muller, Thomas. *Immigrants and the American City.* A Twentieth Century Fund Book. New York: New York University Press, 1993, 372 pp. ISBN 0-8147-5479-1.

In this volume, the author looks at immigration as a source of pride, facilitating urban renewal and decreasing social problems. This book examines how migrants are admitted even while many homeless Americans are sleeping on the streets, in doorways, or in the subways in Los Angeles, New York City, Miami, and other cities. It discusses how immigration has passed through several phases. In the colonial period and until the 1920s, U.S. borders were open to European immigrants. Beginning in the 1920s, the open door policy began to tighten. In the mid-1960s legislation initiatives abandoned the idea of immigration quotas based on nationality; thus immigrants from Southeast Asia, Central America, and Afghanistan were accepted. The aim of the book is to show the effects of immigration on the native population. Since the increased flow of immigrants in the mid-1970s, gateway cities such as Los Angeles, New York, Miami, and San Francisco have built new office towers, added jobs in service industries, and shown signs of urban renewal. A striking change is evident in the racial composition of large cities. The book has bibliographical notes for chapters and several tables.

Papademetriou, Demetrios G., and Mark J. Miller, eds. *The Unavoidable Issue: U.S. Immigration Policy in the 1980s.* Philadelphia, PA: Institute for the Study of Human Issues, 1983, 305 pp. ISBN 0-89727-047-9.

Each of the ten chapters in this volume was written by an expert on various aspects of U.S. immigration. The purpose of the book is to familiarize the reader with the many controversies in the debate over immigration and help the reader understand the immigration issue and the need for reform. Topics of discussion include immigrants and the labor market, immigration and U.S. foreign policy, the international setting of U.S. refugee policy, and the rights of aliens. Chapters have bibliographical notes. Tables are found throughout.

Rivera-Batiz, Francisco L., Selig L. Sechzer, and Ira N. Gang, eds. *U.S. Immigration Policy Reform in the 1980s: A Preliminary Assessment.* New York: Praeger, 1991, 145 pp., ISBN 0-275-93620-1.

This book is compiled from papers presented at a colloquium held at Rutgers University in New Brunswick, New Jersey, on October 14, 1988. It discusses the fact that many illegal immigrants came to the United States in the late 1970s and 1980s and as a result Congress saw that changes had to be made in U.S. immigration policy. Thus, the Immigration Reform and Control Act of 1986 (IRCA) was developed, which provided amnesty to many illegal immigrants and made policies affecting employers who hired aliens. The book has many tables and figures. Information is given about the editors and contributors. Several pages of bibliographical references are included.

Simcox, David E., ed. *U.S. Immigration in the 1980s: Reappraisal and Reform.* Boulder, CO: Westview Press, and Washington, DC: Center for Immigration Studies, 1988, 308 pp. ISBN 0-8133-7542-8.

This volume contains writings of many authors. The authors take the viewpoint that most Americans do not realize the effect immigrants have on our society and culture. This volume examines the effects and problems immigration causes. It discusses how the Immigration Reform and Control Act (IRCA) was passed in 1986 after much deliberation, strengthening the existing 1965 law for legal immigration to reunite families. Court decisions for excluding or deporting aliens or awarding them immigration benefits were left intact. This volume gives an overview and reappraisal of U.S. immigration reform. One section examines U.S. workers and immigration. Also discussed in the book is the history of immigration, California as the United States' immigration laboratory, and the process of building a more rational, enforceable immigration policy. Chapters have notes, several tables, and information about the authors.

Torres, Andres. *Between Melting Pot and Mosaic: African Americans and Puerto Ricans in the New York Political Economy.* Philadelphia, PA: Temple University Press, 1995, 245 pp. ISBN 1-56639-279-9.

This book explores the nature and causes of poverty among the African American and Puerto Rico immigrants in New York City. The question is raised as to how the dominant culture intends to deal with African Americans along with all the new immigrants who have come to New York since the 1970s. By

1990 Colombians, Dominicans, Ecuadorians, Hispanics, other Latin Americans, Chinese, Koreans, other Asians, Jamaicans, Haitians, and other Caribbean people have come to New York. Together they constitute a population of immigrant minorities. The book has several tables. Appendix A gives definitions of variables. Appendixes B and C deal with wage regressions, while Appendix D discusses decomposition analysis. Chapters have bibliographical notes. There are several pages of bibliographical information.

Tucker, Robert W., Charles B. Keely, and Linda Wrigley, eds. *Immigration and U.S. Foreign Policy.* Boulder, CO: Westview Press, 1990, 229 pp. ISBN 0-8133-7853-2.

This volume is the compilation of writings by several authors. Works were prepared under the auspices of the Lehrman Institute, New York City, and funded by the Ford Foundation. The book discusses how the changing character of the nation's population due to immigration will shape foreign policy. Immigration does affect the United States' foreign relations. The United States is the largest receiver of immigrants in the world and its immigration policy will be of interest to other countries. The book has four parts. The first part looks at the period between the two world wars; the second studies the postwar refugee situation of 1945–1965; the third part looks at Latin immigration; and the final part looks at Asian immigration. Chapters have bibliographical notes and most have additional references. Many tables and figures are found throughout.

Ziegler, Benjamin Munn, ed. *Immigration: An American Dilemma.* Problems in American Civilization. Boston, MA: Heath, 1953, 118 pp. No ISBN.

This 1953 book is of interest to show that immigration has always been a problem. The book begins with the historical background of U.S. immigration policy, discussing the kinds of people who came to the United States and why they came both prior to and after World War I. Conflicting views are presented in the book. One writer maintains that immigrants have made the United States great, while another writer feels immigrants have been the cause of crime, low wages, disease, etc. Two other authors discuss the effects immigrants have on politics. Also discussed at length is the McCarran Immigration Bill (1952) and President Truman's message to the House on the veto of this bill. President Truman felt the bill discriminated against many of the peoples of the world. Its purpose was to cut down and virtually eliminate immigration to the United States from southern and eastern Europe; peoples of English, Irish, and German descent got priority. The book gives excerpts from the report by the President's Commission on Immigration and Naturalization. It has a few tables and suggestions for additional reading.

## Economic Considerations

Ascenio, Fernando Lozano. *Bringing It Back Home: Remittances to Mexico from Migrant Workers in the United States.* San Diego, CA: Center for U.S. Mexican Studies, University of California, San Diego, 1993, 77 pp. ISBN 1-878367-11-0.

Traditionally Mexican migrants to the United States have sent money home, though the amounts are difficult to determine because of the lack of personal records. Since 1980 increased research has provided more information through interviews with migrant workers and through projections of the total documented and undocumented migrant population. This study reveals the economic importance of U.S. money to the Mexican economy.

Borjas, George J. *Friends or Strangers: The Impact of Immigrants on the U.S. Economy.* New York: Basic Books, 1990, 274 pp. ISBN 0-465-02567-6.

This book begins with an overview of immigrants in the United States in a discussion of who comes and how the immigration market works. In one chapter the author gives the history of U.S. immigration policy. He shows the economic impact of immigration on earnings and employment and the part played by illegal aliens. He plays on the fact that new immigrants are less skilled than previous ones. Thus, there is higher unemployment, which leads to more poverty. Once an immigrant gets settled in the United States, his or her family members generally follow, so immigration is a family affair. In the last part of the book, the international competition for immigrants is discussed, especially in terms of how the United States competes with Canada and Australia in the immigration market. An appendix shows differences among national-origin groups. Several pages of notes for chapters are found at the end of the book. A few tables are interspersed throughout the book.

Borjas, George J., and Richard B. Freeman., eds. *Immigrantion and the Work Force: Economic Consequences for the United States and Source Areas.* A National Bureau of Economic Research Project Report. Chicago, IL: University of Chicago Press, 1992, 281 pp. ISBN 0-226-06633-9.

This book is the result of a research project organized by the Labor Studies Program of the National Bureau of Economic Research and was funded by the Ford Foundation. Some of the questions discussed in the book include: Who are the immigrants? How do they perform in the U.S. labor market? How do they affect employment chances of U.S. citizens? How does immigration to the United States affect the economies of the countries from which the immigrants come? What are the labor market effects of immigration on trade? There are many tables in the book and bibliographic references at the end of each chapter. There is a subject and author index.

Bouvier, Leon F. *Peaceful Invasions: Immigration and Changing America.* Lanham, MD: University Press of America, 1992, 234 pp. ISBN 0-8191-8402-0.

The first part of the book discusses how the U.S. population grew so large and how big it will get. It concludes with a discussion of population growth in countries that send immigrants to the United States. The second part discusses why immigration should be limited for reasons concerning the labor market, economic growth, cultural adaptation, and population growth. The book's third part poses challenges for the future. In the author's view, the United States must face the fact that it is becoming the first racially heterogeneous industrialized nation. This book is pro-immigration and is concerned with the success of its new residents. It has several tables, notes for each chapter, and a lengthy list of bibliographical references.

Briggs, Vernon M., Jr. *Mass Immigration and the National Interest.* Labor and Human Resources Series. Armonk, NY: M.E. Sharpe, 1992, 275 pp. ISBN 1-56324-170-6.

As discussed in this book, the term *mass immigration* refers to the size of the annual inflow of foreign-born persons in both the population and labor force of the United States. The book discusses how the immigration policy set up by the U.S. government at the national level was the reason for the influx of immigrants in the

1960s. It describes how the Immigration Act of 1965 allowed for an increase in immigration. According to the author, immigration was still out of control despite this act; immigration policy was developed without any thought concerning its economic consequences. Thus, the act had to be revised in the form of the Immigration Act of 1990. The author discusses the notion that immigration policy should be consistent with the changing labor market for economic stability. Three appendixes show the preference system created under the Immigration Act of 1965; the legal immigration system and its preferences that were in effect from 1980 to 1991; and 34 countries whose nationals were eligible for the transitional program for diversity immigrants in 1992–1994. The book has several tables and figures. Chapters have bibliographical notes.

Briggs, Vernon M., Jr., and Stephen Moore. *Still an Open Door? U.S. Immigration Policy and the American Economy.* The American University Public Policy Series. Washington, DC: American University Press, 1994, 167 pp. ISBN 1-879383-31-4.

In this small volume two points of view are discussed. One question is: Do immigrants help or hurt the United States economically? The other is: Have immigrants taken jobs from American workers and thus lowered the U.S. standard of living? One author feels that immigrants definitely hurt the United States economically by taking job from U.S. workers. The other author feels strongly that immigrants bring much-needed talent, skills, and energy. There are illustrations and many references.

Cohen, Robin. *The New Helots: Migrants in the International Division of Labour.* Research in Ethnic Relations Series. Brookfield, VT: Gower, 1987, 290 pp. ISBN 0-566-00932-3.

This book deals with migrant laborers. The author examines such topics as unfair labor practices and modern migrants; theories of how immigration affects the United States and its labor reservoirs; the reproduction of labor power in southern Africa; functions of migrant labor in Europe; policing the frontiers to regulate the supply of migrant labor; and the experience of migrant workers. The book has figures and tables and a long list of references.

Palmer, Ransford W., ed. *In Search of a Better Life: Perspectives on Migration from the Caribbean.* New York: Praeger, 1990, 185 pp. ISBN 0-275-93409-8.

This volume examines immigration from the Caribbean and the cultural, social, and economic adaptation of the immigrants to their new environments. The book also considers illegal immigrants who came to the United States as visitors but violated their visas by remaining. One chapter looks at Caribbean immigrant women in the United States and the important part they play in the labor force. Some tables are used for explanatory purposes. Notes and selected bibliographies are found throughout the book. Several authors collaborated to compile this volume.

## Historical

Commons, John R. *Races and Immigrants in America*. New York: Augustus M. Kelley, 1967, 242 pp. No ISBN.

The first edition of this volume was published in 1907. The second edition was published in 1920 and reprinted in 1967. The volume begins with the introduction to the 1920 edition, with only minor changes. The book discusses how immigrants from northwestern Europe went into agriculture while immigrants from southern and eastern Europe went into manufacturing. Thus, the growth in U.S. food production did not keep up with population, whereas manufactured products exceeded population growth. Therefore, before World War I, the United States was a food importer but in manufactures was an exporting country. World War I changed this situation somewhat; farmers had trouble getting laborers because of manufacturing competition. The author suggests that making agriculture more profitable and attractive, rather than furnishing cheap labor to manufacturers, is the proper course for the United States. The book discusses how proper cultural assimilation of immigrants was a national problem in the late nineteenth and early twentieth centuries, but this problem eased somewhat with the second generation of immigrants. The book has illustrations and a list of references cited in footnotes.

Corcoran, Mary P. *Irish Illegals: Transients between Two Societies*. Contributions in Ethnic Studies, no. 32. Westport, CT: Greenwood Press, 1993, 205 pp. ISBN 0-313-28624-8.

The author begins by giving the history of Irish immigration to the United States and current immigration trends. She then relates the way she gathered statistics in Queens, New York, from August 26, 1987, through August 10, 1988, and analyzes the findings throughout the book. For example, she examined the factors that caused Irish people to embark on a journey to the

United States. She notes that relatives are helpful for short periods but can't necessarily be of assistance in helping the immigrants find work, especially if the immigrants are in the country illegally. Many "New Irish" remain here illegally and seem to be able to exist by working at various jobs such as tending bar or being a nanny. Legally or not, the Irish are an important part of U.S. labor, politics, and sports. The economic situation in Ireland in the 1980s led to a large-scale exodus to the United States, especially New York, where the immigrants were able to find work. The effect of Irish immigration as a result of the Immigration Act of 1990 is discussed in the epilogue. The book has a few tables and many bibliographical references.

Dublin, Thomas, ed. *Immigrant Voices: New Lives in America, 1773–1986.* Urbana, IL: University of Illinois Press, 1993, 319 pp. ISBN 0-252-01769-2.

This book is a compilation of letters, diaries, and oral histories of immigrants from the early nineteenth century to the present day. Some of those reporting are John Harrow (from Shetland Islands); the Hollingworth family (from England); Mary Paik (from Korea); Rosa Cassettari (from Italy); the Galarza family (from Mexico); Kazuko Itoi (from Japan); Piri Thomas (from Puerto Rico); William and Sophie Frank Seyffardt (from Germany); Rose Gollup (from Russia); and the Nguyen family (from Vietnam). This book has a selected bibliography of first-person accounts. A few pictures appear throughout the book.

Gabaccia, Donna. *From the Other Side: Women, Gender, and Immigrant Life in the U.S., 1820–1990.* Bloomington, IN: Indiana University Press, 1994, 192 pp. ISBN 0-253-32529-3.

This volume discusses the experiences of migratory women, but it also mentions men from time to time. The book has three parts. In the first part, the women discuss coming to the United States, telling where they come from. In the second part, each woman discusses being both foreign and female in immigrant life and tells about the work she does. In the last part each woman discusses class and culture in the twentieth century, including the many changes she faces as an immigrant. Chapters have bibliographical notes and several pages of bibliographical essays.

Golden, Hilda H. *Immigrant and Native Families: The Impact of Immigration on the Demographic Transformation of Western*

*Massachusetts, 1850–1900.* Lanham, MD: University Press of America, 1993, 259 pp. ISBN 0-8191-9287-2.

This entire volume deals with western Massachusetts and shows the part that region played in the social and economic transformation of the United States. This region became a center of manufacturing enhanced by technological changes. The region's accessibility was important in the transformation. Another factor important for the manufacturing growth was the ample supply of water power. Immigrants came and settled in the region because they found employment in factories. By 1900 the region had a higher percentage of people who were foreign born and of foreign parentage than the nation as a whole. Early immigrants came from Ireland and French Canada, and by 1900 new immigrants came from Poland, Italy, and other eastern and southern European countries. Nativity and ethnicity are analyzed to show how they have transformed the demographic structure of the region. Many tables and figures are used throughout the book. Appendix A shows a distribution of households, in percentages, by household typology and by nativity in 1900. The book has several pages of cited references.

Hoerder, Dirk, and Horst Rossler, eds. *Distant Magnets: Expectations and Realities in the Immigrant Experience, 1840–1930.* Ellis Island Series. New York: Holmes & Meier, 1993, 312 pp. ISBN 0-8419-1302-1.

These essays were written by authors expressing the desires and wishes of immigrants from different countries. Some of the immigrants were from England, Italy, Hungary, Ireland, and Eastern Europe. Expectations of European and North American immigrants are compared. The word *magnet* in the title describes the irresistible force of attraction represented by job opportunities and a better place to live. Each chapter has bibliographical notes. Information about the contributors is also given.

Namias, June. *First Generation: In the Words of Twentieth-Century American Immigrants.* Revised edition. Urbana, IL: University of Illinois Press, 1992, 278 pp. ISBN 0-252-06170-5.

The first edition of *First Generation* was published in 1978; many changes have occurred in the world and United States since then. The author is interested in conditions in immigrants' homelands that forced them to immigrate—political upheaval, religious intolerance, economic misery, and a desire for new opportunities. The book discusses how immigrants who entered the United States before World War I were mainly from Europe but that, since the 1965 Immigration and Nationality Act, immigrants have come from Asia, Latin America, and island countries in the Western hemisphere and the Middle East. This book examines problems the United States faces regarding immigration policies. Such problems include: Whom shall the United States welcome? What can be done with people entering the United States illegally? How can the United States provide for refugees? How can the social and cultural costs of immigration be solved? The book has three parts. The first part discusses new beginnings in the period 1900–1929. The second part deals with survivors from 1930–1945, and the third part discusses the postwar period 1946–1990. In each part, stories are related by specific individuals from different countries of origin. The book is illustrated with photos. There are notes for each chapter and a bibliography.

Nugent, Walter. *Crossings: The Great Transatlantic Migrations, 1870–1914.* Bloomington, IN: Indiana University Press, 1992, 234 pp. ISBN 0-253-34140-X.

This book is divided into three parts. Part one explores the Atlantic region and its population in the nineteenth century, as well as the patterns and motives for immigration. Part two discusses the European ethnicities departing their homelands: the British, Scandinavians, Germans, Italians, Spanish, Portuguese, etc. In part three, the author discusses the American destinations: the United States, Canada, Brazil, and Argentina. The book has many maps and tables. Bibliographical notes are given for each chapter. Several pages list works the author consulted and cited.

Watkins, Susan Cotts. *After Ellis Island: Newcomers and Natives in the 1910 Census.* New York: Russell Sage Foundation, 1994, 451 pp. ISBN 0-87154-910-7.

Several authors associated with the Population Studies Center of the University of Pennsylvania contributed to this volume, which is based on the 1910 U.S. census. Each chapter focuses on different aspects of the immigrant experience, such as mortality, fertility, households, neighborhoods, schooling, and industrial affiliation. Ellis Island opened on January 1, 1892, so obviously not all immigrants came through Ellis Island. The author discusses how some people did not stay but instead returned to their homeland. Those who stayed sent for their relatives and developed neighborhoods like they had in the old country. The 1910 census was taken prior to World War I, when many immigrants arrived. This influx slowed after restrictions were placed on immigration in the 1920s. This volume aims to describe certain aspects of immigrant life and gives detailed descriptions of various ethnic groups. There are two appendixes and many figures and tables, along with an extensive bibliography.

Yans-McLaughlin, Virginia, ed. *Immigration Reconsidered: History, Sociology, and Politics.* New York: Oxford University Press, 1990, 342 pp. ISBN 0-19-505510-1.

These essays grew out of a conference held at the New York Public Library on October 24–25, 1986, sponsored by the Statue of Liberty Ellis Island Foundation, the Alfred Sloan Foundation, and the New York Council for Humanities. The essays deal with such topics as migration patterns in world history (the tropical world, Asia, and the United States), ethnicity and social structure, the study of immigration, new approaches to the study of immigration, and the politics of immigration. There are a few tables. Essays have bibliographical notes.

## Security

Weiner, Myron, ed. *International Migration and Security.* Boulder, CO: Westview Press, 1993, 333 pp. ISBN 0-81338774-4.

This book was made possible by a grant from the Sloan Foundation. Papers were presented at a conference on security and international migration held at the Center for International Studies of the Massachusetts Institute of Technology (MIT) in December 1991. The conference was organized by the MIT Inter-University Committee on International Migration. The papers in part one analyze immigration flows that make societies either ethnically homogeneous or diverse, and they examine the results on the political and security-related stability of states. The papers in part two examine security implications of international immigration for the Third World. The papers have references and notes. Several tables are found throughout the book.

## Laws and Regulations

Bean, Frank D., Georges Vernez, and Charles B. Keely. *Opening and Closing the Doors: Evaluating Immigration Reform and Control.*

Santa Monica, CA: Rand Corporation, and Washington DC: The Urban Institute, 138 pp. ISBN 0-87766-429-3.

This volume begins by giving the history of immigration. The book is essentially an evaluation of the 1986 Immigration Reform and Control Act (IRCA). This act presented the most sweeping legislation on immigration in more than 20 years and was intended to help reduce illegal immigration. However, the number of immigrants increased greatly because of the reuniting of families. The book discusses how in earlier periods of American history, immigrants came mainly from Europe but that in recent years they have come mainly from Asia and Latin America. Some of the provisions included in IRCA deal with employer requirements, antidiscrimination, a program to reimburse states for additional legislative costs, agricultural issues, and screening programs for welfare eligibility. The book has two appendixes and many tables and figures. Information is given about the authors, and there are several pages of selected references.

Fragomen, Austin T., Jr., and Steven C. Bell. *Immigration Fundamentals: A Guide to Law and Practice.* Basic Practice Skills Series. New York: Practicing Law Institute, 1992, various paging. ISBN 0-87224-047-9.

This book was written to be helpful to those who are interested in immigration and are new to the field. It is up-to-date since it includes the Immigration Act of 1990 in the material discussed. It covers such topics as entry of aliens to the United States, immigrant employment, family-sponsored immigration, nonimmigrants, refugees and asylum, deportation and exclusion, the rights and obligations of aliens, judicial review, naturalization, and citizenship. There are seven appendixes, a table of statutes, and a table of cases. Information is given about the authors.

Lewis, Loida Nicholas, and Len T. Madlansacay. *How to Get a Green Card: Legal Ways to Stay in the U.S.A.* Berkeley, CA: Nolo Press, 1993, various paging. ISBN 0-87337-193-3.

This is an invaluable book for those who want to obtain a visa in the United States. It explains the history, laws, and requirements associated with visas. It explains forms, procedures, and quotas. There are chapters explaining specific situations for an individual requesting a green card, and it explains how to file for oneself or another person. The book ends by discussing what a person should do if he or she loses a green card. The book has four appendixes giving sample filled-in forms; the locations of Immigration and Naturalization Service offices and U.S. embassies and consulates; and a list of nonprofit organizations that assist individuals with immigration.

Montwieler, Nancy Humel. *The Immigration Reform Law of 1986: Analysis, Text and Legislative History.* Washington, DC: Bureau of National Affairs, 1987, 557 pp. ISBN 0-87179-552-3.

The revisions made to immigration policy by the Immigration Reform and Control Act of 1986 were the only major changes in 35 years concerning immigration. This book gives an overview of the 1986 law, gives its history, and discusses the major provisions. The full text of the law is found in the second part, along with reports of committees and President Reagan's message when he signed the bill on November 6, 1986, in the White House Roosevelt Room.

Weissbrodt, David. *Immigration Law and Procedure in a Nutshell.* 3d ed. St. Paul, MI: West Publishing, 1992, 497 pp. ISBN 0-314-01070-X.

This book was written to show what subjects should be covered in a course given on immigration and law procedure in order to show how the immigration process really works in the United States. The author begins by giving the history of U.S. immigration law and policy, followed by discussions on how to obtain a visa, deportation and exclusion, refugee and asylum issues, and ethical issues that confront immigration lawyers. An extensive bibliography includes laws and regulations, cases and decisions, books, treaties, digests, a list of periodicals, and databases. A table of cases and other authorities (e.g., U.S. Code Annotated, Immigration and Nationality Act) are found at the beginning of the book as a source for additional information.

## Immigration

Bogen, Elizabeth. *Immigration in New York.* New York: Praeger, 1987, 268 pp. ISBN 0-275-92199-9.

New York City is largely a city of immigrants. To get material for this book the author set up an office at the City Planning Department in 1984. In this way, the author learned much about the immigrants—who they are, how they live, what they give the United States, and what the country gives them. In addition to this book the Office of Immigrant Affairs was able to make a directory of immigrant service agencies and other materials of use to immigration applicants. The book discusses how immigrants made their mark in politics and the U.S. economy. For example, the garment industry depended on immigrant labor of the late nineteenth and early twentieth centuries. During the same period the subway and sewer system were built with immigrant labor. The book has a lengthy glossary, a list of acronyms used, and bibliographical references. There are many figures and tables.

Bouvier, Leon F., and Lindsey Grant. *How Many Americans? Population, Immigration and the Environment.* San Francisco, CA: Sierra Club Books, 1994, 174 pp. ISBN 0-87156-496-3.

This small volume examines the relationship between population growth and the environmental, social, and resource issues facing the United States. It then projects population patterns for the twenty-first century if the population is not controlled. According to the author, the United States cannot solve Third World population problems by accepting immigrants. The book has many tables and figures to illustrate how immigration has affected the U.S. population and will continue to do so. There is an appendix. Each chapter has notes.

Dashefsky, Arnold, Jan DeAmicis, Bernard Lazerwitz, and Ephraim Tabory. *Americans Abroad: A Comparative Study of Emigrants from the United States.* Environment Development and Public Policy; Public Policy and Social Services. New York: Plenum Press, 1992, 166 pp. ISBN 0-306-43941-7.

This book explores the experience of Americans abroad, specifically those in developed countries with a lower standard of living than the United States. Three questions are investigated: What motivates migrants to move? What are the sources of the adjustment problems migrants encounter? What explains whether migrants remain or return to the United States? This study is distinctive in that it offers a comparative analysis of the experience of a group of migrants moving from one country to another. There are a few tables, four pages of references, and both an author and subject index.

Delgado, Hector L. *New Immigrants, Old Unions: Organizing Undocumented Workers in Los Angeles.* Philadelphia, PA: Temple University Press, 1993, 186 pp. ISBN 1-566639-044-3.

This book is based on interviews with four immigrants who entered the United States surreptitiously and found work in a factory, settled in Los Angeles, and became involved in a labor dispute. It relates their experiences, their relationships to organized labor, and what their undocumented status really meant to them. Notes are found for each chapter, followed by several pages of bibliography.

D'Innocenzo, Michael, and Josef P. Sirefman, eds. *Immigration and Ethnicity: American Society—"Melting Pot" or "Salad Bowl"?* Contributions in Sociology no. 97. Westport, CT: Greenwood Press, 1992, 344 pp. ISBN 0-313-27759-1.

Prepared under the auspices of Hofstra University, this volume is divided into three parts. Part one discusses the problems associated with preserving ethnic identity. Part two explains social and cultural experiences of immigrants and ethnics. The final part discusses ethnic challenges in a maturing United States. Each essay in the volume was written by a different author. Bibliographic notes are found with each essay. A few tables are found. Information is given about the editors and contributors.

Edmonston, Barry, and Jeffrey S. Passel, eds. *Immigration and Ethnicity: The Integration of America's Newest Arrivals.* Washington, DC: The Urban Institute Press, 1994, 360 pp. ISBN 0-87766-578-8.

This Urban Institute book focuses on the integration of immigrants who came to the United States after 1980. The authors examine the ethnic origins of immigrants; adjustments new immigrants have made including language, earnings, and political change; U.S. policy toward immigrants; and the impact of immigrants on the future racial-ethnic composition of the United States. Many tables and figures are found throughout. References and notes are found with each chapter.

Freeman, Gary P., and James Jupp, eds. *Nations of Immigrants: Australia, the United States, and International Migration.* New York: Oxford University Press, 1992, 250 pp. ISBN 0-19-553483-2.

This book is sponsored by the Bureau of Immigration Research in Melbourne and the Center for Australian Studies at the University of Texas at Austin. The two editors exchanged visits to each other's universities and, after much consultation with the contributors, produced this book. The immigration policies of the United States and Australia are compared. Problems controlling immigration as well as illegal immigration are discussed. Another topic the book considers is immigration and the economy. Chapters discuss the settlement policies in each country. Separate bibliographies are given for the United States and Australia. A list of abbreviations and acronyms is given for each country.

James, Daniel. *Illegal Immigration: An Unfolding Crisis.* Lanham, MD: University Press of America, 1991, 155 pp. ISBN 0-8191-8404-7.

This volume concerns illegal immigration and deals with such problems as the burden placed on social services and public assistance, effects on the labor market, increases in border violence, drug traffic; the threat to U.S. security, and possible remedies. Two appendixes discuss categories of aliens excluded under the Immigration Act of 1990 and laws associated with illegal immigration to the United States. The book also explains what the Mexico-United States Institute is. Bibliographic sources are listed for each chapter.

Jones, Maldwyn Allen. *American Immigration.* 2d ed. Chicago History of American Civilization Series. Chicago, IL: University of Chicago Press, 1992, 353 pp. ISBN 0-226-40634-2.

Many changes have occurred since the first edition of this book was published in 1960. This edition covers Third World immigration from 1960 to 1990 in a special chapter to update the book. The book discusses how the history of the United States was molded by continuous waves of immigrants who helped develop the country. Other topics covered include why immigrants choose the United States, how they influence U.S. society, how special communities are developed, and continuing ancestral customs and loyalties. A list of important dates is given. Suggested readings and an additional bibliography cover several pages. A few pictures are used for illustration.

Kane, Hal. *The Hour of Departure: Forces That Create Refugees and Migrants.* Worldwatch Paper, 125. Washington, DC: Worldwatch Institute, 1995, 56 pp. ISBN 1-878071-26-2.

This small volume shows how pressures such as wars, famine, and poverty have forced people to flee their homeland. About 125 million people worldwide live in countries other than the ones in which they were born. Many millions also migrate within their own country. Relief agencies respond to wars and famine with emergency provisions such as food and tents and try to halt immigration with laws and border patrols, but they generally are not able to cope with the crises effectively. The author argues that the refugee problem can be reduced by development of economic and social policies that recognize the problems of refugees.

Nelson, Brent A. *America Balkanized: Immigration's Challenge to Government.* Monterey, VA: The American Immigration Control Foundation, 1994, 148 pp. ISBN 0-936247-14-2.

This book examines some aspects of the problems of governance in the multiethnic state that will appear in the United States if immigration is not placed under control. The author considers public policy, government, and nationhood and states that, if immigration continues in the 1990s, a balkanization of the United States is possible. The last section presents a critique of opponents of immigration control. The author believes that immigration must be controlled. The book has several pages of bibliograhic notes.

Reimers, David M. *Still the Golden Door: The Third World Comes to America.* 2d ed. New York: Columbia University Press, 1992, 362 pp. ISBN 0-231-07680-0.

In this volume, Reimers updates his earlier (1985) edition. He begins with a discussion of the Third World immigration before World War II. The book examines the United States' open door policy of 1943–1945. Different chapters cover temporary workers (braceros) and the "wetbacks" (los Mojados); the Immigration Act of 1965; new Asian immigrants; immigrants from Mexico, Central and South America, and the Caribbean; Third World refugees; undocumented aliens; and the Immigration Reform and Control Act of 1986. Chapters have bibliographical notes and several pages of selected bibliography.

Stolarik, M. Mark, ed. *Forgotten Doors: The Other Ports of Entry to the United States.* Philadelphia, PA: The Balch Institute Press, 1988, 207 pp. ISBN 0-944190-00-6.

Several authors contributed to this volume. Included are essays presented at a conference held at the Balch Institute for Ethnic Studies on June 13–14, 1986. The book includes essays on the following ports of entry: Boston, Philadelphia, Baltimore, Miami, New Orleans, San Francisco, and Los Angeles. A few tables and photos are shown for illustration. Chapters have notes. In the back information is found on the contributors.

## Latin American Immigrants

Bean, Frank D., Jurgen Schmandt, and Sidney Weintraub, eds. *Mexican and Central American Population and U.S. Immigration Policy.* Austin, TX: The Center for Mexican American Studies, University of Texas, 1989, 211 pp. ISBN 0-292-75115-X.

This is a compilation of papers presented at the Southwest Symposium on Mexican and Central American Population Issues, held October 1987 in Austin. In the 1950s most of our immigrants came from Europe, whereas now there is an increased number coming from Latin American and Asian countries. With the changes in immigration patterns came a need for immigration reform, which led to passage of the Immigration Reform Control Act in 1986. Two authors discuss Mexican and Central American demographic situations. One chapter discusses the peoples of Spanish origin in the Southwest. The imbalance between labor supply and demand in the Caribbean is also examined. The last chapter gives the final report of the group. The book has many tables, figures, notes, and references. An appendix lists the participants at the meeting.

Brown, Peter G., and Henry Shue, eds. *The Border That Joins: Mexican Migrants and U.S. Responsibility.* Maryland Studies in Public Philosophy Series. Totowa, NJ: Rowman and Littlefield, 1983, 254 pp. ISBN 0-8476-7072-4.

This volume is a product of the Center for Philosophy and Public Policy sessions held on the Washington area campus of the University of Maryland, as part of a Center Working Group on Mexican Immigrants and U.S. Responsibility. The group was financed by the International Relations Division of the Rockefeller Foundation and the Mexico City office of the Ford Foundation. The book has four parts. Part one describes the philosophical views of Mexican migrants. The second part deals with historical aspects. Part three discusses the current situation, including agricultural and rural development and Mexican immigration to the United States. Part four examines immigration problems, foreign labor problems, and how they can be solved. There are many tables and figures. Each chapter has bibliographical notes.

Browning, Harley L., and Rodolfo O. de la Garza, eds. *Mexican Immigrants and Mexican Americans: An Evolving Relation.* Austin, TX: Center for Mexican American Studies, University of Texas Press, 1986, 256 pp. ISBN 0-292-75094.

This is a compilation of papers presented at the conference "The Impact of Mexican Immigration on the Chicano Population of the United States," held October 1982 at the University of Texas at Austin. This volume shows that Mexican immigrants and Mexican Americans are two distinct groups. It examines the factors that connect and also separate these groups. Both legal and illegal Mexican immigration are discussed. Some papers have tables. Each paper has a list of references.

Calavita, Kitty. *Inside the State: The Bracero Program, Immigration, and the I.N.S.* New York: Routledge, Chapman, and Hall, 1992, 243 pp. ISBN 0-415-90537-0.

In preparing this book the author was helped by the staff of the National Archives and the Freedom of Information and Privacy Act Office of the Immigration and Naturalization Service (INS), as well as by many others. This book tells the story of 500 Mexican farmworkers who were transported to California on September 29, 1942, to help fill a labor shortage in agriculture. These workers bore the name *braceros* and were the start of the bracero program that continued to expand over the years. Such laborers provide growers with a supply of cheap labor but also cause problems for the state. Bibliographic notes are found for each chapter. An appendix contains tables. There are several pages of bibliography.

Hondagneu-Sotelo, Pierrette. *Gendered Transitions: Mexican Experiences of Immigraiton.* Berkeley, CA: University of California Press, 1994, 258 pp. ISBN 0-520-07513-7.

To gather material for this book the author interviewed 44 men and women in 26 families. Most of the people were undocumented when they entered the United States, but many of them became legal citizens. The author discusses in detail how the interviews were conducted. The goal of the study was to elucidate the dynamics of gender in the process of immigration and settlement. Chapter 1 discusses immigration, gender, and settlement. Chapter 2 gives the history of Mexican undocumented settlement in the United States. Chapter 3 describes the Oakview Barrio. Chapter 4 deals with the transitions the interviewees experienced, with an emphasis on gender. Chapter 5 reconstructs gender through immigration settlement. Chapter 6 shows the part women play in consolidating settlement. The last chapter discusses immigration in the context of gender. This study suggests taking a look inside the household and social networks to see how gender relations shape immigration experiences. The book has a table of study participants and many bibliographic references.

Kasinitz, Philip. *Caribbean New York: Black Immigrants and the Politics of Race.* Anthropology of Contemporary Issues, Ithaca, NY: Cornell University Press, 1992, 280 pp. ISBN 0-8014-9951-8.

To get information for the book the author interviewed many Caribbean American New Yorkers. This volume examines how racial and ethnic identities of English-speaking Caribbean immigrants affect those persons' political activity. The author uses many tables and figures to provide information. Many pages of bibliography provide books for additional reading.

Levine, Barry B., ed. *The Caribbean Exodus.* New York: Praeger, 1987, 293 pp. ISBN 0-275-92182-4.

This volume discusses the Caribbean exodus to the United States. It first gives the framework for the exodus: surplus population, history of West Indian immigration, social psychology of immigration, and experiences of immigrants. Immigrants come from Mexico, Puerto Rico, Cuba, Haiti, Dominican Republic, and Central America. Caribbeans also immigrate to Britain, France, Netherlands, and Canada. The book ends with a discussion of the impact of U.S. immigration policy on Caribbean immigration. Bibliographical notes for each chapter are included.

Lowenthal, Abraham F., and Katrina Burgess, eds. *The California-Mexico Connection.* A Twentieth Century Fund Book. Stanford, CA: Stanford University Press, 1993, 364 pp. ISBN 0-8047-2188-2.

This book discusses how the Rio Grande has long been the division between North and South. Latin immigrants are coming so fast that the Latino population is the fastest-growing group in the United States, especially in California. Trade between California and Mexico increased greatly in value from 1988 to 1991—from $6 billion to more than $10 billion. Mexico is

California's second-largest foreign market after Japan and is also a large source of imports. The book is divided into four parts. Part one is an introduction to the California-Mexico situation. Part two explores economic, political, and social changes in Mexico and how they affect California. Part three stresses Mexicans in California and how they affect the economy, society, education, and politics. Part four analyzes what can be done to strengthen the California-Mexico connection. There are two appendixes. Several pages of notes for chapters serve as reference matter. Several figures and tables are used.

Martinez, John. *Mexican Emigration to the U.S. 1910–1930.* (1930) University of California. Reprinted by R and E Research Associates and edited by Adam S. Eterovich. San Francisco and Saratoga, CA: Robert D. Reed, 1971, 100 pp. No ISBN.

The subject of this 1930 dissertation is the departure of Mexican nationals from their homeland because of poor economic conditions and their entrance into the United States. The study begins with the Mexican Revolution of 1910 and ends with the great depression of 1929. The revolution caused a great exodus and an expansion of agricultural development in the United States that opened opportunities for many farm laborers. Chapters in the dissertation are well footnoted, and there is also a selected bibliography.

Massey, Douglas S., Rafael Alarcon, Jorge Durand, and Humberto Gonzalez. *Return to Aztlan: The Social Process of International Migration from Western Mexico.* Studies in Demography vol. 1. Berkeley, CA: University of California Press, 1987, 335 pp. ISBN 0-520-06079-2.

Research for this book was supported by the U.S. National Institute of Child Health and Human Development. Many other colleagues and students gave their support. This book was written to be understood by the average citizen; it skips the technical chapters written for the scientist. The book covers such topics as the historical development of international immigration, current immigration patterns, social organization, migration and the household economy, and integration in the United States. The authors conclude by giving some findings from their study. There are many tables and figures and several pages of references for further reading.

Masud-Piloto, Felix Roberto. *With Open Arms: Cuban Migration to the United States.* Rev. ed. Totowa, NJ: Rowman & Littlefield, 1995, 200 pp. ISBN 0-8476-8037-1.

This book discusses the immigration of Cubans to the United States from 1858 to the mid-1990s. It notes that Cuban immigration since 1959 can be understood only in terms of a long prior history. It discusses the vigorous challenge of the Cuban revolution to the U.S. policies to control the spread of Communism in the world. Although the United States has attempted to control Cuban migration, the Cuban government has also played politics with refugees and political prisoners. Particular emphasis has been placed on the unusual events and episodes that have made the immigration in many ways unique, such as the Cuban Children's Program, the Camarioca boatlift, the Cuban airlift, and the Mariel boatlift. This edition extends the discussion with an examination of the Bush and Clinton administrations' responses to recent events in Cuba. Chapters have bibliographical notes. There are a few tables and several pages of bibliography.

Trueba, Henry T., et al. *Healing Multicultural America: Mexican Immigrants Rise to Power in Rural California.* Washington, DC: Falmer Press, 1993, 194 pp. ISBN 0-75070-150-1.

The book tells the historical and anthropological story of how low-income Mexicans in Woodland, California, managed to use their language and culture to develop economic and political organizations to help them become first-class citizens. The book tells how they accomplished their goals and what contribution they made to U.S. society. It focuses on experiences of inter-ethnic conflict, cultural conflict, poverty, alienation, violence, and self-rejection. It aims to help people to understand what it takes to live in a multicultural democratic society. Chapters have references and a few tables and figures. The last chapter provides annotated references for cultural therapy.

## Far East Immigration

Espiritu, Yen Le. *Asian American Panethnicity: Bridging Institutions and Identities.* Asian American History and Culture Series. Philadelphia, PA: Temple University Press, 1992, 222 pp. ISBN 0-87722-955-4.

The author, a Vietnamese American who married a Filipino American, interviewed more than 25 people to obtain information and views for this book. The book reveals how Asian

Americans are adjusting to American life such as cultural differences, living in a different economic system, and social adjustments. He uses the term *Asian Americans* except in chapters 4 and 5, when he speaks of *Asian Pacific Americans* in the context of government agencies, the census classification, and the politics of social service funding. Chapters have notes. The book includes a list of interviewees, many tables and figures, and several pages of references.

Haines, David W., ed. *Refugees as Immigrants: Cambodians, Laotians and Vietnamese in America.* Totowa, NJ: Rowman & Littlefield, 1989, 198 pp. ISBN 0-8476-7553-X.

The basis for this book was formed at the 1986 annual meeting of the American Association for the Advancement of Science, which had a panel on Southeast Asian refugees. The research done on Southeast Asian refugees documents the process of adjustment for those who have come to the United States, how the immigrants have adapted to U.S. society, and the interaction of refugees in social programs. The book discusses experiences of Cambodians, Laotians, and Vietnamese. One chapter is a case study of an Indochinese refugee in San Diego. Each chapter has tables used for illustration, as well as bibliographical notes. There are several pages of references and information about the contributors.

Hein, Jeremy. *States and International Migrants: The Incorporation of Indochinese Refugees in the United States and France.* Boulder, CO: Westview Press, 1993, 214 pp. ISBN 0-8133-8541-5.

The incorporation of Indochinese refugees into the culture and economy of the United States and France is the basic theme of this volume. The study includes such topics as international immigration, political immigrants, managing ethnic communities, constants and variables in Indochinese immigration, social conflict, the evaluation of social contracts, and social networks. The author constructs a complex generalization about the relationships among history, states, and immigrants' social networks. A list of acronyms used in the book is given. The book has several tables and several pages of bibliography.

Kimura, Yukiko. *Issei: Japanese Immigrants in Hawaii.* Honolulu, HI: University of Hawaii Press, 1988, 283 pp. ISBN 0-8248-1029-5.

This volume deals with the experiences of Japanese immigrants in Hawaii from 1885 through 1970. The first generation, the

Issei, came to Hawaii before July 1, 1924, when the Japanese Exclusion Act became effective. The book is divided into four parts. Part one gives the background of Japanese immigrants as contract laborers. Part two deals with the major occupations of the Issei. Part three discusses the influences on the Japanese community, in terms of family, schools, religion, etc. Part four explores the position of the Issei in the two world wars. The book has a few tables, notes for each chapter, and several pages of bibliography.

Lyons, Adrian, ed. *Voices, Stories, Hopes: Cambodia and Vietnam: Refugees and Volunteers.* North Blackburn, Victoria, Australia: Collins Dove, 1993, 173 pp. ISBN 1-86371-226-7.

This small volume centers on refugees as human beings. It is about the people of Vietnam and Cambodia who sought refuge away from their homelands after severe fighting ended. Stories in the book cover the period 1980 to 1992 and include people speaking from Cambodia, people in Khymer Camps, and Vietnamese at sea. Refugees tell how it feels to face danger, to fail to escape, to be refused entry into a new country, and to experience the death of loved ones. Refugee workers also tell of the suffering and hopes of refugees in their search for a better life.

Mangiafico, Luciano. *Contemporary American Immigrants: Patterns of Filipino, Korean, and Chinese Settlement in the United States.* New York: Praeger, 1988, 211 pp., ISBN 0-275-92726-1.

This book is divided into three parts. Part one gives the history of immigration and studies the ebb and flow of immigration and the sociodemographic characteristics of immigrants living in the United States. Part two looks at immigration to the United States from the Philippines, Korea, and China by discussing history, current immigration trends, problems, and the social and demographic characteristics for immigrants from each country. Part three surveys the immigration situation during the period 1980–1985. Chapters have notes, many tables throughout, and a selected bibliography.

Strand, Paul J. and Woodrow Jones, Jr. *Indochinese Refugees in America: Problems of Adaptation and Assimilation.* Duke Press Policy Studies Series. Durham, NC: Duke University Press, 1985, 182 pp. ISBN 0-8223-0629-8.

This study was conducted jointly in 1981 by the Social Science Research Laboratory (SSRL) of San Diego State University and

ACCESS, a San Diego private organization providing services to Indochinese refugees. The study covers such subjects as resettlement of immigrants and refugees, living conditions, experiences of arrivals, health, education, language, employment, and successful assimilation into the country of asylum. There are two appendixes. Chapters have bibliographical notes. Tables are found in most chapters.

Yu, Eui-Young, and Earl H. Phillips, eds. *Korean Women in Transition: At Home and Abroad.* Korean-Americans and Korean Studies Publication Series, no. 5. Los Angeles, CA: Center for Korean American and Korean Studies, University of California, Los Angeles, 1987, 304 pp. ISBN 0-942831-00-4.

Many authors contributed to this volume to illuminate the immigration experience of Korean women. The first few articles focus on women in Korea and the remaining ones focus on Korean women's transition in the United States. Five waves of Korean women have come to the United States in the twentieth century. The first wave was from 1903 to 1910 and included urban wives and students. The next, from 1910 to 1924, included the educated and politically active. The next, in the 1950s, included the poor, less-educated wives of servicemen. This was followed by educated professionals in the 1960s. The last influx since 1974 included single and married urban women from various economic backgrounds. Chapters have bibliographic notes. Many tables are found throughout the book.

## Refugees

Gold, Steven J. *Refugee Communities: A Comparative Field Study.* Sage Series on Race and Ethnic Relations, vol. 4. Newbury Park, CA: Sage Publications, 1992, 257 pp. ISBN 0-8039-3796-2.

This is a sociological study of the refugee adaptation experiences of Soviet Jews and Vietnamese, two of the largest groups of refugee immigrants since 1980. The author examines the diversity and complexity within the two groups, studying ethnic group solidarity, use of social services, entrepreneurship, barriers to success, and assimilation. The volume reveals that there are several different Jewish and Vietnamese immigrant communities that have reacted differently to being transplanted to a new environment. Chapters have bibliographical notes and a few photos. There are several pages of references, an index, and a note about the author.

Gorman, Robert F. *Mitigating Misery: An Inquiry Into the Political and Humanitarian Aspects of U.S. and Global Refugee Policy.* Lanham, MD: University Press of America, 1993, 347 pp. ISBN 0-8191-9175-2.

This interesting volume deals with issues related to the number of refugees, refugee protection, emergency relief, development assistance, repatriation, and resettlement. The author visited many refugee camps and got firsthand information for the book. The book is written in an easy-to-understand manner for the scholar and layperson. There is a bibliographic essay for each chapter and a list of acronyms and abbreviations used in the book.

Koehn, Peter H. *Refugees from Revolution: U.S. Policy and Third World Migration.* Boulder, CO: Westview Press, 1991, 463 pp. ISBN 0-8133-7719-6.

This volume dealing with refugees is divided into five parts. The first part discusses conditions that lead to Third World refugees, showing how these people leave their homeland because of danger or dire political and economic circumstances. Emphasis is placed on Cuban and Vietnamese refugees. The second part discusses the routes of immigration and the hardships refugees face to get to the country they desire. The third part discusses Third World exiles in industrial societies, their reception in the United States, and the social and economic adjustments they make. The fourth part discusses repatriation. The last part presents conclusions regarding refugee origins, U.S. admissions policy, reception issues, and repatriation. Each chapter has many bibliographical notes, as well as many tables and figures. The appendix lists the approach and sampling results for the author's studies in both Washington, D.C., and Los Angeles. Books are listed for further reading.

Loescher, Gil, and John A. Scanlan. *Calculated Kindness: Refugees and America's Half-Open Door, 1945 to the Present.* New York: The Free Press, 1986, 346 pp. ISBN 0-02-927340-4.

The authors served as consultants to the Select Commission on Immigration and Refugee Policy in 1980. They discuss how no one knows how many refugees there are. Refugees are desperate people who have been pushed out of their native country because of wars, disasters, or persecution. Thousands of refugees are admitted to the United States each year and afforded resettlement benefits. This book discusses the humanitarian policies of the United States and the selection of refugees by the U.S. government. It describes the resentment and other problems immigration has historically created. Chapters have extensive bibliographical information

Nackerud, Larry G. *The Central American Refugee Issue in Brownsville, Texas: Seeking Understanding of Public Policy Formulation from Within a Community Setting.* San Francisco, CA: Mellen Research University Press, 1993, 255 pp. ISBN 0-7734-2240-4.

In this volume the author relates how Brownsville, Texas, an impoverished community, reacted to the influx of thousands of asylum seekers from Central America. The appearance of these asylum seekers took a heavy toll on the people of the city and wreaked havoc on public and private institutions for providing social services. The author lived in Brownsville to conduct research on Central Americans coming to the town; he learned their stories of being sponsored by a friend or relative and going on to Miami or elsewhere in the United States. Appendix A lists the questions he asked in his interviews, and Appendix B describes procedures used to interview individuals. There are several pages of bibliographical items.

Ong, Paul, Edna Bonacich, and Lucie Cheng, eds. *The New Asian Immigration in Los Angeles and Global Restructuring.* Asian American History and Culture Series. Philadelphia, PA: Temple University Press, 1994, 330 pp. ISBN 1-56639-217-9.

Research for this book was done before the Los Angeles riots of April 29 to May 1, 1992. The authors decided to focus on Asian immigrants in Los Angeles so they could combine the global or regional level with the local level and consider how the two interact. They stress how social forces affect immigration and the economic and political adaptation of immigrants. The first part discusses the issues studied. The second part analyzes developments in Asia since World War II and how they affect immigration conditions and policy in the United States. The book's third part looks at the economy of Los Angeles and the role immigrants have played. The final part of the book examines political issues and effects with respect to Asian immigration. Each chapter includes bibliographical notes and a list of references.

Rivera, Mario Antonio. *Decision and Structure: U.S. Refugee Policy in the Mariel Crisis.* Lanham, MD: University Press of America, 1991, 263 pp. ISBN 0-8191-8389-X.

This book's author served as a research analyst with the Cuban-Haitian Task Force, and when it disbanded he continued working with the Cuban-Haitian Entrant Program in the Office of Refugee Resettlement of the Department of Health and Human Services. The book begins by giving the history of Cuban immigration and the Mariel boatlift, showing how the Carter administration was not prepared for such an event. Federal legislation at the time was ineffective, and as a result states and various localities shouldered the fiscal and social burdens of the boatlift. The Reagan administration's policies were similar. Acronyms are used throughout the book and are explained. Notes follow each chapter. A list of bibliographical references is also found.

Sutter, Valerie O'Connor. *The Indochinese Refugee Dilemma.* Political Traditions in Foreign Policy Series. Baton Rouge, LA: Louisiana State University, 1990, 256 pp. ISBN 0-8071-1556-8.

Refugees from the Indochina countries have been leaving for more than a decade. This book discusses the foreign policy interests related to problems with these refugees. The author investigates social, economic, and political factors in Indochina to show how these internal interests have affected or are affected by refugees. She also considers the national interests of Indochinese refugees and compares these individuals to other refugees. She discusses the relationship between national interests and humanitarian efforts to assist refugees. The book concludes with an investigation of national interests and the implications for resolution, stalemate, or expansion of the Indochinese crisis. The book is footnoted and has a list of bibliographical references.

Yarnold, Barbara M. *Refugees without Refuge: Formation and Failed Implementation of U.S. Political Asylum Policy in the 1980s.* Lanham, MD: University Press of America, 1990, 270 pp. ISBN 0-8191-7845-4.

This book offers a wealth of information on the United States Refugee Act of 1980 and its impact on refugees. The act provided political asylum and aimed to prevent bias in favor of aliens from hostile countries. The histories of U.S. immigration, refugee, and asylum policies are detailed in full. Specific cases are used for explanation. The book has six appendixes, a few tables, and bibliographical references.

Zucker, Norman L., and Naomi Flink Zucker. *The Guarded Gate: The Reality of American Refugee Policy.* San Diego, CA: Harcourt Brace Jovanovich, 1987, 342 pp. ISBN 0-15-137575-5.

These authors look at the circumstances associated with refugees and give recommendations for admitting refugees to the United States. They suggest upgrading the importance of refugees. In their view, the United States should be the leader with respect to assisting refugees and should help further the international system for protecting refugees. The book discusses how the Refugee Act of 1980 helped aliens become citizens and gives them temporary protection. Bibliographical notes are found for each chapter.

# Journal Articles and Government Documents

## General

"America and the Immigrant." *Proteus* 11 (Fall 1994): 5–65.

Andreas, Peter. "Border Troubles: Free Trade, Immigration and Cheap Labour." *Ecologist* 24 (November–December 1994): 230–234.

Bentivegna, Joseph. "A Study of the San Cataldesi Who Emigrated to Dunmore, Pennsylvania." *Pennsylvania Folklife* 45 (Autumn 1995): 22–30.

Blace, Francine D. *The Fertility of Immigrant Women: Evidence from High Fertility Source Countries.* NBER Working Paper no. 3608. Cambridge, MA: National Bureau of Economic Research, 1991, 58 pp.

Black, J. S., Hal G. Gregersen, and Mark E. Mendenhall. "Toward a Theoretical Framework of Repatriation Adjustment." *Journal of International Business Studies* 23, 4 (1992): 737–760.

Cerrone, Catherine. "An Aura of Toughness, Too?: Italian Immigration to Pittsburgh and Vicinity." *Pennsylvania Folklife* 45 (Autumn 1995): 37–42.

Cisneros, Henry, and Ryzard Kapuscinski. "American Dynamism & the New World Culture." *New Perspectives Quarterly* 5 (Summer 1988): 36–46.

Coates, J. F. "Immigration Then, Now and in the Future." *Technological Forecasting and Social Change* 39 (July 1995): 411–415.

DeLeo, Nicholas V. "A Look at the Early Years of Philadelphia's 'Little Italy'." *Pennsylvania Folklife* 45 (Autumn 1995): 31–36.

Dowty, Alan. "The Assault on Freedom of Emigration." *World Affairs* 151 (Fall 1988): 85–92.

Espenshade, Thomas J. "Does the Threat of Border Apprehension Deter Undocumented U.S. Immigration?" *Population and Development Review* 20 (December 1994): 871–892.

Fawcett, James T. "Networks, Linkages, and Migration Systems" *International Migration Review* 23 (Fall 1989): 671–680.

Frey, William H. "Immigration and Internal Migration 'Flight': A California Case Study." *Population and Environment* 16 (March 1995): 353–375.

———. "Immigration and Internal Migration Flight from U.S. Metropolitan Areas: Toward a New Demographic Balkanisation." *Urban Studies* 32 (May 1995): 733–757.

"The Future of Migration." *International Migration Review* 21 (Spring 1987): 128–154.

Garson, Jean-Pierre. "International Migration: Facts, Figures, Policies." *OECD (Org Econ Coop and Development) Observer* (June–July 1992): 18–23.

Garvin, Glenn. "No Fruits, No Shirts, No Service: The Real-World Consequences of Closed Borders." *Reason* (April 1995): 18–26.

Gordon, Jennifer L. "Out of the Spotlight and into the Shadows." *Migration World* 17, 5 (1989): 10–17.

Hardin, Garrett. "There Is No Global Population Problem: Can Humanists Escape the 'Catch-22' of Population Control?" *Humanist* 49 (July–August 1989): 11–13+.

Hatton, Timothy J., and Jeffrey G. Williamson. *The Impact of Immigration on American Labor Markets Prior to the Quotas.* Cambridge, MA: National Bureau of Economic Research, 1995, 59 pp.

Hing, Bill Ong. "Immigration Policies: Messages of Exclusion to African Americans." *Howard Law Journal* 37 (Winter 1994): 237–282.

"Immigration Commission Proposals: An Analysis." *Migration World Magazine* 22, 5 (1994): 24–26.

"Immigration Debate." *Foreign Policy* (Summer 1994): 139–150.

"International Migration: Perspectives from Three Continents." *Regional Development Dialogue* 12 (Autumn 1991): 3–209.

Jamison, Tena. "Immigration On-line: The Privacy Implications of a National Registry." *Human Rights (American Bar Association)* (Winter 1995): 12–15.

Jefferson, Jon. "Alienation: Is There a Legal Solution to the Immigration Mess?" *ABA (American Bar Association) Journal* 79 (September 1993): 54–59.

Jost, Kenneth. "Cracking Down on Immigration: Should Government Benefits and Services Be Cut Off?" *CQ Researcher* 5 (February 3, 1995): 99–119.

Joyce, Carmel. "Playing the Green Card." *Business and Finance (Ireland)* 27 (August 1, 1991): 18–19.

Legomsky, Stephen H. "Forum Choices for the Review of Agency Adjudication: A Study of the Immigration Process." *Iowa Law Review* 71 (July 1986): 1297–1403.

Leimberg, S. R., and T. Kurlowicz. "Liquidity Planning Considerations for the Resident Alien." *Journal of the American Society of CLU & ChFC* 44 (November 1990): 58–67; 45 (January 1991): 44–50.

Lemann, N. "The Underclass and the Great Migration." *Public Interest*, no. 105 (Fall 1991): 107–122.

Mahtesian, Charles. "Immigration: The Symbolic Crackdown." *Governing* 7 (May 1994): 52–55+.

Marotto, Robert A. "Are Those Streetpeople Part of the New Poor, Too? Toward an Applied Sociology of Social Problems." *American Sociologist* 20 (Summer 1989): 111–122.

Martin, Philip L. "The Migration Issues." *Migration World Magazine* 20, 5(1992): 10–15.

Massey, Douglas S. "The Social and Economic Origins of Immigration." *Annals of the American Academy of Political and Social Science* 510 (July 1990): 60–72.

McCarthy, Donald. "This Land Is Not Your Land: The Propagating of Proposition 187." *Business Mexico* 5 (May 1995): 24–27.

McConnell, S. "The New Battle Over Immigration." *Fortune* 117 (May 9, 1988): 89–91+.

McDaniel, Antonio. "The Dynamic Racial Composition of the United States." *Daedalus* 124 (Winter 1995): 179–198.

Morrison, Peter A. *Demographic Factors Reshaping Ties to Family and Place.* (Rand Note N-3271-RC). Santa Monica, CA: Rand Corporation, 1990, 10 pp.

Neuman, Gerald L. "We Are the People: Alien Suffrage in German and American Perspective." *Michigan Journal of International Law* 13 (Winter 1992): 259–335.

Nowak, J. E. "Managing in a City of Changing Demographics." *Public Management* 73 (April 1991): 3–7.

"123 Million People on the Move: The Tides of Humanity." *World Press Review* 41 (October 1994): 8–13.

Organization for Economic Cooperation and Development. *The Changing Course of International Migration.* Paris, France: 1993, 263 pp.

Portes, Alejandro, and Min Zhou. "Should Immigrants Assimilate?" *Public Interest (Washington)* (Summer 1994): 18–33.

Rex, Tom R. "Migration Patterns Stabilize During 80s." *Arizona Business* 33 (December 1986): 1–5.

Robey, Bryant. "Locking up Heaven's Door." *American Demographics* 9 (February 1987): 24–29+.

Saverino, Joan. "'Domani Ci Zappa': Italian Immigration and Ethnicity in Pennsylvania." *Pennsylvania Folklife* 45 (Autumn 1995): 2–22.

Schuck, Peter H. "The Message of 187: Facing up to Illegal Immigration." *American Prospect* (Spring 1995): 85–92.

Simon, Julian L. "The Case for Greatly Increased Immigration." *Public Interest (Washington)* (Winter 1991): 89–103.

Skerry, P. "Individualist America and Today's Immigrants." *Public Interest* 2 (Winter 1991): 104–118.

"Special Report: The Challenge of Immigration." *World and I* 7 (October 1992): 22–49.

Stokes, Bruce. "Millions on the Move: State-Controlled Economics and Authoritarian Political Systems Are Collapsing around the World." *National Journal* 23 (November 23, 1991): 2850–2854.

Svorny, S. "Consumer Gains from Physician Immigration to the U.S.: 1966–1971." *Applied Economics* 23 (February 1991): 331–337.

"Symposium: Challenges in Immigration Law and Policy: An Agenda for the Twenty-first Century." *New York Law School Journal of Human Rights* 11 (Symposium 1994): 451–601.

"Symposium on Immigration." *American Philosophical Society Proceedings* 136 (June 1992): 157–225.

"Temporary Worker Programs: Mechanisms, Conditions, Consequences: Special Issue." *International Migration Review* 20 (Winter 1986): 740–1019.

Theophano, Janet. "Expressions of Love, Acts of Labor: Women's Work in an Italian American Community." *Pennsylvania Folklife* 45 (Autumn 1995): 43–49.

U.S. Commission on Immigration Reform. U.S. *Immigration Policy: Restoring Credibility: 1994 Report to Congress.* Washington, DC: Government Printing Office, 1994, 250 pp.

U.S. Congress. House. Committee on Government Operations. Information, Justice, Transportation and Agriculture Subcommittee. *Controlling the Flow of Illegal Immigration at U.S. Land Borders: Hearing, December 10, 1993.* 103d Cong., 1st sess. Washington, DC: Government Printing Office, 1994, 137 pp.

———. *The Impact of Federal Immigration Policy and INS Activities on Communities: Hearings, June 2, 1993–March 28, 1994.* 103d Cong., 1st and 2d sess. Washington, DC: Government Printing Office, 1995, 644 pp.

U.S. Congress. House. Committee on the Judiciary. Subcommittee on Immigration and Claims. *Foreign Visitors Who Violate the Terms of Their Visas by Remaining in the United States Indefinitely: Hearing, February 24, 1995.* 104th Cong., 1st sess. Washington, DC: Government Printing Office, 1995, 49 pp.

———. *Management Practices of the Immigration and Naturalization Service: Hearing, February 8, 1995.* 104th Cong., 1st sess. Washington, DC: Government Printing Office, 1995, 50 pp.

U.S. Congress. House. Committee on the Judiciary. Subcommittee on International Law, Immigration and Refugees. *Haitian Asylum–Seekers: Hearing, June 15, 1994, on H.R. 3663, H.R. 4114, and H.R. 4264.* 103d Cong., 2d sess. Washington, DC: Government Printing Office, 1994, 504 pp.

U.S. President. *Comprehensive Triennial Report on Immigration, January 1989.* Washington, DC: Government Printing Office, 1990, various paging.

Weiner, Myron. "Security, Stability and International Migration." *International Security* 17 (Winter 1992/1993): 91–126.

"Why Excess Immigration Damages the Environment." *Population and Environment* 13 (Summer 1992): 303–312.

Widgren, Jonas. "International Migration and Regional Stability." *International Affairs (London)* 66 (October 1990): 749–766.

Zlolnik, Hania. "South-to-North Migration Since 1960: The View from the North." *Population Bulletin of the United Nations*, no. 31/32 (1991): 17–37.

## History

Coates, J. F. "Immigration Then, Now, and in the Future." *Technological Forecasting and Social Change* 39 (July 1991): 411–415.

Mutzbauer, Monica. "Leaving the Old World for the New: Rules Governing Emigration from Landau in the Palatinate." *Pennsylvania Folklife* 44 (Spring 1995): 137–144.

Salt, John. "A Comparative Overview of International Trends and Types, 1950–80." *International Migration Review* 23 (Fall 1989): 431–456.

## Laws and Regulations

Arp, William, Marilyn K. Dantico, and Marjorie S. Zatz. "The Immigration Reform and Control Act of 1986: Differential Impacts on Women?" *Social Justice (San Francisco)* 17 (Summer 1990): 23–39.

Baker, Susan Gonzalez. *The Cautious Welcome: The Legalization Programs of the Immigration Reform and Control Act*. Santa Monica, CA: Rand Corporation, 1990, 196 pp.

Bean, Frank D., Georges Vernez, and Charles B. Keely. *Opening and Closing the Doors: Evaluating Immigration Reform and Control*. Santa Monica, CA: Rand Corporation; Washington, DC: Urbana Institute, 1989, 138 pp.

Bessette, Diane M. "Getting Left Behind: The Impact of the 1986 Immigration Reform and Control Act Amnesty Program on Single Women with Children." *Hastings International and Comparative Law Review* 13 (Winter 1990) 287–314.

Biskupic, Joan. "Immigration and Legislation." *Congressional Quarterly Weekly Report* 48 (December 8, 1990): 4105–4112.

Boswell, Richard A. "The Immigration Reform Amendments of 1986: Reform or Rehash?" *Journal of Legislation* 14, 1 (1987): 23–40.

Briggs, V. M., Jr. "Immigration Reform and the Urban Labor Force [with Discussion]." *Labor Law Journal* 42 (August 1991): 537–545.

Brownstein, Amy R. "Why Same-Sex Spouses Should Be Granted Preferential Immigration Status: Reevaluating Adams v. Howerton." *Loyola of Los Angeles International and Comparative Law Journal* 16 (June 1994): 763–798.

Cathcart, D. A., and J. K. Lilly. "The Immigration Reform and Control Act of 1986—Key Compliance Issues [Nondiscrimination Provisions of the Frank Amendment]." *Employee Relations Law Journal* 13 (Autumn 1987): 224–248.

Clinton, William J. "Statement on Signing the Immigration and Nationality Technical Corrections Act of 1994, October 24, 1994." *Weekly Compilation of Presidential Documents* 30 (October 31, 1994): 152–153.

Cornelius, Wayne A. "Impacts of the 1986 U.S. Immigration Law on Emigration from Rural Mexican Sending Communities." *Population and Development Review* 15 (December 1989): 689–705.

Donato, Katharine M., Jorge Durand, and Douglas S. Massey. "Stemming the Tide? Assessing the Deterrent Effects of the Immigration Reform and Control Act." *Demography (Population Association of America)* 29 (May 1992): 139–157.

Finch, Wilbur A., Jr. "The Immigration Reform and Control Act of 1986: A Preliminary Assessment." *Social Service Review* 64 (June 1990): 244–260.

Frierson, James G. "National Origin Discrimination: The Next Wave of Lawsuits." *Personnel Journal* 66 (December 1987): 97–98+.

Groban, R. S., Jr. "The Immigration Act of 1990: An Employee's Primer of Its New Provisions." *Employee Relations Law Journal* 17 (Winter 1991–1992): 357–387.

Guendelsberger, John, "The Right to Family Unification in French and United States Immigration Law." *Cornell International Law Journal* 21 (Winter 1988): 1–102.

Guskind, Robert. "Border Backlash: Facing a Tough Reelection Battle, California Governor Pete Wilson Is Mounting a Harshly Worded Campaign Against Illegal Immigrants; in the Process, He's Making National Issues of the Costs of Providing for the 'Illegals' and the Federal Government's Responsibilities." *National Journal* 26 (June 4, 1994): 1296–1299.

Helton, Arthur C. "U.S. Refugee Policy: African and Caribbean Effects." *TransAfrica Forum* 9 (Summer 1992): 93–102.

"Immigration Law: United States and International Perspectives on Asylum and Refugee Status." *Loyola of Los Angeles International and Comparative Law Journal* 16 (Symposium Issue 1994): 1–269.

Juffras, Jason. *Impact of the Immigration Reform and Control Act on the Immigration and Naturalization Service.* RAND/JRI–09. Santa Monica, CA: Rand Corporation, 1991, 93 pp.

Kanstroom, Daniel. "Judicial Review of Amnesty Denials: Must Aliens Bet Their Lives to Get into Court?" *Harvard Civil Rights–Civil Liberties Law Review* 25 (Winter 1990): 53–100.

Kirschten, Dick. "Second Thoughts: After Election Day, It Appeared the Stage Was Set for a Radical Overhaul of the Nation's Immigration Policies; Suddenly It's No Longer Clear That the Republican Party Is Itching for an Inflammatory and Partisan Confrontation." *National Journal* 27 (January 21, 1995): 150–155.

"Law and Human Resources in the Canada–U.S. Context: Proceedings of the Canada–United States Law Institute Conference, Cleveland, Ohio, April 20–22, 1990." *Canada–United States Law Journal* 16 (1990): 1–332.

Loken, Gregory A., and Lisa R. Bambino. "Harboring Sanctuary and the Crime of Charity under Federal Immigration Law." *Harvard Civil Rights–Civil Liberties Law Review* 28 (Winter 1993): 119–184.

Mann, Marilyn. "Timeliness of Petitions for Judicial Review under Section 106(a) of the Immigration and Nationality Act." *Michigan Law Review* 86 (April 1988): 990–1023.

Marshall, Patrick G. "The Politics of American Refugee Policy: Critics of U.S. Refugee Policy Say the Government Unfairly Favors Those Fleeing Communist Countries or Other Nations with Which the United States Is at Odds: The Refugee Act of 1980 Was Meant to Depoliticize the Process, but as Recent Disputes over Soviet Emigrés Indicate, the Legislation Hasn't Had the Intended Effect." *Editorial Research Reports* (October 27, 1989): 602–615.

Matlack, Carol. "Working around a Law: As U.S. Officials Start Enforcing New Rules Covering up to Five Million Illegal Aliens, They Confront an Economy Still Using Such Workers to Do Hard Jobs at Low Pay." *National Journal* 19 (July 1, 1987): 1776–1781.

McDonald, J. J., Jr. "IRCA and the Fourth Amendment: Constitutionality of Warrantless Access Provisions." *Employee Relations Law Journal* 13 (Winter 1987–1988): 426–444.

McGrath Dale, Susan, Michael C. LeMay, and Al E. Mariam. "Breaching the Barriers: Migrating Ethnic Groups and Immigration Policy." *Southeastern Policy Review* 22 (December 1994): 729–752.

Moore, Stephen. "Mixed Blessings—The New Immigration Law Will Be Good for Some Businesses, Bad for Others; The Larger Question: Is This Infusion of Human Capital Really Necessary?" *Across the Board* 28 (March 1991): 45–49.

Muñoz, Rosalio. "The Simpson-Rodino Immigration Law: An Assault on the Working Class." *Political Affairs* 66 (June 1987): 12–18.

New Jersey. General Assembly. Labor Committee. *Public Hearing: "Testimony on Undocumented Aliens in New Jersey and Their Impact on Jobs and Money Spent for Them in Health Care, Education, Prisons, and other Services": Trenton, New Jersey, April 11, 1994.* Trenton, NJ, 1994, 222 pp.

Papademetriou, D. G., and B. L. Lowell. "Immigration Reform and the Skill Shortage Issue [with Discussion]." *Labor Law Journal* 42 (August 1991): 520–527, 544–545.

Patterson, Judith, Gina G. Palmer, and Elizabeth Brandes. "IRCA, IMFA, and SDCEA: What Does This Immigration Alphabet Soup Spell?" *Baylor Law Review* 39 (Spring 1987): 413–468.

Perotti, Rosanna. "IRCA's Antidiscrimination Provisions: What Went Wrong?" *International Migration Review* 26 (Fall 1992): 732–753.

Pilotte, Hannah L. D. "IRCA: A Double-Edged Sword for Unwary Employers." *Employment Relations Today* 17 (Summer 1990): 121–126.

Pirie, Sophie H. "The Need for a Codified Definition of 'Persecution' in United States Refugee Law." *Stanford Law Review* 39 (November 1986): 187–234.

"Reexamining the Constitutionality of INS Workplace Raids after the Immigration Reform and Control Act of 1986." *Harvard Law Review* 100 (June 1987): 1979–2000.

Robinson, Robert K., and Diana L. Gilbertson. "The Immigration Reform and Control Act of 1986: Employer Liability in the Employment of Undocumented Aliens." *Labor Law Journal* 38 (October 1987): 658–664.

Rolph, Elizabeth, and Abby Robyn. *A Window on Immigration and Reform: Implementing the Immigration Reform and Control Act in Los Angeles.* RAND/JRI–06. Santa Monica, CA: Rand Corporation, 1990, 117 pp.

Schuck, Peter H., and Theodore Hsien Wang. "Continuity and Change: Patterns of Immigration Litigation in the Courts, 1979–1990." *Stanford Law Review* 45 (November 1992): 115–183.

Sculnick, Michael W. "Immigration Reform: What It Means for Employers—The Immigration Reform and Control Act of 1986 Imposes Significant New Monitoring and Recordkeeping Burdens on Employers." *Employment Relations Today* 14 (Spring 1987): 3–7.

"Selected Comments on 1986 Immigration Reforms." *University of Miami Law Review* 41 (May 1987): 997–1116.

Siegel, Martha S., and Laurence A. Canter. *The Insiders' Guide to the New Immigration Act of 1990.* Tucson, AZ: Sheridan Chandler Co., 1990, 44 pp.

Skrentny, Roger. "Immigration Reform: What Cost to Business." *Personnel Journal* 66 (October 1987): 52–60.

"Symposium: Challenges in Immigration Law and Policy—An Agenda for the Twenty-first Century." *New York Law School Journal of Human Rights* 11 (1994): 451–601.

Thompson, G. D., and P. L. Martin. "Immigration Reform and the Agricultural Labor Force [with Discussion]." *Labor Law Journal* 42 (August 1991): 528–536, 544–545.

Tysse, G. John. *The New Immigration Law: An Employer's Handbook.* Publication no. 7009. Washington, DC: Chamber of Commerce of the United States, 1987, 60 pp.

U.S. Congress. House. *Immigration Act of 1989, Joint Hearings: Pts. 1–3, September 27, 1989–March 14, 1990, on S. 358 and Other Bills Before the Subcommittee on Immigration, Refugees and International Law of the Committee on the Judiciary and the Immigration Task Force of the Committee on Education and Labor.* 101st Cong., 2d sess. Washington, DC: Government Printing Office, 1989–1990, 3 parts.

————. *Impact of an Alien Verification System on Assisted Housing Programs: Joint Hearing, August 6, 1986, Before the Subcommittee on Housing and Community Development of the Committee on Banking, Finance and Urban Affairs and the Select Committee on Aging, on H.R. 3810, a Bill to Amend the Immigration and Nationality Act to Revise and Reform the Immigration Laws, and for Other Purposes.* 99th Cong., 2d sess. Washington, DC: Government Printing Office, 1986, 336 pp.

————. *Processing of Soviet Refugees: Joint Hearing, September 14, 1989, Before the Subcommittee of Europe and the Middle East of the Committee on Foreign Affairs, and the Subcommittee on Immigration, Refugees, and International Law of the Committee on the Judiciary.* 101st Cong., 1st sess. Washington, DC: Government Printing Office, 1990, 221 pp.

U.S. Congress. House. Committee on Education and Labor. Subcommittee on Employment Opportunities. *Hearing on Employment Discrimination under the Immigration Reform and Control Act: Hearing, October 30, 1989.* 101st Cong., 1st sess. Washington, DC: Government Printing Office, 1989, 181 pp.

U.S. Congress. House. Committee on Energy and Commerce. Subcommittee on Health and the Environment. *HHS Authority over Immigration and Public Health: Hearing, June 27, 1990, on H.R. 4506, a Bill to Require the Secretary of Health and Human Services to Review and Revise the List of Contagious Diseases Used in the Exclusion of Aliens from the United States.* 101st Cong., 1st sess. Washington, DC: Government Printing Office, 1991, 114 pp.

U.S. Congress. House. Committee on Foreign Affairs. *U.S. Policy toward Haitian Refugees: Joint Hearing and Markup, June 11 and 17, 1992, Before the Subcommittee on Western Hemisphere Affairs and International Operations.* 102d Cong., 2d sess. Washington, DC: Government Printing Office, 1992, 172 pp.

U.S. Congress. House. Committee on Foreign Affairs. Subcommittee on Asian and Pacific Affairs. *Indochinese Refugees at Risk: The Boat People, Cambodians under Khmer Rouge Control, and Re-education–Camp Detainees: Hearing, February 8, 1989.* 101st Cong., 1st sess. Washington, DC: Government Printing Office, 1989, 170 pp.

U.S. Congress. House. Committee on Foreign Affairs. Subcommittee on International Operations. *Funding Alternatives for Refugee Resettlement: Hearing, July 31, 1990.* 101st Cong., 2d sess. Washington, DC: Government Printing Office, 1990, 118 pp.

———. *The Refugee Dilemma in Europe and Asia and the United States' Response: Hearing, June 20, 1990.* 101st Cong., 2d sess. Washington, DC: Government Printing Office, 1990, 104 pp.

U.S. Congress. House. Committee on Government Operations. Government Information, Justice, and Agriculture Subcommittee. *Immigration and Nationalization Service and U.S. Border Control: Agency Mission and Pursuit Policies: Hearing, July 30, 1992.* 102d Cong., 2d. sess. Washington, DC: Government Printing Office, 1993, 311 pp.

U.S. Congress. House. Committee on Government Operations. Information, Justice, Transportation and Agriculture Subcommittee. *The Impact of Federal Immigration Policy and INS Activities on Communities: Hearings, June 2, 1993–March 28, 1994.* 103d Cong., 1st and 2d sess. Washington, DC: Government Printing Office, 1995, 644 pp.

U.S. Congress. House. Committee on the Judiciary. *Immigration and Nationality Act (Reflecting Laws Enacted as of April 1, 1992) with Notes and Related Laws, April 1992.* 102d Cong., 2d sess. Washington, DC: Government Printing Office, 1992, 617 pp.

———. *The "Immigration Reform and Control Act of 1986" (P.L. 99-603): A Summary and Explanation.* 99th Cong., 2d sess. Washington, DC: Government Printing Office, 1986, 35 pp.

U.S. Congress. House. Committee on the Judiciary. Subcommittee on Immigration, Refugees, and International Law. *Central America, Asylum-Seekers: Hearing, March 9, 1989.* 101st Cong., 1st sess. Washington, DC: Government Printing Office, 1989, 335 pp.

———. *Criminal Aliens: Hearing, November 1, 1989; on H.R. 3333, to Amend the Immigration and Nationality Act to Expand and Arrest Authority of Officers and Employees of the Immigration and Naturalization Service.* 101st Cong., 1st sess. Washington, DC: Government Printing Office, 1990, 152 pp.

———. *Eastern European Refugees: Hearing, November 2, 1989.* 101st Cong., 1st sess. Washington, DC: Government Printing Office, 1990, 116 pp.

———. *Exclusion and Deportation of Aliens: Hearing, June 23, 1987, on H.R. 1119.* 100th Cong., 1st sess. Washington, DC: Government Printing Office, 1987, 394 pp.

———. *Haitian Detention and Interdiction: Hearing, June 8, 1989.* 101st Cong., 1st sess. Washington, DC: Government Printing Office, 1989, 250 pp.

———. *Immigration Reform and Control Act of 1986 Oversight: Hearings, May 10 and 17, 1989.* 101st Cong., 1st sess. Washington, DC: Government Printing Office, 1990, 661 pp.

———. *Immigration Status of Chinese Nationals Currently in the United States: Hearing, July 20, 1989, on H.R. 2929 [and Other Bills].* 101st Cong., 1st sess. Washington, DC: Government Printing Office, 1989, 253 pp.

———. *Legal Immigration—Occupational Preferences: Hearing, July 21, 1987.* 100th Cong., 1st sess. Washington, DC: Government Printing Office, 1987, 109 pp.

———. *Orderly Departure Program and U.S. Policy Regarding Vietnamese Boat People: Hearing, June 28, 1989.* 101st Cong., 1st sess. Washington, DC: Government Printing Office, 1990, 100 pp.

———. *Reform of Legal Immigration: Hearings, September 7 and 16, 1988, on H.R. 5115 and S. 2104.* 100th Cong., 2d sess. Washington, DC: Government Printing Office, 1989, 622 pp.

———. *Soviet Refugees: Hearing, April 6, 1989, on H.R. 1605 and H. Con. Res. 73, Emergency Refugee Act of 1989.* 101st Cong., 1st sess. Washington, DC: Government Printing Office, 1989, 371 pp.

———. *Stay of Deportation for Undocumented Salvadorans and Nicaraguans: Hearing, May 20, 1987, on H.R. 618.* 100th Cong., 1st sess. Washington, DC: Government Printing Office, 1987, 139 pp.

U.S. Congress. House. Committee on the Judiciary. Subcommittee on International Law, Immigration, and Refugees. *Access to Public Assistance Benefits by Illegal Aliens: Hearing, May 11, 1994, on H.R. 3594 and H.R. 3860 (Title IV).* 103d Cong., 2d sess. Washington, DC: Government Printing Office, 1994, 223 pp.

————. *Administration's Proposed Refugee Admissions Program for Fiscal Year 1993: Hearing, July 30, 1992.* 102d Cong., 2d sess. Washington, DC: Government Printing Office, 1992, 194 pp.

————. *Alien Smuggling: Hearing, June 30, 1993.* 103d Cong., 1st sess. Washington, DC: Government Printing Office, 1993, 187 pp.

————. *Asylum and Inspections Reform: Hearing, April 27, 1993, on H.R. 1153, H.R. 1355 and H.R. 1679, Asylum Reform Act of 1993.* 103d Cong., 1st sess. Washington, DC: Government Printing Office, 1993, 452 pp.

————. *Cuban and Haitian Immigration: Hearing, November 20, 1991.* 102d Cong., 1st sess. Washington, DC: Government Printing Office, 1992, 241 pp.

————. *Employer Sanctions: Hearing, June 16, 1993.* 103d Cong., 1st sess. Washington, DC: Government Printing Office, 1994, 566 pp.

————. *Operations of the Border Patrol: Hearing August 5, 1992.* 102d Cong., 2d sess. Washington, DC: Government Printing Office, 1992, 269 pp.

————. *Refugee Admissions: Hearing, September 23, 1991.* 102d Cong., 1st sess. Washington, DC: Government Printing Office, 1992, 69 pp.

————. *Refugee Admissions Program for Fiscal Year 1994: Hearing, September 23, 1993.* 103d Cong., 1st sess. Washington, DC: Government Printing Office, 1994, 172 pp.

U.S. Congress. House. Committee on Small Business. Subcommittee on Regulation and Business Opportunities. *Impact of 1986 Immigration Law Reforms on Small Business: Hearing, June 22, 1987.* 100th Cong., 1st sess. Washington, DC: Government Printing Office, 1987, 138 pp.

U.S. Congress. House. Select Committee on Aging. *After 30 Years, America's Continuing Harvest of Shame: Hearing, April 24, 1990.*

101st Cong., 2d sess. Washington, DC: Government Printing Office, 1990, 288 pp.

U.S. Congress. Senate. Committee on Commerce, Science and Transportation. Subcommittee on Foreign Commerce and Tourism. *Visitor Facilitations: Hearing, July 18, 1990.* 101st Cong., 2d sess. Washington, DC: Government Printing Office, 1990, 114 pp.

U.S. Congress. Senate. Committee on Finance. Subcommittee on Social Security and Family Policy. *Tamper-Proof Social Security Cards: Hearing, April 18, 1990, and S. 214.* 101st Cong., 2d sess. Washington, DC: Government Printing Office, 1990, 38 pp.

U.S. Congress. Senate. Committee on the Judiciary. *Consultation on Refugee Admissions for the Fiscal Year 1990: Hearing, September 15, 1989.* 101st Cong., 1st sess. Washington, DC: Government Printing Office, 1990, 227 pp.

U.S. Congress. Senate. Committee on the Judiciary. Subcommittee on Immigration and Refugee Affairs. *Immigration Reform: Hearing, March 3, 1989, on S. 358 and S. 448.* 101st Cong., 1st sess. Washington, DC: Government Printing Office, 1990, 601 pp.

————. *Legal Immigration to the United States: A Demographic Analysis of Fifth Preference Visa Permissions: A Staff Report, April 1987.* 100th Cong., 1st sess. Washington, DC: Government Printing Office, 1987, 89 pp.

————. *Naturalization Procedures: Hearing, June 15, 1989, on Proposed Legislation to Modify Immigration and Naturalization Requirements.* 101st Cong., 1st sess. Washington, DC: Government Printing Office, 1990, 107 pp.

————. *Options for an Improved Employment Verification System: A Staff Report, September 1992.* 102d Cong., 2d sess. Washington, DC: Government Printing Office, 1992, 84 pp.

————. *Terrorism, Asylum Issues, and U.S. Immigration Policy: Hearing, May 28, 1993, on S. 667, a Bill to the Immigration and Nationality Act to Improve Procedures for the Exclusion of Aliens to Enter the United States by Fraud.* 103d Cong., 1st sess. Washington, DC: Government Printing Office, 1994, 209 pp.

————. *Torture Victim Protection Act of 1989: Hearing June 22, 1990, on S. 1629, a Bill to Establish Clearly a Federal Right of Action* by *Aliens and United States Citizens Against Persons Engaging In Torture or Extrajudicial Killing, and for Other Purposes, and H.R. 1662, a Bill to Amend the United Nations Participation Act of 1945 to Carry out Obligations of the United States under the United Nations Charter and Other International Agreements Pertaining to the Protection of Human Rights by Providing a Civil Action for Recovery from Persons Engaging in Torture and for Other Purposes.* 101st Cong., 2d sess. Washington, DC: Government Printing Office, 1991, 84 pp.

———. *U.S. Immigration Law and Policy, 1952–1986: A Report December 1987, by Joyce Vialet.* 100th Cong., 1st sess. Washington, DC: Government Printing Office, 1988, 138 pp.

U.S. Department of Justice. Civil Rights Division. Task Force on IRCA Related Discrimination. *Report and Recommendations, September 1990.* Washington, DC: 1990, 106 pp.

U.S. General Accounting Office. *Border Patrol: Southwest Border Enforcement Affected by Mission Expansion and Budget: Briefing Report to the Honorable Dennis Deconcini, U.S. Senate.* Report B-243386. Gaithersburg, MD: 1991, 21 pp.

———. *Nonimmigrant Visas: Requirements Affecting Artists, Entertainers, and Athletes: Report to Congressional Committees.* Report B-250554. Gaithersburg, MD: 1992, 23 pp.

———. *Refugee Program: The Orderly Departure Program from Vietnam: Report to the Chairman, Subcommittee on Immigration, Refugees, and International Law, Committee on the Judiciary, House of Representatives.* Report B-238006. Gaithersburg, MD: 1990, 12 pp.

———. *Soviet Refugees: Processing and Admittance to the United States: Report to Congressional Requesters.* Report B-238005. Gaithersburg, MD: 1990, 26 pp.

———. *State Department: 1991 Immigrant Visa Lottery: Report to the Honorable Brian Donnelly, House of Representatives.* Report B-248123. Gaithersburg, MD: 1992, 18 pp.

"U.S. Immigration Act of 1990 (November 29, 1990)." *International Legal Materials* 30 (March 1991): 298–381.

U.S. Immigration and Naturalization Service. *Immigration Reform and Control Act: Report on the Legalized Alien Population.* (M-375). Washington, DC: 1992, various paging.

White, Michael J., Frank D. Bean, and Thomas J. Espenshade. "The U.S. 1986 Immigration Reform and Control Act and Undocumented Migration to the United States." *Population Research and Policy Review* 9 (May 1990): 93–116.

Yale-Loehr, Stephen, ed. *Understanding the Immigration Act of 1990.* Washington, DC: Federal Publications, Inc., 1991, various paging.

Yarnold, Barbara M. "Federal Court Outcomes in Asylum-Related Appeals 1980–1987: A Highly 'Politicized' Process." *Policy Sciences (Amsterdam)* 23 (November 1990): 291–306.

———. "The Refugee Act of 1980 and the Depoliticization of Refugee/Asylum Admissions: An Example of Failed Policy Implementation." *American Politics Quarterly* 18 (October 1990): 527–536.

## Immigration—Policy

Anderson, Michelle J. "A License to Abuse: The Impact of Conditional Status on Female Immigrants." *Yale Law Journal* 102 (April 1993): 1401–1430.

Briggs, Vernon M., Jr. "Efficiency and Equity as Goals for Contemporary U.S. Immigration Policy." *Population and Environment* 11 (Fall 1989): 7–24.

———. "Immigration Policy: Political or Economic?" *Challenge* 34 (September–October 1991): 12–19.

Chiswick, Barry R. "Legal Aliens: Toward a Positive Immigration Policy." *Regulation (American Enterprise Institute)* 12, 1 (1988): 17–22.

Cooper, Mary H. "Immigration Reform: Do Immigration Policies Need a Radical Overhaul?" *CQ Researcher* 3 (September 24, 1993): 843–863.

Crown, William H., and Charles F. Longino, Jr. "State and Regional Policy Implications of Elderly Migration." *Journal of Aging and Social Policy* 3, 1–2 (1991): 185–207.

"The 'Explosiveness' of Chain Migration: Research and Policy Issues." *International Migration Review* 23 (Winter 1989): 797–903.

Graham, Otis L., Jr. *Re-thinking the Purposes of Immigration Policy,* CIS Paper no. 6. Washington, DC: Center for Immigration Studies, 1991, 36 pp.

"Immigration Reform: Pro and Con." *Congressional Digest* 65 (October 1989): 225–256.

Junk, Virginia W., and Joyce J. Dillman. *Public Policy and Housing and the Migration of the Maturing Population: A Working Bibliography.* CPL Bibliography no. 245. Chicago, IL: Council Planning Librarians, 1989, 47 pp.

Laude, Stephen, and Nellis Crigler. *Trade Policy Measures as a Means to Reduce Immigration in the 1990s: An Update.* Working Paper no. 28, Washington, DC: U.S. Committee for the Study of International Migration and Cooperation, 1990, 41 pp.

Martin, Philip L. "The Migration Issue." *Migration World Magazine* 20, 5 (1992): 10–15.

Moore, S. "Immigration Policy: Open Minds on Open Borders." *Business and Society Review,* no. 77 (Spring 1991): 35–40.

Rolph, Elizabeth S. *Immigration Policies: Legacy from the 1980s and Issues for the 1990s.* Santa Monica, CA: Rand Corporation, 1992, 58 pp.

Siegel, Martha S., and Laurence A. Canter. *U.S. Immigration Made Easy, 1991–1992: The Insiders' Guide.* Tucson, AZ: Sheridan Chandler Co., 1991, various paging.

Simon, Rita J., ed. "Immigration and American Public Policy." *Annals of the American Academy of Political and Social Science* 487 (September 1986): 9–217 (13 articles).

Skerry, Peter. "Borders and Quotas: Immigration and the Affirmative-Action State." *Public Interest (Washington)* (Summer 1989): 86–102.

Solomon, C. M. "Managing Today's Immigrants." *Personnel Journal* 72 (February 1993): 56–65.

Tichenor, Daniel J. "The Policy of Immigration Reform in the United States, 1981–1990." *Polity* 26 (Spring 1994): 333–362.

U.S. Bureau of International Labor Affairs. Division of Immigration Policy and Research. *Employer Sanctions and U.S. Labor Markets: First Report.* Washington, DC: 1991, 142 pp.

U.S. Committee for the Study of International Migration and Cooperation. Economic Development. *U.S. Policy and the Caribbean Basin Sugar Industry: Implications for Migration.* Washington, DC: 1990, 32 pp.

## Naturalization

Baker, Susan González. *The Cautious Welcome: The Legalization Programs of the Immigration Reform and Control Act.* RAND/ JRI–05. Santa Monica, CA: Rand Corporation, 1990, 196 pp.

Frelick, Bill. *Refugees at Our Border: The U.S. Response to Asylum Seekers.* Washington, DC: U.S. Committee for Refugees, 1989, 20 pp.

Guendelsberger, John W. "Access to Citizenship for Children Born within the State to Foreign Parents." *American Journal of Comparative Law* 40 (Spring 1992): 379–429.

Juffras, Jason. *Impact of the Immigration Reform and Control Act on the Immigration and Naturalization Service.* RAND/JRI–09. Santa Monica, CA: Rand Corporation, 1991, 93 pp.

Kirschten, Dick. "Border Traffic Cop: As Commissioner of the Immigration and Naturalization Service, Gene McNary Inherited an Agency in Distress; INS Watchers Say That He Has Been a Calming Influence." *National Journal* 22 (June 30, 1990): 1597–1600.

Stanfield, Rochelle L. "Cracking 'el Sistema': Latin American Immigrants, in Increasing Numbers, Are Turning to the Political System in Quest of Empowerment—Citizenship Is a Hurdle to Be Cleared on the Way to the Vote." *National Journal* 23 (June 1, 1991): 1284–1287.

U.S. Congress. House. Committee on Government Operations. Information, Justice and Agriculture Subcommittee. *Immigration and Naturalization Service and U.S. Border Patrol: Agency Mission and Pursuit Policies: Hearing, July 30, 1992.* 102d Cong., 2d sess. Washington, DC: Government Printing Office, 1992, 311 pp.

————. *The Immigration and Naturalization Service: A Mandate for Change: Hearing, March 30, 1993.* 103d Cong., 1st sess. Washington, DC: Government Printing Office, 1993, 299 pp.

U.S. Congress. House. Committee on the Judiciary. *Grounds for Exclusion of Aliens under the Immigration and Nationality Act: Historical Background and Analysis, September 1988.* 100th Cong., 2d sess. Washington, DC: Government Printing Office, 1988, 155 pp.

U.S. Congress. House. Committee on the Judiciary. Subcommittee on Immigration, Refugees and International Law. *Criminal Aliens: Hearing, November 1, 1989, on H.R. 3333, to Amend the Immigration and Naturalization Act to Expand the Arrest Authority of Officers and Employees of the Immigration and Naturalization Service.* 101st Cong., 1st sess. Washington, DC: Government Printing Office, 1990, 152 pp.

U.S. Congress. Senate. Committee on the Judiciary. Subcommittee on Immigration and Refugee Affairs. *Naturalization Procedures: Hearing, June 15, 1989, on Proposed Legislation to Modify Immigration and Naturalization Requirements.* 101st Cong., 1st sess. Washington, DC: Government Printing Office, 1990, 107 pp.

U.S. Immigration and Naturalization Service. *The Immigration of Adopted and Prospective Adoptive Children.* Washington, DC: Government Printing Office, 1990, 31 pp.

## Mathematical Models

Crane, Keith, et al. *The Effect of Employer Sanctions on the Flow of Undocumented Immigrants to the United States.* JRI-03. UI Report 90-8. Santa Monica, CA: Rand Corporation: Washington, DC: Urban Institute, 1990, 85 pp.

Graves, P. E., and T. A. Knapp. "Mobility Behavior of the Elderly." *Journal of Urban Economics* 24 (July 1988): 1–8.

Graves, P. E., and D. M. Waldman. "Multimarket Amenity Compensation and the Behavior of the Elderly [Retirement Migration]." *American Economic Review* 81 (December 1991): 1374–1381.

Greenwood, M. J., Gary L. Hunt, Dan S. Rickman, and George I. Treyz. "Migration, Regional Equilibrium, and the Estimation of Compensating Differentials." *American Economic Review* 81 (December 1991): 1382–1390.

Huang, W-C. "A Pooled Cross-Section and Time Series Study of Professional Indirect Immigration to the United States." *Southern Economic Journal* 54 (July 1987): 95–109.

Lake, M. B., and L. R. Conway. "Avoiding Discriminatory Immigration-Related Employment Practices." *Employment Relations Today* 15 (Spring 1988): 49–55.

Mathur, V. K., and S. H. Stein. "A Dynamic Interregional Theory of Migration and Population Growth." *Land Economics* 67 (August 1991): 292–298.

## Immigration—Trends

Blot, D. "The Demographics of Migration." *OECD Observer*, no. 163 (April–May 1990): 21–25.

Frey, William H. "Lifecourse Migration and Redistribution of the Elderly Across U.S. Regions and Metropolitan Areas." *Economic Outlook USA* 13, 2 (1986): 10–16.

————. "Migration and Depopulation of the Metropolis: Regional Restructuring or Rural Renaissance?" *American Sociological Review* 52 (April 1987): 240–257.

Garson, J. P. International Migration: Facts, Figures, Policies [OECD Countries]." *OECD Observer* 176 (June–July 1992): 18–24.

Green, Marshall. "Stop, All Ye Who Enter Here: U.S. Needs Annual Immigration Cap to Stem Tide of Illegal Aliens." *Foreign Service Journal* 71 (December 1994): 48–52.

Greenwood, Michael J., and Shannon E. Ragland. "Measuring the Net Migration of Immigrants to U.S. Metropolitan Areas." *Journal of Economics and Social Measurement* 17, 3–4 (1991): 233–248.

Haub, Carl. "World and United States Population Prospects." *Population and Environment* 12 (Spring 1991): 297–310.

Kahley, William J. "Measuring Interstate Migration." *Federal Reserve Bank of Atlanta* 75 (March–April 1990): 26–40.

Kraly, Ellen Percy. "Long-Term Immigration to the United States: New Approaches to Measurements." *International Migration Review* 25 (Spring 1991): 60–92.

Kraly, Ellen Percy, and Robert Warren. "Estimates of Long-Term Immigration to the United States: Moving U.S. Statistics toward United Nations Concepts." *Demography (Population Association of America)* 29 (November 1992): 613–626.

Kulkarni, Milind, and Louis G. Pol. "Migration Expectancy Revisited: Results for the 1970s, 1980s, and 1990s." *Population Research and Policy Review* 13 (June 1994): 195–202.

Luger, M. L. "Federal Tax Reform and the Interjurisdictional Mobility Impulse." *Journal of Urban Economics* 23 (March 1988): 235–250.

"Measuring International Migration: Theory and Practice— Special Issue." *International Migration Review* 21 (Winter 1987): 925–1550.

Morrill, Richard L. "Aging in Place, Age Specific Migration and Natural Decrease." *Annals of Regional Science* 29, 1 (1995): 41–66.

Roberts, Steven V. "Shutting the Golden Door: Economic Fear, Ethnic Prejudice and Politics as Usual Make the Melting Pot a Pressure Cooker." *U.S. News and World Report* 117 (October 3, 1994): 36–40.

Rosenwaike, Ira, and Katherine Hempstead. "Differential Mortality by Ethnicity: Foreign-Born Irish, Italians, and Jews in New York City, 1979–81." *Social Science and Medicine* 29, 7 (1989): 885–889.

Simon, J. L. "The Case for Greatly Increased Immigration." *Public Interest*, no. 102 (Winter 1991): 89–103.

U.S. General Accounting Office. *Illegal Aliens: Despite Data Limitations, Current Methods Provide Better Population Estimates: Report to the Chairman, Information, Justice, Transportation and Agriculture Subcommittee, Committee on Government Operations, House of Representatives.* Report B-253652. Gaithersburg, MD, 1993, 93 pp.

Warren, Robert, and Jeffrey S. Passel. "A Count of the Unaccountable: Estimates of Undocumented Aliens Counted in the

1980 United States Census." *Demography (Population Association of America)* 24 (August 1987): 375–393.

"Why Excess Immigration Damages the Environment." *Population and Environment* 13 (Summer 1992): 303–312.

Williams, Greg. "Population Growth and Migration in Alaska." *Alaska Economic Trends* 7 (February 1987): 1–9.

## Control of Immigration

Adarkar, Sachin D. "Political Asylum and Political Freedom: Moving towards a Just Definition of 'Persecution on Account of Political Opinion' under the Refugee Act." *UCLA (University of California-Los Angeles) Law Review* 42 (October 1994): 181–220.

Brownstein, Amy R. "Why Same-Sex Spouses Should Be Granted Preferential Immigration Status: Reevaluating Adams v. Howerton." *Loyola of Los Angeles International and Comparative Law* 16 (June 1994): 763–798.

Clinton, William J. "Proclamation 6636: Suspension of Entry as Immigrants and Nonimmigrants of Persons Who Formulate, Implement or Benefit from Policies That Are Impeding the Transition to Democracy in Nigeria, December 10, 1993." *Weekly Compilation of Presidential Documents* 29 (December 20, 1993): 2567.

Miller, Mark J., ed. "Strategies for Immigration Control: An International Comparison." *Annals of the American Academy of Political and Social Science* 524 (July 1994): 17–177.

Shughart, William F., II, Robert D. Tollison, and Mwangi S. Kimenyi. "The Political Economy of Immigration Restrictions." *Yale Journal of Regulation* 4 (Fall 1986): 79–97.

Skerry, P. "Borders and Quotas: Immigration and the Affirmative-Action State." *Public Interest*, no. 96 (Summer 1989): 86–102.

## Illegal Immigrants

Andreas, Peter. "The Making of Amerexico: (Mis)handling Illegal Immigration." *World Policy* 11 (Summer 1994): 45–56.

Arp, William, III. "The Exclusion of Illegal Hispanics in Agenda-Setting: The Immigration Reform and Control Act of 1986." *Policy Studies Review* 9 (Winter 1990): 327–338.

Bean, Frank D., Barry Edmonston, and Jeffrey S. Passel. *Undocumented Migration to the United States: IRCA and the Experience of the 1980s.* Santa Monica, CA: Rand Corporation, 1990, 271 pp.

Bratsberg, Brent. "Legal Versus Illegal U.S. Immigration and Source Country Characteristics." *Southern Economic Journal* 61 (January 1995): 715–727.

Clark, Rebecca L., Jeffrey S. Passel, Wendy N. Zimmerman, and Michael E. Fix. "Fiscal Impacts of Undocumented Immigrants." *Government Finance Review* 11 (February 1995): 20–22.

Clinton, William J. "Memorandum on Illegal Immigration, February 7, 1995." *Weekly Compilation of Presidential Documents* 31 (February 13, 1995): 200–204.

Cosco, J. "Bringing Illegal Aliens out of the Shadows [to Apply for Amnesty]." *Public Relations Journal* 44 (October 1988): 16–20+.

Crane, Keith, Donald P. Henry, and Katharine W. Webb. *The Effect of Employer Sanctions on the Flow of Undocumented Immigrants to the United States.* JRI-03. Santa Monica, CA: Rand Corporation, 1990, 85 pp.

DeParle, Jason. "Why Amnesty Failed: How to Make It Work for Illegal Immigrants." *Washington Monthly* 20 (April 1988): 11–14+.

Espenshade, Thomas J. "Does the Threat of Border Apprehension Deter Undocumented U.S. Immigration?" *Population and Development Review* 20 (December 1994): 871–892.

Farley, Christopher John. "Dangerous Tides: A New Wave of Illegal Aliens Is Finding a Perilous and Expensive Route into the United States." *Time* 145 (April 10, 1995) 56–57.

Gordon, Jennifer L. "Out of the Spotlight and into the Shadows." *Migration World* 17, 5 (1989): 10–17.

Griffin, Rodman D. "Illegal Immigration: Does It Damage the Economy and Strain Social Services?" *CQ Researcher* 2 (April 24, 1992): 363–383.

Henckaerts, Jean-Marie. "The Current Status and Content of the Prohibition of Mass Expulsion of Aliens." *Human Rights Law Journal* 15 (November 30, 1994): 301–317.

Hill, John K., and James E. Pearce. "Enforcing Sanctions Against Employers of Illegal Aliens." *Federal Reserve Bank of Dallas Economic Review* (May 1987): 1–15.

Idelson, Holly. "Immigration: Bridging Gap between Ideas and Action: Tightened Borders Are Gaining Support; Experts Debate Costs, Benefits of Newest Arrivals." *Congressional Quarterly Weekly Report* 53 (April 15, 1995): 1065–1066+.

Kirschten, Dick. "Catch-up Ball: Report of Terrorist Plots and Alien Smuggling, Combined with High Unemployment and Economic Uncertainty, Are Fanning Flames of Anti-Immigrant Sentiment; Scrambling to Respond, the White House Is Getting Tough on Political Asylum." *National Journal* 25 (August 7, 1993): 1976–1979.

——. "Second Thoughts: After Election, It Appeared the Stage Was Set for a Radical Overhaul of the Nation's Immigration Policies; Suddenly It's No Longer Clear That the Republican Party Is Itching for an Inflammatory and Partisan Confrontation." *National Journal* 27 (January 21, 1995): 150–155.

Long, Stewart, and Andrew Gill. "The Gender Gap in the Wages of Illegal Aliens." *Social Science Journal (Fort Worth)* 26, 1 (1989): 65–74.

Matlack, Carol. "Working around a Law: As U.S. Officials Start Enforcing New Rules Covering up to Five Million Illegal Aliens; They Confront an Economy Still Using Such Workers to Do Hard Jobs at Low Pay." *National Journal* 19 (July 11, 1987): 1776–1781.

Mitchell, Charles E. "Illegal Aliens, Employment Discrimination, and the 1986 Immigration Reform and Control Act." *Labor Law Journal* 40 (March 1989): 177–182.

Passel, Jeffrey S. "Undocumented Immigrants." *Annals of the American Academy of Political and Social Science* 487 (September 1986): 181–200.

Piatt, Bill. "Born as Second Class Citizens in the U.S.A.: Children of Undocumented Parents." *Notre Dame Law Review* 63, 1 (1988): 35–54.

"Refugees and International Population Flows." *Journal of International Affairs* 47 (Winter 1994): 341–588.

Siegel, Mark A., et al. *Immigration and Illegal Aliens: Burden or Blessing?* Information Series on Current Topics, Wylie, TX: Information Plus, 1989, 112 pp.

Smith, Paul J. "The Strategic Implications of Chinese Emigration." *Survival* 36 (Summer 1994): 60–77.

Solomon, Kay S. "An Alien Minor's Ability to Seek Asylum in the United States Against Parental Wishes." *Loyola of Los Angeles International and Comparative Law Journal* 9, 1 (1986): 169–191.

U.S. Committee for the Study of International Migration and Cooperation. Economic Development. *Unauthorized Migration: Addressing the Root Causes: Research Addendum, vol. 1–2, 1987–1990.* Washington, DC: 1990, 2 vols.

———. *Unauthorized Migration: An Economic Development Response: Report, July 1990.* Washington, DC: 1990, 110 pp.

U.S. Congress. House. Committee on Government Operations. Information, Justice, Transportation and Agriculture Subcommittee. *Controlling the Flow of Illegal Immigration at U.S. Land Borders: Hearing, December 10, 1993.* 103d Cong., 1st sess. Washington, DC: Government Printing Office, 1994, 137 pp.

U.S. Congress. House. Committee on the Judiciary. Subcommittee on International Law, Immigration, and Refugees. *Access to Public Assistance Benefits by Illegal Aliens: Hearing, May 11, 1994, on H.R. 3594 and H.R. 3860 (Title IV).* 103d Cong., 2d sess. Washington, DC: Government Printing Office, 1994, 223 pp.

———. *Alien Smuggling: Hearing June 30, 1993.* 103d Cong., 1st sess. Washington, DC: Government Printing Office, 1993, 187 pp.

———. *Border Violence: Hearing, September 29, 1993, on H.R. 2119, Immigration Enforcement Review Commission Act.* 103d Cong., 1st sess. Washington, DC: Government Printing Office, 1994, 366 pp.

U.S. Congress. Senate. Committee on Appropriations. *Increasing Costs of Illegal Immigration, Hearing.* 103d Cong., 2d sess. Washington, DC: 1994, 174 pp.

U.S. Congress. Senate. Committee on Governmental Affairs. Subcommittee on Federal Spending, Budget, and Accounting.

*Illegal Alien Felons: A Federal Responsibility: Hearing, March 12, 1987.* 100th Cong., 1st sess. Washington, DC: Government Printing Office, 1988, 145 pp.

U.S. General Accounting Office. *Illegal Aliens: Despite Data Limitations, Current Methods Provide Better Population Estimates; Report to the Chairman, Information, Justice, Transportation and Agriculture Subcommittee, Committee on Government Operations, House of Representatives.* Report B-253652. Gaithersburg, MD: 1993, 93 pp.

Warren, Robert, and Jeffrey S. Passel. "A Count of the Uncountable: Estimates of Undocumented Aliens Counted in the 1980 United States Census." *Demography (Population Association of America)* 24 (August 1987): 375–393.

White, Michael J., F. D. Bean, and T. S. Espenshade. "The U.S. 1986 Immigration Reform and Control Act and Undocumented Migration to the United States." *Population Research and Policy Review* 9 (May 1990): 93–116.

Wolf, Daniel. *Undocumented Aliens and Crime: The Case of San Diego County, Monograph Series 29.* La Jolla, CA: Center for U.S.-Mexican Studies. University of California, San Diego, 1988, 54 pp.

## Return Migration and Repatriation

Black, J. S., and H. B. Gregersen. "When Yankee Comes Home: Factors Related to Expatriate and Spouse Repatriation Adjustment." *Journal of International Business Studies* 22, 4 (1991): 671–694.

Getschman, Gregory J. "The Uncertain Role of Innocence in United States Efforts to Deport Nazi War Criminals." *Cornell International Law Journal* 21 (Summer 1988): 287–316.

Gonzalez, Rosalinda Mendez. "Operation Wetback and Operation Guatemala: The Cold War Objectives of Domestic Racism." In Zarembka, Paul, ed. *Research in Political Economy.* Greenwich, CT: JAI Press, 1987, 197–219.

Gregersen, H. B. "Commitments to a Parent Company and a Local Work Unit During Repatriation [American Expatriate Managers]." *Personnel Psychology* 45 (Spring 1992): 29–54.

Griffith, Elvin. "Asylum and Withholding of Deportation: Challenges to the Alien After the Refugee Act of 1989." *Loyola of Los Angeles International and Comparative Law Journal* 12 (March 1990): 515–577.

Harvey, M. G. "Repatriation of Corporate Executives: An Empirical Study." *Journal of International Business Studies* 20 (Spring 1989): 131–144.

Human Rights Watch. Americas Watch Committee. *Half the Story: The Skewed U.S. Monitoring of Repatriated Haitian Refugees.* New York: 1992, 16 pp.

Human Rights Watch. Asia Watch Committee. *Refugees at Risk: Forced Repatriation of Vietnamese from Hong Kong.* New York: 1992, 11 pp.

Napier, N. K., and R. B. Peterson. "Expatriate Re-entry: What Do Repatriates Have to Say." *Human Resource Planning* 14, 1 (1991): 19–28.

Rogers, Rosemarie. *Return Migration, Migrants' Savings and Sending Countries' Economic Development: Lessons from Europe.* Working Paper no. 30. Washington, DC: U.S. Commission for the Study of International Migration and Cooperation. 1990, 29 pp.

U.S. Congress. House. Committee on the Judiciary. Subcommittee on Immigration, Refugees, and International Law. *Exclusion and Deportation of Aliens: Hearing, June 23, 1987, on H.R. 1119.* 100th Cong., 1st sess. Washington, DC: Government Printing Office, 1987, 394 pp.

———. *Stay of Deportation for Undocumented Salvadorans and Nicaraguans: Hearing, May 20, 1987, on H.R. 618.* 100th Cong., 1st sess. Washington, DC: Government Printing Office, 1987, 139 pp.

U.S. Congress. House. Committee on Rules. Subcommittee on Rules of the House. *Central American Studies and Temporary Relief Act of 1987: Hearings, May 13–June 17, 1987, on H.R. 618 and H.R. 1409, to Temporarily Suspend the Deportation of Certain Salvadorans and Nicaraguans.* 100th Cong., 1st sess. Washington, DC: Government Printing Office, 1987, 297 pp.

White, Stephen E. "Interstate Return Migration: Regional Differences and Implications." *Social Science Journal* (Fort Worth) 29, 3 (1992): 347–362.

Winicki, Norine M. "The Denaturalization and Deportation of Nazi Criminals: Is It Constitutional?" *Loyola of Los Angeles International and Comparative Law Journal* 11, 1 (1989): 117–143.

## Economic Aspects

Berger, M. C., and P. E. Gabriel. "Risk Aversion and the Earnings of U.S. Immigrants and Natives." *Applied Economics* 23 (February 1991): 311–318.

Bleasdale, J. A. "Think Globally, Sell Locally [Real Estate Brokers; Working with Buyers from Other Countries]." *Real Estate Today* 25 (June 1992): 14–19.

Borjas, George J. *Assimilation and Changes in Cohort Quality Revisited: What Happened to Immigrant Earnings in the 1980s?* NBER Working Paper no. 4866, Cambridge, MA: National Bureau of Economic Research, 1994, 34 pp.

———. "Self-Selection and the Earnings of Immigrants." *American Economic Review* 77 (September 1987): 531–553. Discussion 80 (March 1990): 298–308.

Borjas, George J., Stephen G. Bronars, and Stephen J. Trejo. "Assimilation and the Earnings of Young Internal Migrants." *Review of Economics and Statistics* 74 (February 1992): 170–175.

Butcher, K. F., and D. Card. "Immigration and Wages: Evidence from the 1980s." *American Economic Review* 81 (May 1991): 292–296.

Clark, Rebecca L., Jeffrey S. Passel, Wendy N. Zimmerman, and Michael E. Fix."Fiscal Impacts of Undocumented Immigrants." *Government Finance Review* 11 (February 1995): 20–22.

Cohen, Yinon. "Socioeconomic Dualism: The Case of Israeli-Born Immigrants in the United States." *International Migration Review* 23 (Summer 1989): 267–288.

Daneshvary, N., Henry W. Herzog, Jr., Richard A. Hofler, and Alan M. Schlottmann. "Job Search and Immigrant Assimilation: An Earnings Frontier Approach." *Review of Economics and Statistics* 74 (August 1992): 482–492.

Field-Hendrey, E., and E. Balkan. "Earnings and Assimilation of Female Immigrants." *Applied Economics* 23 (October 1991): 1665–1672.

Freeman, Richard B. *Immigration, Trade and the Labor Market: Summary Report.* Cambridge, MA: National Bureau of Economic Research, 1988, 38 pp.

Gabriel, P. E., and S. Schmitz. "The Relative Earnings of Native and Immigrant Males in the United States." *Quarterly Review of Economics and Business* 27 (Autumn 1987): 91–101.

Giella, Catherine R. "Visas for Sale: A Comparison of the U.S. Investor Provision with the Australian Business Migration Program." *Northwestern Journal of International Law and Business* 13 (Spring–Summer 1992): 209–238.

Griffin, Rodman D. "Illegal Immigration: Does It Damage the Economy and Strain Social Services?" *CQ Researcher* 2 (April 24, 1992): 363–383.

Hensley, David. "The Impacts of Immigration Reform on the California Economy." *Labor Law Journal* 40 (August 1989): 527–535.

"How Much for How Many? Population and Consumption." *Environmental Action* 26 (1994): 15–26.

"The Immigrants: How They're Helping to Revitalize the U.S. Economy." *Business Week* (July 13, 1992): 114–118+.

"Immigration: Boon or Bane to the U.S.?" *World and I* 9 (January 1994): 359–393.

"It's Really Two Immigrant Economies: Refugees and Illegals Cost the U.S. Money; But Other Immigrants More Than Pay Their Way." *Business Week* (June 20, 1994): 74+.

King, Allan G., B. Lindsay Lowell, and Frank D. Bean. "The Effects of Hispanic Immigration on the Earnings of Native Hispanics Americans." *Social Science Quarterly* 67 (December 1986): 673–689.

Lee, Sharon M. "Poverty and the U.S. Asian Population." *Social Science Quarterly* 75 (September 1994): 541–559.

Light, Ivan, et al. "Beyond the Ethnic Enclave Economy." *Social Problems (Society for the Study of Social Problems)* 41 (February 1994): 65–80.

Massey, Douglas S. "Economic Development and International Migration in Comparative Perspective." *Population and Development Review* 14 (September 1988): 383–413.

Organization for Economic Co-operation and Development. *The Changing Course of International Migration*. Paris, France: 1993, 263 pp.

Peñaloza, Lisa. "Immigrant Consumers: Marketing and Public Policy Considerations in the Global Economy." *Journal of Public Policy and Marketing* 140 (Spring 1995): 83–94.

Perkins, John. "Immigration and Scale Economies: A Macro Analysis." *National Economic Review* (April 1992): 28–48.

Rahman, M. Azizur. "Self-Selection and Earnings: A Cross Section Analysis of U.S. Immigrants." *Bangladesh Development Studies* 19 (December 1991): 1–26.

Rauch, J. E. "Reconciling the Pattern of Trade with the Pattern of Migration [Skilled Labor Migration]." *American Economic Review* 81 (September 1991): 775–796.

Roberts, Steven P., Paul Glastris, and Jim Impoco: "Shutting the Golden Door: Economic Fear, Ethnic Prejudice and Politics as Usual Make the Melting Pot a Pressure Cooker." *U.S. News & World Report* 117 (October 3, 1994): 36–40.

Rothman, Eric S., and Thomas J. Espenshade. "Fiscal Impacts of Immigration to the United States." *Population Index (Princeton)* 58 (Fall 1992): 381–415.

Stanfield, Rochelle L. "Melting Pot Economics: With Immigration on the Rise and State Budget Balances in Decline, Generous Federal Policies for Admitting Refugees and Other Foreigners Are Being Questioned, But the Economic Costs and Benefits of Immigrants Are Far from Easy to Sort Out." *National Journal* 24 (February 22, 1992): 442–446.

Taylor, J. E. "Earnings and Mobility of Legal and Illegal Immigrant Workers in Agriculture." *American Journal of Agricultural Economics* 74 (November 1992): 889–896.

U.S. Committee for the Study of International Migration and Cooperation. Economic Development. *Unauthorized Migration*

*Addressing the Root Causes: Research Addendum, vols. 1–2, 1987–1990.* Washington, DC: 1990, 2 vols.

———. *Unauthorized Migration: An Economic Development Response: Report, July 1990.* Washington, DC: 1990, 110 pp.

U.S. Congress. House. Committee on Government Operations. Information, Justice, Transportation and Agriculture Subcommittee. *Charging a Fee to Enter the United States at a Land Border Post: Hearing August 3, 1993.* 103d Cong., 1st sess. Washington, DC: Government Printing Office, 1994, 167 pp.

U.S. Congress. House. Committee on the Judiciary. Subcommittee on International Law, Immigration, and Refugees. *Immigration-Related Issues in the North American Free Trade Agreement: Hearing, November 3, 1993.* 103d Cong., 1st sess. Washington, DC: Government Printing Office, 1994, 316 pp.

U.S. Congress. Joint Economic Committee. Subcommittee on Economic Resources, Competitiveness, and Security Economics. *Economic and Demographic Consequences of Immigration: Hearings, May 21–29, 1986.* 99th Cong., 2d sess. Washington, DC: Government Printing Office, 1987, 653 pp.

U.S. National Commission for Employment Policy. *U.S. Employment in an International Economy.* Report no. 24. Washington, DC: 1988, 69 pp.

Waldinger, Roger. "Structural Opportunity or Ethnic Advantage? Immigrant Business Development in New York." *International Migration Review* 23 (Spring 1989): 48–72.

# Labor and Employment

Abowd, John M., and Richard B. Freeman. *The Internationalization of the U.S. Labor Market.* NBER Working Paper no. 3321. Cambridge, MA: National Bureau of Economic Research, 1990, 41 pp.

Andreas, Peter. "Border Troubles: Free Trade, Immigration and Cheap Labour." *Ecologist* 24 (November–December 1994): 230–234.

Berry, D. P. "Policing the Hiring of Foreign Workers: Employers Get the Job." *Personnel* 64 (March 1987): 48–51.

Black, J. S., and H. B. Gregersen. "Serving Two Masters: Managing the Dual Alliance of Expatriate Employees." *Sloan Management Review* 33 (Summer 1992): 61–71.

Borjas, George J. "Immigrants in the U.S. Labor Market: 1940–80." *American Economic Review* 81 (May 1991): 287–291.

————. *Long-Run Convergence of Ethnic Skill Differentials.* NBER Working Paper no 4641. Cambridge, MA: National Bureau of Economic Research, 1994, 28 pp.

————. "Long-Run Convergence of Ethnic Skill Differentials: The Children and Grandchildren of the Great Migration." *Industrial and Labor Relations Review* 47 (July 1994): 553–573.

Borjas, George J., and Marta Tienda. "The Employment and Wages of Legalized Immigrants." *International Migration Review* 27 (Winter 1993): 712–747.

Borjas, George J., Richard B. Freeman, and Lawrence F. Katz. *On the Labor Market Effects of Immigration and Trade.* NBER Working Paper no. 3761. Cambridge, MA: National Bureau of Economic Research, 1991, 33 pp.

Bouvier, Leon F., and David Simcox. "Foreign-Born Professionals in the United States." *Population and Environment* 16 (May 1995): 429–444.

Briggs, Vernon M., Jr. "Mass Immigration, Free Trade, and the Forgotten American Worker." *Challenge* 33 (May–June 1995): 37–44.

Cain, Bruce E., D. Roderick Kieweit, and Carole J. Uhlaner. "The Acquisition of Partnership by Latinos and Asian Americans." *American Journal of Political Science* 35 (May 1991): 390–422.

Daneshvary, Nasser, and R. Keith Schwer. "Black Immigrants in the U.S. Labor Market: An Earnings Analysis." *Review of Black Political Economy* 22 (Winter 1994): 77–98.

Dicken, B., and R. Blomberg. "Immigrants—Can They Provide the Future Labor Force?" *Public Personnel Management* 20 (Spring 1991): 91–100.

Donato, Katharine M., J. Durand, and D. S. Massey. "Changing Conditions in the U.S. Labor Market: Effects of the Immigration

Reform and Control Act of 1986." *Population Research and Policy Review* 11, 2 (1992): 93–115.

Duffield, J. A., and R. Coltrane. "Testing for Disequilibrium in the Hired Farm Labor Market." *American Journal of Agricultural Economics* 74 (May 1992): 412–420.

Emerson, R. D. "Migratory Labor and Agriculture [Influence of Economic Incentives and Participation in the Migratory Stream." *American Journal of Agricultural Economics* 71 (August 1989): 617–629.

Fix, Michael, and Paul T. Hill. *Enforcing Employer Sanctions: Challenges and Strategies*. JRI-04. UI Report 90-6. Santa Monica, CA: Rand Corporation, Washington, DC: Urban Institute, 1990, 148 pp.

Funkhouser, E. "Do Immigrants Have Lower Unionization Propensities Than Natives?" *Industrial Relations* 32 (Spring 1993): 248–261.

Gordon, Danielle. "Horse Racing's Ghetto: Workers Who Care for Million-Dollar Thoroughbreds at Fancy Race Tracks Find Life in the Backstretch Anything but Horseplay." *Issues* 21 (June 1995): 18–22.

Grasmick, J. C. "How to Work in the U.S. under the Free Trade Agreement." *Business Quarterly* 54 (Summer 1989): 63–66.

Greenwood, M. J., and J. M. McDowell. "Differential Economic Opportunity, Transferability of Skills, and Immigration to the United States and Canada." *Review of Economics and Statistics* 73 (November 1991): 612–623.

Grossman, Eliot Lee. "Day Laborers and Street Vendors in Los Angeles: Survival Strategies in the Times of Simpson-Rodino." *Guild Practitioner* 47 (Fall 1990): 97–108.

Gunter, L. F., Joseph C. Jarrett, and James A. Duffield. "Effect of U.S. Immigration Reform on Labor-Intensive Agricultural Commodities." *American Journal of Agricultural Economics* 74 (November 1992): 897–906.

Hartstein, B. A. "IRCA Violations—A Procedural Guide for Employers." *Employment Relations Today* 16 (Spring 1989): 43–50.

Haus, Leah. "Openings in the Wall: Transnational Migrants, Labor Unions, and U.S. Immigration Policy." *International Organization* 49 ( Spring 1995): 285–313.

Keely, Charles B., and Bao Nga Tran. "Remittances from Labor Migration: Evaluations, Performance, and Implications." *International Migration Review* 23 (Fall 1989): 500–525.

Kirschten, Dick. "'Citizens-Only' Hiring: Evidence Is Growing That the Immigration Reform Law Has Prompted Employers to Avoid Hiring Anyone Who Looks or Sounds Like a Foreigner, Irrespective of Citizenship Status." *National Journal* 22 (January 27, 1990): 191–194.

———. "The Melting-Pot Recipe: As Congress Embarks on Another Immigration Reform Debate, It Faces Tough Choices on Such Issues as Needed Job Skills and Family Unification: There Are Racial and Ethnic Overtones." *National Journal* 21 (March 1989): 514–517.

Kwong, Peter. "Chinese Staff and Workers' Association: A Model for Organizing in the Changing Economy?" *Social Policy* 25 (Winter 1994): 30–38.

LaLonde, R. J., and R. H. Topel. "Immigrants in the American Labor Market: Quality, Assimilation, and Distributional Effects." *American Economic Review* (May 1991): 297–302.

Massey, Douglas S., and Zai Liang. "The Long-Term Consequences of a Temporary Worker Program: The U.S. Bracero Experience." *Population Research and Policy Review* 8 (September 1989): 199–226.

McConnell, Scott. "The New Battle over Immigration: America Needs Skills; So Should It Admit People from Abroad Because They Have These Skills or Because They Have Relatives Who Are Citizens?" *Fortune* 117 (May 9, 1988): 89–91+.

Meisenheimer, Joseph R., II. "How Do Immigrants Fare in the U.S. Labor Market?" *Monthly Labor Review* 115 (December 1992): 3–19.

Mitchell, C. E. "Illegal Aliens, Employment Discrimination, and the 1986 Immigration Reform and Control Act." *Labor Law Journal* 40 (March 1989): 177–182.

Ong, P. M. "Immigrant Wives' Labor Force Participation [Chinese Immigrant Wives]." *Industrial Relations* 26 (Fall 1987): 296–303.

Parliman, Gregory C., and Rosalie J. Shoeman. "National Origin Discrimination or Employer Prerogative? An Analysis of Language Rights in the Workplace." *Employee Relations Law Journal* 19 (Spring 1994): 551–565.

Reid, M. E. "The Paper Chase [Obtaining Work Authorization for Alien Employees]." *Small Business Reports* 18 (February 1993): 45–49.

Reubens, Edwin P. "Temporary Foreign Workers in the U.S.: Myths, Facts, and Policies."*International Migration Review* 20 (Winter 1986): 677–696.

Rose, M. "From the Fields to the Picket Line: Huelga Women and the Boycott." *Labor History* 31 (Summer 1990): 271–293.

Simcox, David E. "Immigration and Free Trade with Mexico: Protecting American Workers Against Double Jeopardy." *Population and Environment* 14 (November 1992): 159–175.

Stuart, P. "A Better Future for Migrant Workers." *Personnel Journal* 71 (December 1992): 65–74.

"Symposium: Economic Justice in America's Cities: Visions and Revisions of a Movement." *Harvard Civil Rights–Civil Liberties Law Review* 30 (Summer 1995): 299–506.

Taylor, J. E., and D. Thilmany. "Worker Turnover, Farm Labor Contractors, and IRCA's Impact on the California Farm Labor Market." *American Journal of Agricultural Economics* 75 (May 1993): 350–360.

Tran, Thanh V. "Sponsorship and Employment Status among Indochinese Refugees in the United States." *International Migration Review* 25 (Fall 1991): 536–550.

U.S. Bureau of International Labor Affairs. Division of Immigration Policy and Research. *Employer Sanctions and U.S. Labor Markets: First Report.* Immigration Policy Research Report no. 2, Washington, DC: 1991, 142 pp.

U.S. Congress. House. Committee on Science, Space, and Technology. Subcommittee on Science Research and Technology. *Increasing U.S. Scientific Manpower: Hearing, July 31, 1990.* 101st Cong., 2d sess. Washington, DC: Government Printing Office, 1990, 181 pp.

U.S. Congress. Senate. Committee on the Judiciary. *The GAO Report on Employer Sanctions and Discrimination: Hearings, March 30 and April 20, 1990, on the Implementation of the Immigration Reform and Control Act of 1986.* 101st Cong., 2d sess. Washington, DC: Government Printing Office, 1990, 338 pp.

U.S. Congress. Senate. Committee on the Judiciary. Subcommittee on Immigration and Refugee Affairs. *The Implementation of Employer Sanctions: Hearings, April 3 and 10, 1992 on S. 1734, to Repeal Provisions of Law Regarding Employer Sanctions and Unfair Immigration-Related Employment Practices, to Strengthen Enforcement of Law Regarding Illegal Entry into the United States, and for Other Purposes.* 102d Cong., 2d sess. Washington, DC: Government Printing Office, 1993, 437 pp.

U.S. General Accounting Office. *Immigration and the Labor Market: Nonimmigrant Alien Workers in the United States Report to the Chairman, Subcommittee on Immigration and Refugee Affairs, the Judiciary, U.S. Senate.* Report B-245126. Gaithersburg, MD: 1992, 96 pp.

Vernez, Georges, and Kevin McCarthy. *Meeting the Economy's Labor Needs through Immigration: Rationale and Challenges.* Rand Note N-3052-FF. Santa Monica, CA: Rand Corporation, 1990, 75 pp.

Walker, Robert, Mark Ellis, and Richard Barff. "Linked Migration Systems: Immigration and Internal Labor Flows in the United States." *Economic Geography* 68 (July 1992): 234–248.

Way, P. "Shovel and Shamrock: Irish Workers and Labor Violence in the Digging of the Chesapeake and Ohio Canal [1830s]." *Labor History* 30 (Fall 1989): 489–517.

Whitman, D. "The Great Sharecropper Success Story." *Public Interest*, no. 104 (Summer 1991: 3–19.

Wildasin, D. E. "Income Redistribution in a Common Labor Market." *American Economic Review* 81 (September 1991): 757–774.

Wingarden, C. R., and L. B. Khor. "Undocumented Immigration and Unemployment of U.S. Youth and Minority Workers: Econometric Evidence." *Review of Economics and Statistics* 73 (February 1991): 105–112.

## Agriculture and Migrant Labor

Ferran, Fernando I., and Patricia R. Pessar. *Dominican Agriculture and the Effect of International Migration.* Working Paper no. 29, Washington, DC: U.S. Commission for the Study of International Migration and Cooperation, 1990, 33 pp.

Martin, Philip L. "Harvest of Confusion: Immigration Reform and California Agriculture." *International Migration Review* 24 (Spring 1990): 69–95.

"Status of Migrant Farmworkers in the United States: Helsinki Commission Briefing." *Migration World Magazine* 20, 4 (1992): 29–33.

Thompson, Gary, Ricardo Amón, and Philip L. Martin. "Agricultural Development and Emigration: Rhetoric and Reality." *International Migration Review* 20 (Fall 1986): 575–597.

U.S. General Accounting Office. Human Resources Division. *Foreign Farm Workers in the U.S.: Department of Labor Action Needed to Protect Florida Sugar Cane Workers.* Report B-247239. Gaithersburg, MD: 1992, 24 pp.

Vaupel, S., and P. L. Martin. "Evaluating Employer Sanctions Farm Labor Contractor Experience." *Industrial Relations* 26 (Fall 1987): 304–313.

## Taxation of Immigrants

Bissell, Thomas St. G. "Problems of Green Card Aliens Living Abroad." *International Tax Journal* 13 (Winter 1987): 39–51.

Buchanan, J. M., and R. L. Faith. "Succession and the Limits of Taxation: Toward a Theory of Internal Exit." *American Economic Review* 77 (December 1987): 1023–1031.

Curtis, Ned P. "U.S.–West Germany Tax Treaty and the Section 7701(b) Definition of 'Resident Alien.'" *International Tax Journal* 13 (Winter 1987): 53–63.

Karlin, M. J. A. "Duty through the Eye of the Withholder [Withholding Taxes on Amount Paid to Foreign Persons]." *Taxes* 70 (July 1992): 492–516.

Wilson, J. D. "Optimal Income Taxation and International Personal Mobility." *American Economic Review* 82 (May 1992): 191–196.

Zak, Barbara M. "Determination of Residency of Alien Individuals for U.S. Federal Income Tax Purposes." *Bulletin of International Fiscal Documentation* 40 (August–September, 1986): 369–373.

## Human Rights

Alarcon, Evelina. "Anti-immigrant Racism and the Fight for Unity." *Political Affairs* 74 (April 1995): 6–11+.

Anderson, Michelle J. "A License to Abuse: The Impact of Conditional Status on Female Immigrants." *Yale Law Journal* 102 (April 1993): 1401–1430.

Collins, Allyson, and Lee Tucker. "United States: Crossing the Line—Human Rights Abuses along the U.S. Border with Mexico Persists Amid Climate of Impunity." *Human Rights Watch* 7, 4 (April 1995): 1–37.

Espenshade, Thomas J., and Vanessa E. King. "State and Local Fiscal Impacts of U.S. Immigrants: Evidence from New Jersey." *Population Research and Policy Review* 13 (September 1994): 225–236.

Foner, Nancy. "Race and Ethnic Relations in Immigrant New York." *Migration World Magazine* 23, 3 (1995): 14–18.

Goodwin-Gill, Guy S. "International Law and Human Rights: Trends Concerning International Migrants and Refugees." *International Migration Review* 23 (Fall 1989): 526–546.

Grove, C. "An Ounce of Prevention: Supporting International Job Transitions [Human and Economic Costs of Expatriate Failure]." *Employment Relations Today* 17 (Summer 1990): 111–119.

Hing, Bill Ong. "Beyond the Rhetoric of Rhetoric of Assimilation and Cultural Pluralism: Addressing the Tension of Separatism and Conflict in an Immigration-Driven Multiracial Society." *California Law Review* 81 (July 1993): 863–925.

Loken, Gregory A., and Lisa R. Bambino. "Harboring, Sanctuary and the Crime of Charity under Federal Immigration Law." *Harvard Civil Rights–Civil Liberties Law Review* 28 (Winter 1993): 119–184.

Morrison, Peter A. *Demographic Factors Reshaping Ties to the Family and Place.* Santa Monica, CA: Rand Corporation, 1990, 14 pp.

Perotti, Rosanna. "IRCA's Antidiscrimination Provisions: What Went Wrong?" *International Migration Review* 26 (Fall 1992): 732–753.

Schuck, Peter H. "The New Immigration and the Old Civil Rights." *American Prospect* (Fall 1993): 102–111.

U.S. Congress. Senate. Committee on Governmental Affairs. Permanent Subcommittee on Investigations. *Criminal Aliens in the United States: Hearings, November 10 and 16, 1993.* 103d Cong., 1st sess. Washington, DC: Government Printing Office, 1994, 106 pp.

Valenzuela, Abel, Jr. "California's Melting Pot Boils Over: The Origins of a Cruel Proposition." *Dollars and Sense* (March–April 1995): 28–31.

## Welfare Benefits

Borjas, George J. *Immigration and Welfare, 1970–1990.* NBER Working Paper no. 4872, Cambridge, MA: National Bureau of Economic Research, 1994, 31 pp.

Borjas, George, and S. J. Trejo. Immigrant Participation in the Welfare System." *Industrial and Labor Relations Review* 44 (January 1991): 195–211.

———. *Immigration Participation in the Welfare System.* NBER Working Paper 3423. Cambridge, MA: National Bureau of Economic Research, 1990, 29 pp.

Duleep, Harriet Orcutt. "Social Security and the Emigration of Immigrants." *Social Security Bulletin* 57 (Spring 1994): 37–52.

Gelfand, Donald E., and Rebecca Bialik-Gilad. "Immigration Reform and Social Work." *Social Work (National Association of Social Workers)* 34 (January 1989): 23–27.

Jensen, Leif. "Patterns of Immigration and Public Assistance Utilization, 1970–1980." *International Migration Review* 22 (Spring 1988): 51–83.

Jost, Kenneth. "Cracking Down on Immigration: Should Government Benefits and Services Be Cut Off?" *CQ Researcher* 5 (February 3, 1955): 99–119.

Kirschten, Dick. "Tempest-Tossed Task: A New Surge of Migration Sorely Tests the Capabilities of the Much-Criticized Immigration and Naturalization Service; But the Agency May Benefit from the High-Level Attention It Is Finally Receiving." *Government Executive* 25 (October 1993): 34–38.

Long, Larry. "Changing Residence: Comparative Perspectives on Its Relationship to Age, Sex, and Marital Status." *Population Studies (London)* 46 (March 1992): 141–158.

Siddharthan, K. "Health Insurance Coverage of the Immigrant Elderly." *Inquiry* 28 (Winter 1991): 403–412.

U.S. Congress. House. Committee on Ways and Means. Subcommittee on Human Resources. *Impact of Immigration on Welfare Programs: Hearing, November 15, 1993.* 103d Cong., 1st sess. Washington, DC: Government Printing Office, 1994, 189 pp.

U.S. Immigration and Naturalization Service. *The Immigration of Adopted and Prospective Adoptive Children.* Washington, DC: Government Printing Office, 1990, 31 pp.

Zuvekas, Ann. "Health Care Reform and Recent Arrivals." *Migration World Magazine* 22, 5 (1994): 18–23.

## Education—Brain Drain

Barnathan, J. "The Soviet Brain Drain Is the U.S. Brain Gain." *Business Week* (November 4, 1991): 94–96+.

"Break the Language Barrier [Safety Training in More Than One Language]." *Safety and Health* 144 (October 1991): 32–37.

Dunn, William. "Educating Diversity." *American Demographics* 15 (April 1993): 38–43.

Kirschten, Dick. "Spending to Assimilate: Federal Funds Intended to Help States Absorb Newly Legalized Aliens Are Being Used to Educate the Newcomers; But Critics Worry That States View the Money as a Welfare Windfall." *National Journal* 21 (September 2, 1989): 2146–2149.

"Mandatory HIV Testing of Immigration Applicants: New York State Responds with an Educational Program for INS Civil Surgeons." *AIDS and Public Policy Journal* 6 (Summer 1991): 64–68.

Margo, R. A. "Segregated Schools and the Mobility Hypothesis: A Model of Local Government Discrimination [Southern States]." *Quarterly Journal of Economics* 106 (February 1991): 61–73.

McConnell, Lorraine M., and Paul T. Hill. *Newcomers in American Schools: Meeting the Educational Needs of Immigrant Youth.* Santa Monica, CA: Rand Corporation, 1993, 117 pp.

National Coalition of Advocates for Students. *New Voices: Immigrant Students in U.S. Public Schools: An NCAS Research and Policy Report.* Boston, MA: 1988, 176 pp.

Nguyen, Beatrice Bich-Dao. "Accent Discrimination and the Test of Spoken English: A Call for an Objective Assessment of the Comprehensibility of Nonnative Speakers." *California Law Review* 81 (October 1993): 1325–1361.

Oberle, J. "Teaching English as a Second Language [Foreign-Born Workers]." *Training* 27 (April 1990): 61–67.

Ogbu, John U. "Minority Education in Comparative Perspective." *Journal of Negro Education* 59 (Winter 1990): 45–57.

Ramsey, Kimberly, and Abby Robyn. *Preparing Adult Immigrants for Work: The Educational Response in Two Communities.* Santa Monica, CA: Rand Corporation, 1992, 62 pp.

"Small Business and the Coming Labor Shortage: Issues of Education, Work Force Participation, and Immigration." *Journal of Labor Research* 13 (Winter 1992): 1–178.

Spener, David. "Transitional Bilingual Education and the Socialization of Immigrants." *Harvard Education Review* 58 (May 1988): 133–153.

Thiederman, S. "Training the Foreign-Born Worker: Maximizing Classroom Participation." *Supervisory Management* 34 (June 1989): 27–32.

U.S. Congress. House. Committee on Education and Labor. *Hearing on H.R. 2235, Workforce 2000 Employment Readiness Act of 1989: Hearing, November 3, 1989.* 101st Cong., 1st sess. Washington, DC: Government Printing Office, 1990, 128 pp.

————. *Hearing to Review Issues Relating to Immigration and Education: Hearing, September 28, 1987.* 100th Cong., 1st sess. Washington, DC: Government Printing Office, 1988, 250 pp.

————. *Immigration Reform and Control Act (IRCA): Hearing, November 30, 1988.* 100th Cong., 2d sess. Washington, DC: Government Printing Office, 1989, 313 pp.

U.S. Department of Education. Office of Vocational and Adult Education. Division of Adult Education and Literacy. *Teaching Adults with Limited English Skills: Progress and Challenges.* Washington, DC: 1991, 80 pp.

U.S. National Committee on Migrant Education. *Keeping up With Our Nation's Migrant Students: A Report on the Migrant Student Record Transfers (MSRTS).* Bethesda, MD: 1991, 25 pp.

Vasegh-Daneshvary, Nasser, Alan M. Schlottmann, and Henry W. Herzog, Jr. "Immigration of Engineers, Scientists, and Physicians and the U.S. High Technology Renaissance." *Social Science Quarterly* 63 (June 1987): 311–325.

Voth, Donald E., Frank L. Farmer and Diane M. Danforth. "The Impact of Migration upon the Educational Levels of the Arkansas Population by Age." *Arkansas Business and Economic Review* 22 (Fall 1989): 11–19.

Zimmermann, Wendy. "Teaching Immigrants English: Growing Needs and Shrinking Resources." *Migration World Magazine* 22, 2/3 (1994): 13–16.

## Women and Immigration

Anderson, Michelle J. "A License to Abuse: The Impact of Conditional Status on Female Immigrants." *Yale Law Journal* 102 (April 1993): 1401–1430.

Arp, William, Marilyn K. Dantico, and Marjorie S. Zatz. "The Immigration Reform and Control Act of 1986: Differential Impacts on Women?" *Social Justice (San Francisco)* 17 (Summer 1990): 23–39.

Donato, Katharine M. "Current Trends and Patterns of Female Migration: Evidence from Mexico." *International Migration Review* 27 (Winter 1993): 748–771.

Duleep, H. O., and S. Sanders. "The Decision to Work by Married Immigrant Women." *Industrial Labor Relations Review* 46 (July 1993): 677–690.

Field-Hendrey, E., and E. Balkan. "Earnings and Assimilation of Female Immigrants." *Applied Economics* 23 (October 1991): 1665–1672.

"How the Other Half Moves." *Populi (UN)* 20 (July–August 1993): 8–11.

Koenig, R. C., and J. Williams. "Marital Deduction Loss for Noncitizens Provides Life Insurance Opportunities [Considerations under Technical and Miscellaneous Revenue Act of 1988]." *Journal of the American Society of CLU & ChFC* 45 (May 1991): 66–70.

MacPherson, D. A., and J. B. Stewart. "The Labor Force Participation and Earnings Profiles of Married Female Immigrants." *Quarterly Review of Economics and Business* 29 (Autumn 1989): 57–72.

Magaram, P. S., and S. Abraham. "Transfer to Noncitizen Spouses Significantly Affected by RRA'89 [Qualified Domestic Trust]." *Journal of Taxation* 72 (May 1990): 266–270+.

Moyce, David. "Petitioning on Behalf of an Alien Spouse: Due Process under the Immigration Laws." *California Law Review* 74 (October 1986): 1747–1776.

U.S. Congress. Senate. Committee on the Judiciary. *The GAO Report on Employer Sanctions and Discrimination: Hearings, March 30 and April 20, 1990, on the Implementation of the Immigration Reform and Control Act of 1986.* 101st Cong., 2d sess. Washington, DC: Government Printing Office, 1990, 338 pp.

## United States

Allen, James P., and Eugene J. Turner. "Where to Find the New Immigrants: Look for Koreans in Baltimore, Mexicans in Chicago, Laotians in Minneapolis and Fresno, and Cambodians in Providence and Seattle." *American Demographics* 10 (September 1988): 22–27+.

Bean, Frank D., Barry Edmonston, and Jeffrey Passel, eds. *Undocumented Migration to the United States: IRCA and the Experience of the 1980s.* Santa Monica, CA: Rand Corporation, 1990, 271 pp.

———. "Undocumented Migration to the United States: Perception and Evidence." *Population and Development Review* 13 (December 1987): 675–690.

Briody, Elizabeth K. "Patterns of Household Immigration into South Texas." *International Migration Review* 21 (Spring 1987): 27–47.

Bunke, H. C. "The Heartland from Afar." *Business Horizons* 30 (September–October 1987): 3–12.

Burns, Allan. "The Maya of Florida." *Migration World* 17, 3–4 (1989): 20–26.

Carlson, Alvar W. "America's New Immigration: Characteristics, Destinations, and Impact, 1970–1989." *Social Science Journal (Fort Worth)* 31, 3 (1994): 213–236.

Cohen, Yinon. "Socioeconomic Dualism: The Case of Israeli-Born Immigrants in the United States." *International Migration Review* 23 (Summer 1989): 267–288.

Cohen, Yinon, and Andrea Tyree. "Palestinian and Jewish Israeli-Born Immigrants in the United States." *International Migration Review* 28 (Summer 1994): 243–255.

Conway, Denis. "Emigration in North America: The Continuing Option for the Caribbean." *Caribbean Affairs* 3 (April–June 1990): 109–119.

Davis, Mike. "Chinatown, Part Two? The 'Internationalization' of Downtown Los Angeles." *New Left Review* (July–August 1987): 65–86.

Denton, Barbara H., et al. "Net Migration in Louisiana, 1980–90." *Louisiana Business Survey* 22 (Spring 1991): 9–12.

Donato, Katharine M., Jorge Durand, and Douglas S. Massey. "Stemming the Tide? Assessing the Deterrent Effects of the Immigration Reform and Control Act." *Demography (Population Association of America)* 29 (May 1992): 139–157.

Durand, Jorge, and Douglas S. Massey. "Mexican Migration to the United States: A Critical Review." *Latin American Research Review* 27, 2 (1992): 3–42.

Gilboy, Janet A. "Deciding Who Gets in: Decisionmaking by Immigration Inspectors." *Law and Society Review* 25, 3 (1991): 571–599.

Greenwood, Michael J., and Shannon E. Ragland. "Measuring the Net Migration of Immigrants to U.S. Metropolitan Areas." *Journal of Economic and Social Measurement* 17, 3–4 (1991): 233–248.

Greenwood, Michael J., and Eloise Trabka. "Temporal and Spatial Patterns of Geographically Indirect Immigration to the United States." *International Migration Review* 25 (Spring 1991): 93–112.

Guarnizo, Luis E. "Los Dominicanyorks: The Making of a Binational Society." *Annals of the American Academy of Political and Social Science* 533 (May 1994): 70–86.

Gurwitt, Rob. "Back to the Melting Pot: A Million Immigrants a Year Add up to a Huge New Challenge for Communities All over America: And They Will Have to Meet It without Much Help From Washington." *Governing* 5 (June 1992): 30–35.

———. "How We Spent the 1980s: A Pre-Census Look at a Changing America: Immigration, Inner City Decline and an Aging Population Create Issues That Will Preoccupy Local Policy Makers for Years." *Governing* 2 (August 1989): 26–33.

Hartman, Robert W. "Can Immigration Slow U.S. Population Aging?" *Journal of Policy Analysis and Management* 13 (Fall 1994): 759–768.

Harwood, Edwin. "American Public Opinion and U.S. Immigration Policy." *Annals of the American Academy of Political and Social Science* 487 (September 1986): 201–212.

Hing, Bill Ong. "Immigration Policies: Messages of Exclusion to African Americans." *Harvard Law Journal* 37 (Winter 1994): 237–282.

Human Rights Watch. America's Watch Committee. *United States Frontier Injustice: Human Rights Abuses along the U.S. Border with Mexico Persist amid Climate of Impunity.* New York: 1993, 46 pp.

"Immigration and the Changing Face of America." *National Forum* 74 (Summer 1994): 8–45.

"Immigration: Boon or Bane to the U.S.?" *World and I* 9 (January 1994): 359–393.

Jefferson, Jon. "Alienation: Is There a Legal Solution to the Immigration Mess?" *ABA (American Bar Association) Journal* 79 (September 1993): 54–59.

Kahley, William J. "Population Migration in the United States: A Survey of Research." *Federal Reserve Bank of Atlanta Economic Review* 76 (January–February 1991): 2–11.

Kennedy, James T., ed. "Updating Local Area Population Projections with Current Migration Estimates." *Journal of Economic and Social Measurement* 14 (July 1986): 107–120.

Kirschten, Dick. "Come in! Keep out! Open America's Door, Say an Unusual Mix of Pro-Growth Conservatives and Liberal Advocates; Don't Do It, Says and Equally Odd Coalition: The Issue Is Recasting Domestic Politics." *National Journal* 22 (May 19, 1990): 1206–1211.

———. "Immigration, and Rancor, Are Soaring." *National Journal* 26 (June 18, 1994): 16–20.

Kraly, Ellen Percy, and Robert Warren. "Estimates of Long-Term Immigration to the United States: Moving U.S. Statistics toward United Nation Concepts." *Demography (Population Association of America)* 29 (November 1992): 13–26.

Libbey, Marie McGrath. "Another Road Story: Net Migration in Georgia." *Georgia Business and Economic Conditions* 51 (September–October 1991): 1–10+.

Mangum, Garth, and Gaylen Chandler. "Immigration and the Utah Economy." *Utah Economic and Business Review* 47 (September 1987): 1–16.

McLarty, Carol L., and Janet Galvez. "A Profile of Florida's Temporary Residents." *Economic Leaflets (Florida University)* 53 (December 1994): 1–6.

Melendez, Edwin. "Puerto Rican Migration and Occupational Selectivity, 1982–1988." *International Migration Review* 28 (Spring 1994): 49–57.

Mitchell, Christopher. "From Policy Frontier to Policy Dilemmas: The United States and Caribbean Migration, 1960–1990." *European Review of Latin American and Caribbean Studies*, no. 52 (June 1992): 75–89.

Modarres, Ali. "Ethnic Community Development: A Spatial Examination." *Journal of Urban Affairs* 14, 2 (1992): 97–107.

Moore, Stephen. "Flea Market: More Refugees at Lower Cost." *Policy Review* (Spring 1990): 64–68.

———. "Who Should America Welcome?" *Society* 27 (July–August 1990): 55–62.

Nielsen, John T. "Immigration and the Low-Cost Housing Crisis: The Los Angeles Area's Experience." *Population and Environment* 11 (Winter 1989): 123–139.

Piatt, Bill. "Born as Second Class Citizens in the U.S.A.: Children of Undocumented Parents." *Notre Dame Law Review* 63, 1 (1988): 35–54.

Rex, Tom R. "U.S. Migration Patterns Much Different in Early 90s." *Arizona Business* 42 (February 1995): 5–7.

Rivera-Batiz, Francisco L. "The Characteristics of Recent Puerto Rican Migrants: Some Further Evidence." *Migration World* 17, 2 (1989): 6–13.

Rolph, Elizabeth, and Abby Robyn. *A Window on Immigration Reform: Implementing the Immigration Reform and Control Act in Los Angeles.* Rand/JRI-06. Santa Monica, CA: Rand Corporation, 1990, 117 pp.

Sassen, Saskia. "America's Immigration 'Problem.'" *World Policy Journal* 6 (Fall 1989): 811–832.

Schreiner, T. "Foreign Workers [California] *American Demographics* 9 (December 1987): 47–48.

Schuck, Peter H., and Theodore Hsien Wang. "Continuity and Change: Patterns of Immigration Litigation in the Courts, 1979–1990." *Stanford Law Review* 45 (November 1992): 115–183.

Simon, Rita J. "Immigration and American Attitudes." *Public Opinion (American Enterprise Institute)* 10 (July–August 1987): 47–50.

Tanton, John, and Wayne Lutton. "Immigration and Criminality in the U.S.A." *Journal of Social, Political and Economic Studies* 18 (Summer 1993): 217–234.

Vernez, Georges. *After Amnesty: The New Migration Movement in the United States*. P-7786. Santa Monica, CA: Rand Corporation, 1992, 7 pp.

Weintraub, Daniel M. "California Closes Its Doors: Chafing under the Costs of Caring for Illegal Immigrants, Californians Have Approved a Measure That Is Probably Unconstitutional." *State Legislatures* 20 (December 1994): 16–17.

## U.S. Internal Migration

Alba, Richard D., and Katherine Trent. "Population Loss and Change in the North: An Examination of New York's Migration to the Sunbelt." *Social Science Quarterly* 67 (December 1986): 690–706.

Borjas, George J., and Bernt Bratsberg. *Who Leaves? The Outmigration of the Foreign Born*. NBER Working Paper no. 4913. Cambridge, MA: National Bureau of Economic Research, 1994, 40 pp.

Cody, Scott K., and Ravi S. Bayya. "Migration in Florida: Still a 'Northern' South and a 'Southern' North." *Economic Leaflets (Florida University)* 50 (April 1991): 1–4.

Ellson, Richard W., and Brian A. Gilley. "Comings and Goings." *Business and Economic Review (University of South Carolilna)* 33 (January–March 1987): 3–7.

Frey, William H. "Immigration and Internal Migration 'Flight': A California Case Study." *Population and Environment* 16 (March 1995): 353–375.

Friedli, Eric A. "Migration of the Poor." *Population Research and Policy Review* 5, 1 (1986): 47–61.

Klumpp, Scott. "Louisiana Annual Net Migration, 1969–1992." *Louisiana Business Survey* 24 (Fall 1993): 5–9.

Kruse, Jack, and Karen Foster. "Changes in Rural Alaska Settlement Patterns." *Alaska Review of Social and Economic Conditions* 23 (March 1986): 1–19.

Maruggi, Vincent, and Charles R. Wartenberg. "Louisiana Migration: Age, Race and the Economy." *Louisiana Business Survey* 25 (Fall 1994): 7–11.

————. "People on the Move: Trends and Prospects in District Migration Flows." *Federal Reserve Bank of Kansas City Economic Review* 79, 3 (1994): 39–54.

Miller, Glenn H., Jr. "Dynamics of the U.S. Interstate Migration System, 1975–1992." *Growth and Change* 26 (Winter 1995): 139–160.

Rivera-Batiz, Francisco L. "The Characteristics of Recent Puerto Rican Migrants: Some Further Evidence." *Migration World* 17, 2 (1989): 6–13.

Shields, M. P., and G. M. Shields. "A Theoretical and Empirical Analysis of Family Migration and Household Production, 1980–1985." *Southern Economic Journal* 59 (April 1993): 768–782.

Smith, Stanley K., and Mohammed Shahidullah. "Mobility and Migration in Florida and the U.S., 1985–1990." *Economic Leaflets (Florida University)* 52 (October 1993): 1–6.

South, Scott J. "Metropolitan Migration and Social Problems." *Social Science Quarterly* 68 (March 1987): 3–18.

# Canada

Buttrick, John. "Migration between Canada and the United States, 1970–85: Some New Estimates." *International Migration Review* 26 (Winter 1992): 1448–1456.

Fox, Kristine M. "Gender Persecutor: Canadian Guidelines Offer a Model for Refugee Determination in the United States." *Arizona Journal of International and Comparative Law* 11, 1 (1994): 117–144.

## Cuba

"Agreement with Cuba to Control the Flow of Refugees." *Foreign Policy Bulletin* 5 (November–December 1994): 96–100.

Benenson, Bob. "Dissonant Voices Urge Clinton to Revise Policy on Cuba." *Congressional Quarterly Weekly Report* 52 (August 27, 1994): 2498.

Card, D. "The Impact of the Mariel Boatlift on the Miami Labor Market." *Industrial and Labor Relations Review* 43 (January 1990): 245–257.

Doherty, Carrol J. "Influx of Cubans Forces Clinton to Halt Automatic Asylum: Moving to Prevent a Replay of 1980 Mariel Boatlift, President Orders Refugees Taken to Guantanamo." *Congressional Quarterly Weekly Report* 52 (August 20, 1994): 2464–2465.

Funkhouser, Edward, and Fernando A. Ramos. "The Choice of Migration Destination: Dominican and Cuban Immigrants to the Mainland United States and Puerto Rico." *International Migration* 27 (Fall 1993): 537–536.

Kirschen, Dick. "No Refuge: From Cuba to Bosnia to Rwanda, a Surging Tide of Refugees Is Creating a Global Crisis; During the Cold War, Refugees Often Were Welcomed as Pawns in Propaganda Battles, but Now Most Nations Seem Inclined to Pull up the Drawbridges." *National Journal* 26 (September 10, 1994): 2068–2073.

Larzelere, Alex D. *Castro's Ploy—America's Dilemma: The 1980 Cuban Boatlift*. Washington, DC: U.S. National Defense University, 1988, 545 pp.

Robinson, Linda. "Holding Back the Tide: Clinton's Policy Shift toward Cuban Refugees Finesses a Bigger Problem." *U.S. News and World Report* 117 (September 5, 1994): 35–36.

Skoug, Kenneth N., Jr. "The U.S.-Cuba Migration Agreement: Resolving Mariel." *Department of State Bulletin* 88 (May 1988): 76–81.

Tucker, Lee, and David Nachman. "Cuba: Repression, the Exodus of August 1994, and the U.S. Response." *Americas Watch Committee, Human Rights Watch* 6, 12 (October 1994): 1–19.

U.S. Congress. House. Committee on Foreign Affairs. Subcommittee on Human Rights and International Organizations. *Cubans Political Prisoners: Hearing, September 24, 1986.* 99th Cong., 2d sess. Washington, DC: Government Printing Office, 1986, 107 pp.

## Mexico

Acevedo, Dolores, and Thomas J. Espenshade. "Implications of a North American Free Trade Agreement for Mexican Migration into the United States." *Population and Development Review* 18 (December 1992): 729–744.

Anderson, Annelise, and Alan K. Simpson. "Employer Sanctions or Open Borders?" *Cato Policy Report* 8 (September–October 1986): 6–9.

Bean, Frank D., B. L. Lowell, and L. J. Taylor. "Undocumented Mexican Immigrants and the Earnings of Other Workers in the United States." *Demography (Population Association of America)* 25 (February 1988): 35–52.

Coates, J. F. "America 2001 [Influx of Mexicans, Muslims and Other Groups]." *Across the Board* 29 (April 1992): 38–41.

Cornelius, Wayne A. "Impacts of the 1986 U.S. Immigration Law on Emigration from Rural Mexican Sending Communities." *Population and Development Review* 15 (December 1989): 689–705.

Cornelius Wayne A., and Philip L. Martin. "The Uncertain Connection: Free Trade and Rural Mexican Migration to the United States." *International Migration Review* 27 (Fall 1993): 484–512.

Cornwell, T. B., Alan D. Bligh, and Emin Babakus. "Compliant Behavior of Mexican–American Consumers to a Third-Party Agency [Better Business Bureau of South Plains, Tex.]." *Journal of Consumer Affairs* 25 (Summer 1991): 1–18.

Davila, Alberto, and Rogelio Saenz. "The Effect of Maquiladora Employment on the Monthly Flow of Mexican Undocumented Migration to the U.S., 1978–1982." *International Migration Review* 24 (Spring 1990): 96–107.

Donato, Katharine M. "U.S. Policy and Mexican Migration to the United States, 1942–1992." *Social Science Quarterly* 75 (December 1994): 705–740.

Donato, Katharine M., Jorge Durand, and Douglas S. Massey. "Stemming the Tide? Assessing the Deterrent Effects of the Immigration Reform and Control Act." *Demography (Population Association of America)* 29 (May 1992): 139–157.

Durand, Jorge, and Douglas S. Massey. "Mexican Migration to the United States: A Critical Review." *Latin American Research Review* 27, 2 (1992): 3–42.

Faist, Thomas. "States, Markets, and Immigrant Minorities: Second-Generation Turks in Germany and Mexican-Americans in the United States in the 1980s." *Comparative Politics* 26 (July 1994): 439–460.

Farquharson, M. "The Best and the Bravest [Mexican Migrants Take Big Risks to Get to the Other Side]." *Business Mexico* 1 (June 1991): 42–44.

Human Rights Watch. America's Watch Committee. *United States Frontier Injustice: Human Rights Abuses along the U.S. Border with Mexico Persist amid Climate of Impunity.* New York: 1993, 46 pp.

Kossoudji, Sherrie A. "Playing Cat and Mouse at the U.S.-Mexican Border." *Demography (Population Association of America)* 25 (May 1992): 159–180.

Martinez, Roberto L. "The U.S.-Mexico Border: A Legacy of Violence." *Guild Practitioner* 50 (Fall 1993): 102–106.

Massey, Douglas F., and Emilio Parrado. "Migradollars: The Remittances and Savings of Mexican Immigrants in the USA." *Population Research and Policy Review* 13 (March 1994): 3–30.

Massey, Douglas S. "The Settlement Process among Mexican Migrants to the United States." *American Sociological Review* 51 (October 1986): 670–684.

———. "Understanding Mexican Migration to the United States." *American Journal of Sociology* 92 (May 1987): 1372–1402.

"Mexico: Political Movements, Social Movements, and Migration." *Latin American Perspectives* 20 (Summer 1993): 6–75+.

Saenz, Rogelio. "Interregional Migration Patterns of Chicanos: The Core, Periphery, and Frontier." *Social Science Quarterly* 72 (March 1991): 135–148.

Taylor, J. E. "Undocumented Mexico-U.S. Migration and the Returns to Households in Rural Mexico." *American Journal of Agricultural Economics* 69 (August 1987): 626–638.

Tucker, Lee. *United States: Crossing the Line—Human Rights Abuses along the U.S. Border with Mexico Persist amid Climate of Immunity.* New York: Human Rights Watch/America, vol. 7, 1995, 37 pp.

U.S. Congress. House. Committee on the Judiciary. Subcommittee on International Law, Immigration, and Refugees. *Operations of the Border Patrol: Hearing, August 5, 1992.* 102d Cong., 2d sess. Washington, DC: Government Printing Office, 1992, 269 pp.

Vejar, Jesus Romo, and Lisa Weseman Larkin. "Abating Migration of Mexico's Rural Poor: A Legal, Practical and Technical Examination." *Arizona Journal of International and Comparative Law* (1988): 105–151.

Vernez, Georges, and David Ronfeldt. *The Current Situation in Mexican Immigration.* R-4099-FF. Santa Monica, CA: Rand Corporation, 1991, 5 pp.

White, Thomas U. *Mexican Immigrant Labor: An Alternative Analysis and Policy Proposal.* Research Paper Series no. 23. Albuquerque, NM: Latin American Institute, University of New Mexico, 1989, 77 pp.

## Haiti

Feen, Richard H. "The Never Ending Story: The Haitian Boat People." *Migration World Magazine* 21, 1 (1993): 12–15.

Helton, Arthur C. "The United States Government Program of Intercepting and Forcibly Returning Haitian Boat People to Haiti: Policy Implications and Prospects." *New York Law School Journal of Human Rights* 10, part 2 (Spring 1993): 325–349.

Human Rights Watch. America's Watch Committee. *Half the Story: The Skewed U.S. Monitoring of Repatriated Haitian Refugees.* New York: 1992, 16 pp.

———. *No Port in a Storm: The Misguided Use of In-Country Refugee Processing in Haiti*. New York: 1993, 37 pp.

Johnson, Creola. "Quarantining HIV-Infected Haitians: United States' Violations of International Law at Guantanamo Bay." *Harvard Law Journal* 37 (Winter 1994): 305–331.

Jones, Thomas David. "Haitian Refugee Center, Inc. v. James Baker, III: The Dred Scott Case of Immigration Law." *Dickinson Journal of International Law* 11 (Fall 1992): 1–48.

———. "The Haitian Refugee Crisis: A Quest for Human Rights." *Michigan Journal of International Law* 15 (Fall 1993): 77–125.

Koh, Harold Hongju. "The Haitian Centers Council Case." *Harvard International Law Journal* 35 (Winter 1994): 1–47.

Lennox, Malissia. "Refugees, Racism, and Reparations: A Critique of the United States' Haitian Immigration Policy." *Stanford Law Journal* 45 (February 1993): 687–724.

Little, Cheryl. "United States Haitian Policy: A History of Discrimination." *New York Law School Journal of Human Rights* 10, part 2 (Spring 1993): 269–324.

Navajas, Emma D. "Haitian Interdiction: An Overview of U.S. Policy and Practice." *Migration World Magazine* 20, 1 (1992): 38–41.

Ralph, David E. "Haitian Interdiction on the High Seas: The Continuing Saga of the Rights of Aliens Outside United States Territory." *Maryland Journal of International Law and Trade* 17 (Fall 1993): 227–251.

U.S. Congress. House. Committee on Government Operations. Legislation and National Security Subcommittee. *U.S. Human Rights Policy Toward Haiti: Hearing, April 9, 1992.* 102d Cong., 2d sess. Washington, DC: Government Printing Office, 1993, 215 pp.

U.S. Congress. House. Committee on the Judiciary, Subcommittee on Immigration, Refugees, and International Law. *Haitian Detention and Interdiction: Hearing, June 8, 1989.* 101st Cong., 1st sess. Washington, DC: Government Printing Office, 1989, 250 pp.

U.S. Congress. House. Committee on the Judiciary, Subcommittee on International Law, Immigration, and Refugees. *Haitian Asylum-Seekers: Hearing, June 15, 1994, on H.R. 3663, H.R. 4114, and H.R. 4264.* 103d Cong., 2d sess. Washington, DC: Government Printing Office, 1994, 504 pp.

"United States: Supreme Court Opinion in Sale v. Haitian Centers Council (Right to Intercept and Interdict Haitian Refugees: UN Protocol Relating to Status of Refugees: U.S. Refugee Act of 1980), (June 21, 1993)." *International Legal Materials* 32 (July 1993): 1039–1068.

## Caribbean

"Coming North: Latino and Caribbean Immigration." *Report on the Americas.* 26 (July 1992): 13–49.

Conway, Denis. "Emigration to North America: The Continuing Option for the Caribbean." *Caribbean Affairs* 3 (April–June 1990): 104–119.

Duany, Jorge. "Beyond the Safety Valve: Recent Trends in Caribbean Migration." *Social and Economic Studies* 43 (March 1994): 95–122.

Ferran, Fernando I., and Patricia R. Pessar. *Dominican Agriculture and the Effect of International Migration.* Working Paper no. 29. Washington, DC: U.S. Committee for the Study of International Migration and Cooperation. Economic Development, 1990, 33 pp.

Ricketts, Erol. "U.S. Investment and Immigration from the Caribbean." *Social Problems (Society for the Study of Social Problems)* 34 (October 1987): 374–387.

Thomas, Bert J. "Caribbean American Associations: Activism or Parochialism?" *TransAfrica Forum* 5 (Spring 1988): 45–59.

U.S. Commission for the Study of International Migration and Cooperation. Economic Development. *U.S. Policy and the Caribbean Basin Sugar Industry: Implications for Migration.* Washington, DC: 1990, 32 pp.

## Central America

Frelick, Bill. *Running the Gauntlet: The Central American Journey through Mexico.* Washington, DC: U.S. Committee for Refugees, 1991, 24 pp.

Funkhouser, Edward. "Migration from Nicaragua: Some Recent Evidence." *World Development* 20 (August 1992): 1209–1218.

Kowalewski, David. "The Historical Structure of a Dissident Movement: The Sanctuary Case." In *Research in Social Movements, Conflict and Change.* Greenwich, CT: JAI Press, 1990, pp. 89–110.

McGuire, John I. "Sanctuary." *New York University Journal of International Law and Politics* 19 (Spring 1987): 631–657.

Menjivar, Cecelia. "History, Economy and Politics: Macro and Micro-level Factors in Recent Salvadorean Migration to the U.S." *Journal of Refugee Studies* 6, 4 (1993): 350–371.

Rodriguez, Nestor P. "Undocumented Central Americans in Houston: Diverse Populations." *International Migration Review* 21 (Spring 1987): 4–26.

U.S. Congress. House. Committee on the Judiciary. Subcommittee on Immigration, Refugees, and International Law. *Central American Asylum-Seekers: Hearing, March 9, 1989.* 101st Cong., 1st sess. Washington, DC: Government Printing Office, 1989, 335 pp.

Wallace, Steven P. "The New Urban Latinos: Central Americans in a Mexican Immigrant Environment." *Urban Affairs Quarterly* 25 (December 1989): 239–264.

## Soviet Union

Aronson, Geoffrey. "Soviet Jewish Emigration, the United States, and the Occupied Territories." *Journal of Palestine Studies* 19 (Summer 1990): 30–45.

Cullen, Robert B. "Soviet Jewry." *Foreign Affairs* 65 (Winter 1986–1987): 252–266.

Elving, Ronald D. "U.S.-Soviet Pact May Falter over Baltic Emigration." *Congressional Quarterly Weekly Report* 48 (May 19, 1990): 1537–1540.

Gregory, P. R., and I. L. Collier. "Unemployment in the Soviet Union: Evidence from the Soviet Interview Project [Interviews of Soviet Immigrants Living in the U.S.]." *American Economic Review* 78 (September 1988): 613–632.

U.S. Congress. Commission on Security and Cooperation in Europe. *Implementation of the Helsinki Accords: Hearing, April 22, 1986, Soviet and East European Emigration Policies.* 99th Cong., 2d sess. Washington, DC: Government Printing Office, 1986, 70 pp.

U.S. Congress. House. Committee on Armed Services. Investigations Subcommittee. *Security Clearances for Soviet Emigres: Hearings, February 9 and September 15, 1988.* 100th Cong., 2d sess. Washington, DC: Government Printing Office, 1988, 109 pp.

U.S. Congress. House. Committee on the Judiciary. Subcommittee on Immigration, Refugees, and International Law. *Soviet Refugees: Hearing, April 6, 1989, on H.R. 1605 and H.Con.Res. 73, Emergency Refugee Act of 1989.* 101st Cong., 1st sess. Washington, DC: Government Printing Office, 1989, 371 pp.

U.S. Congress. Senate. Committee on the Judiciary. Subcommittee on Immigration and Refugee Affairs. *Soviet Jews Arriving in Israel: The Humanitarian Needs: Staff Report, February 1992.* 102d Cong., 2nd sess. Washington, DC: Government Printing Office, 1992, 18 pp.

U.S. General Accounting Office. *Soviet Refugees: Processing and Admittance to the United States: Report to Congressional Requesters.* Report B-238005. Gaithersburg, MD: 1990, 26 pp.

## China

Kwong, Peter. "Chinese Staff and Workers' Association: A Model for Organizing in the Changing Economy. *Social Policy* 25 (Winter 1994): 30–38.

Smith, Paul J. "The Strategic Implications of Chinese Emigration." *Survival* 36 (Summer 1994): 60–77.

U.S. Congress. Senate. Committee on the Judiciary. Subcommittee on Immigration and Refugee Affairs. *Chinese Students in America and Human Rights in China: Hearing, January 23, 1990 on H.R. 2712, a Bill to Facilitate the Adjustment or Change of Status of Chinese Nationals in the United States by Waiving the 2-Year Foreign Residence Requirement for "J" Nonimmigrants and by Treating Nonimmigrants, Whose Departure Has Been Deferred by the Attorney General, as Remaining in Legal Nonimmigrant Status for Purposes of Adjustment or Change of Status.* 101st Cong., 2d sess. Washington, DC: Government Printing Office, 1991, 192 pp.

Wang, Zheng. "Some New Crime Trends in China: Their Impacts on the United States." *Police Studies* 16 (Spring 1993): 11–19.

## Other Countries

Barnathan, Joyce. "Passage Back to India: Expatriates Seek a Motherlode in the Motherland." *Business Week* (July 17, 1995): 44–46.

Berthelsen, John. "Politics of Exclusion: Anti-immigrant Lobbyists Target Asians Again." *Far Eastern Economic Review* 156 (November 18, 1993): 27–28.

Carino, Benjamin V., et al. *The New Filipino Immigrants to the United States: Increasing Diversity and Change.* Papers of the East-West Population Institute no. 115. Honolulu, HI: Distribution Office. East-West Center, 1990, 92 pp.

Cohen, Yinon. "Socioeconomic Dualism: The Case of Israeli-Born Immigrants in the United States." *International Migration Review* 23 (Summer 1989): 267–288.

DeJong, Gordon F., et al. "Family Reunification and Philippine Migration to the United States: The Immigrants' Perspective." *International Migration Review* 20 (Fall 1986): 598–611.

Giella, Catherine R. "Visas for Sale: A Comparison of the U.S. Investor Provision with the Australian Business Migration Program." *Northwestern Journal of International Law and Business* 13 (Spring–Summer 1992): 209–238.

Kirschten, Dick. "Shock Waves: The World Trade Center Bombing Has Raised Concerns About Islamic Fundamentalist Terrorism: That, in Turn, Has Set Nerves on Edge Among America's Fast Growing but Politically Weak, Arab and Muslim Communities." *National Journal* 25 (June 5, 1993): 1349–1352.

Koehn, Peter, and Girma Negash. "Iranian Emigres and Non-Returners: Political Exiles or Economic Migrants?" *Scandinavian Journal of Development Alternatives* 8 (June 1989): 79–109.

Levi, Robin S. "Legacies of War: The United States' Obligation toward Amerasians." *Stanford Journal of International Law* 29 (Summer 1993): 459–502.

Liu, John M., Paul M. Ong, and Carolyn Rosenstein. "Dual Chain Migration: Post-1965 Filipino Immigration to the United States." *International Migration Review* 25 (Fall 1991): 487–513.

Lucas, Alice. *Cambodians in America: Courageous People from a Troubled Country.* New Focus of Liberty. San Francisco, CA: Many Cultures Publishing, 1993, 25 pp.

Lucas, R. E. B. "Emigration to South Africa's Mines." *American Economic Review* 77 (June 1987): 313–330.

O'Donnell, Daniel. "Resettlement or Repatriation: Screened-Out Vietnamese Child Asylum Seekers and the Convention on Human Rights of the Child." *International Commission of Jurists Review* (June 1994): 16–33.

Park, Insook Han, et al. *Korea Immigrants and U.S. Immigration Policy: A Predeparture Perspective.* Papers of the East-West Population Institute no. 114. Honolulu, HI: Distribution Office, East-West Population Institute, East-West Center, 1990, 119 pp.

Parra Sandoval, Rodrigo. "The Missing Future: Colombian Youth." *CEPAL Review* (August 1986): 79–92.

Phillips, Olivia. "Congress and Immigrants of the Future: Immigration Ceilings and New Admission Criteria Could Reduce the Flow of Newcomers from the Third World." *Focus (Joint Center Pol Studies)* 16 (August 1988): 5–6.

Sarbaugh, Timothy J. "Irish America at the Crossroads: A New Beginning or the Last Gasp of Irish Immigration in the Twenty-First Century." *Migration World Magazine* 19, 3 (1991): 4–8.

Sexton, J. J. "Recent Changes in the Irish Population and in the Pattern of Emigration." *Irish Banking Review* (Autumn 1987): 31–44.

U.S. Congress. House. Committee on Foreign Affairs. Subcommittee on Asian and Pacific Affairs. *The Political Situation in Hong Kong and Issues Relating to Emigration: Hearing and Markup, October 25, 1989, on H.Con.Res. 227.* 101st Cong., 1st sess. Washington, DC, Government Printing Office, 1990, 71 pp.

Wolf, Daniel, and Shep Lowman. "Toward a New Consensus on the Vietnamese Boat People." *SAIS (School Advanced International Studies) Review* 10 (Summer–Fall 1990): 101–119.

# Refugees

Aleinikoff, T. Alexander. "State–Centered Refugee Law: From Resettlement to Containment." *Michigan Journal of International Law* 14 (Fall 1992): 120–138.

Bivins, Jeffrey Scott. "The Refugee Act of 1990: What Burden of Proof—Controversy Lives On After Stevic." *Vanderbilt Journal of Transnational Law* 18 (Fall 1985): 875–913.

Carillo, Carmen. "The Application of Refugee Laws to Central Americans in the United States." *Boston College Third World Law Journal* 9 (Winter 1989): 1–14.

Chu, Jeannette L. "Alien Smuggling: Alien Smuggling Syndicates Are Increasingly Involved in Other Criminal Activities, Infiltrating Legitimate Businesses and Deriving Millions of Dollars in Illicit Proceeds." *Police Chief* 61 (June 1994): 20–25+.

Cravens, Richard B., and Thomas Bornemann. "The Refugee Assistance Program (RAP-MH)." *Information and Referral* 9 (Summer–Fall 1987): 27–44.

Garvin, Glenn. "America's Economic Refugees." *Reason* 25 (November 1993): 18–26.

Gibney, Mark, et al. "USA Refugee Policy: A Human Rights Analysis Update." *Journal of Refugee Studies* 5, 1 (1992): 33–46.

Gozdziak, Elzbieta. "New Branches, Distant Roots: Older Refugees in the United States." *Aging* 359 (1989): 2–7.

Hartigan, Kevin. "Matching Humanitarian Norms with Cold, Hard Interests: The Making of Refugee Policies in Mexico and Honduras, 1980–89." *International Organization* 46 (Summer 1992): 709–730.

Helton, Arthur C. "U.S. Refugee Policy: African and Caribbean Effects." *TransAfrica Forum* 9 (Summer 1992): 93–102.

Howland, Todd. "A Comparative Analysis of the Changing Definition of a Refugee." *New York Law School Journal of Human Rights* 5, part 1 (Fall 1987): 33–70.

Human Rights Watch. America's Watch Committee. *No Port in a Storm: The Misguided Use of In-Country Refugee Processing in Haiti.* New York: 1993, 37 pp.

"Immigration Law: United States and International Perspectives on Asylum and Refugee Status." *Loyola of Los Angeles International and Comparative Law Journal* 16 (August 1994): 1–269.

Lassailly-Jacob, Veronique, and Michael Zmolek. "Environmental Refugees." *Refuge* 12 (June 1992): 1–39.

Lennox, Malissia. "Refugees, Racism and Reparations: A Critique of the United States' Haitian Immigration Policy." *Stanford Law Review* 45 (February 1993): 687–724.

Majka, Lorraine. "Assessing Refugee Assistance Organizations in the United States and the United Kingdom." *Journal of Refugee Studies* 4, 3 (1991): 267–283.

Mattson, Susan. "Health Care Delivery to Southeast Asian Refugees." *Migration World* 17, 1 (1989): 28–35.

Moore, Jonathan. "Perspectives on U.S. Refugee Programs." *Department of State Bulletin* 87 (September 1987): 54–58.

Nelson, Michael J. "Halting a National Sacrilege: Aliens Should Be Given Notice of Their Right to Apply for Political Asylum." *Loyola of Los Angeles International and Comparative Law Journal* 9, 1 (1986): 91–116.

Pho, Hai B. "The Politics of Refugee Settlements in Massachusetts." *Migration World Magazine* 19, 4 (1991): 4–10.

Sexton, Robert C. "Political Refugees, Nonrefoulement and State Practice: A Comparative Study." *Vanderbilt Journal of Transnational Law* 18 (Fall 1985): 731–806.

Shultz, George. "Proposed Refugee Admissions for FY 1987." *Department of State Bulletin* 86 (November 1986): 14–19.

Stastny, Charles. "Sanctuary and the State." *Contemporary Crises* 11, 3 (1987): 279–301.

U.S. Congress. House. Committee on Foreign Affairs. Subcommittee on Asian and Pacific Affairs. *Refugee Protection and*

*Resettlement Issues Relating to Southeast Asia and Hong Kong: Hearing and Markup, June 21, 1990.* 101st Cong., 2d sess. Washington, DC: Government Printing Office, 1992, 226 pp.

U.S. Congress. House. Committee on the Judiciary. Subcommittee on Immigration, Refugees, and International Law. *Extension of the Legalization Program: Hearing, March 30, 1988 on H.R. 4222 and H.R. 3816.* 100th Cong., 2d sess. Washington, DC: Government Printing Office, 1988, 413 pp.

————. *Family Unification, Employer Sanctions, and Anti-Discrimination under IRCA: Hearing, August 23, 1988.* 100th Cong., 2d sess. Washington, DC: Government Printing Office, 1989, 150 pp.

U.S. Congress. House. Committee on the Judiciary. Subcommittee on International Law, Immigration, and Refugees. *Administration's Proposed Refugee Admissions Program for Fiscal Year 1993: Hearing, July 30, 1992.* 102d Cong., 2d sess. Washington, DC: Government Printing Office, 1992, 194 pp.

————. *Alien Smuggling: Hearing, June 30, 1993.* 103d Cong., 1st sess. Washington, DC: Government Printing Office, 1993, 187 pp.

————. *Operations of the Border Patrol: Hearing, August 5, 1992.* 102d Cong., 2d sess. Washington, DC: Government Printing Office, 1992, 269 pp.

U.S. Congress. Senate. Committee on the Judiciary. Subcommittee on Immigration and Refugee Affairs. *Cambodia: Toward Peace and Relief: A Staff Report, November 25, 1991.* 102d Cong., 1st sess. Washington, DC: Government Printing Office, 1992, 49 pp.

————. *Chinese Students in America and Human Rights in China: Hearing, January 23, 1990 on H.R. 2712, a Bill to Facilitate the Adjustment or Change of Status of Chinese Nationals in the United States by Waiving the 2-Year Foreign Residence Requirement for "J" Nonimmigrants and by Treating Nonimmigrants, Whose Departure Has Been Deferred by the Attorney General, as Remaining in Legal Nonimmigrant Status for Purposes of Adjustment or Change of Status.* 101st Cong., 2d sess. Washington, DC: Government Printing Office, 1991, 192 pp.

Van Arsdale, Peter W. "Accessing Human Services: Ethnographic Perspectives on Refugee Communities and Mutual

Assistance Associations." *Information and Referral* 9 (Summer–Fall 1987): 1–25.

Vandu Kroef, Justus M. "The Endless Aftermath of Conquest: Indochina's Refugees and Their World." *Crossroads*, no. 23 (1987): 15–27.

Vandyk, Anthony. "No Entry: Airlines Are Being Fined and Forced to House, Feed and Guard Political Asylum-Seeking Passengers, Who 'Lose' Their Travel Documents." *Air Transport World* 29 (October 1992): 46–49.

Violet, Joyce C. "Immigration and Refugees." *Migration World* 18, 1 (1990): 27–33.

Wilbanks, Dana W. "The Moral Debate between Humanitarianism and National Interest About U.S. Refugee Policy: A Theological Perspective." *Migration World Magazine* 21, 5 (1993): 15–18.

## Political Asylum

Charlton, Roger, et al. "Identifying the Mainsprings of U.S. Refugee and Asylum Policy: A Contextual Interpretation." *Journal of Refugee Studies* 1, 3–4 (1988): 237–259.

Cooper, Davalene. "Promised Land or Land of Broken Promises? Political Asylum in the United States." *Kentucky Law Journal* 76 (Summer 1987–1988) 923–947.

Doherty, Carroll J. "Influx of Cubans Forces Clinton to Halt Automatic Asylum: Moving to Prevent a Replay of 1980 Mariel Boatlift, President Orders Refugees Taken to Guantanamo." *Congressional Quarterly Weekly Report* 52 (August 20, 1994): 2464–2465.

Griffith, Elwin. "Asylum and Withholding Deportation: Challenges to the Alien After the Refugee Act of 1980." *Loyola of Los Angeles International and Comparative Law Journal* 12 (March 1990): 215–277.

Hurley, Maureen O'Connor. "The Asylum Process: Past, Present and Future." *New England Law Review* 26 (Spring 1992): 995–1049.

McSpadden, Lucia Ann, and Helene Moussa. "I Have a Name: The Gender Dynamics in Asylum and in Resettlement of

Ethiopian and Eritrean Refugees in North America." *Journal of Refugee Studies* 6, 3 (1993): 203–225.

Mulligan, Maureen. "Obtaining Political Asylum: Classifying Rape as a Well-Founded Fear of Persecution on Account of Political Opinion." *Boston College Third World Law Journal* 10 (Spring 1990): 355–380.

"Prisoners of Foreign Policy: An Argument for Ideological Neutrality in Asylum." *Harvard Law Review* 104 (June 1991): 1878–1897.

Riordan, Dennis P. "The Sanctuary Movement: Above the Law or Beyond Its Reach?" *New York Law School Human Rights Annual* 4 (Fall 1986): 137–162.

Silk, James. *Despite a Generous Spirit: Denying Asylum in the United States.* Washington, DC: U.S. Committee for Refugees, 1986, 48 pp.

Yarnold, Barbara M. "Federal Court Outcomes in Asylum-Related Appeals 1980–1987: A Highly 'Politicized' Process." *Policy Sciences (Amsterdam)* 23 (November 1990): 291–306.

———. "The Refugee Act of 1980 and the Depoliticization of Refugee/Asylum Admissions: An Example of Failed Policy Implementation." *American Politics Quarterly* 18 (October 1990): 527–536.

## Selected Journal Titles

Information on immigration is found in a wide variety of journals. The following journals publish articles on many subjects related to immigration. New journals are continually appearing. For other journals and additional information, please consult *Ulrich's International Periodicals Directory 1994–1995*, 3d ed. (New York: R.R. Bowker Company, 1994. Information on the journals listed is arranged in the following manner:

Journal Title
1. Editor
2. Year first published
3. Frequency of publication
4. Code

5. Special features
6. Address of publisher

*Across the Board*

1. A. J. Vogl
2. 1939
3. 10 issues per year
4. ISSN 0147-1554
5. Advertising, charts, illustrations, index
6. Conference Board, Inc.
   845 Third Avenue
   New York, NY 10022

*American Demographics*

1. Brad Edmonson
2. 1979
3. Monthly
4. ISSN 0163-4089
5. Book reviews, charts, illustrations, statistics, index, cumulative index
6. American Demographics, Inc.
   Box 68
   Ithaca, NY 14851-0068

*American Economic Review*

1. —
2. 1911
3. Quarterly
4. ISSN 0002-8282
5. Advertising, charts, illustrations, statistics, index
6. American Economic Association
7. 2014 Broadway
   Suite 305
   Nashville, TN 37203

*American Journal of Agricultural Economics*

1. Richard Adams and Steven Buccola
2. 1919
3. 5 issues per year
4. ISSN 0002-9092
5. Advertising, book reviews, bibliography, charts, illustrations, statistics, index

6. American Agricultural Economics Association
   c/o Secretary-Treasurer
   80 Heady Hall
   Iowa State University
   Ames, IA 50011-1070

*Applied Economics*

1. Maurice H. Preston
2. 1969
3. 16 issues per year
4. ISSN 0003-6846
5. Advertising, charts
6. Chapman & Hall
   29 W. 35th Street
   New York, NY 10001-2291

*Cornell International Law Journal*

1. Editorial Board
2. 1968
3. 3 issues per year
4. ISSN 0010-8812
5. Advertising, book reviews, bibliography, index
6. Cornell University Law School
   Myron Taylor Hall
   Ithaca, NY 14853

*CQ Researcher*

1. Sandra Stencil
2. 1923
3. 4 times a month
4. ISSN 1056-2036
5. Book reviews, charts, index
6. Congressional Quarterly, Inc.
   1414 22nd Street, N.W.
   Washington, DC 20037

*Demography*

1. —
2. 1964
3. Quarterly
4. ISSN 0070-3370
5. —

6. Population Association of America
   1722 N. Street, N.W.
   Washington, DC 20036-2983

*Fortune Magazine*

1. Marshall Loeb
2. 1930
3. Biweekly
4. ISSN 0015-8259
5. Advertising, book reviews, illustrations
6. Time, Inc.
   Time & Life Building
   Rockefeller Center
   New York, NY 10020-1393

*Immigration and Nationality Law Review*

1. Maurice A. Roberts
2. 1986
3. Annual
4. ISSN 0149-9807
5. —
6. William S. Hein & Co., Inc.
   1285 Main Street
   Buffalo, NY 14209

*Immigration Newsletter*

1. Dan Kesselbrenner
2. 1972
3. Quarterly
4. ISSN 0145-3416
5. Book reviews
6. National Lawyers Guild
   National Immigration Project
   14 Beacon Street, Suite 506
   Boston, MA 02108

*Immigration Report*

1. Louise Parker
2. 1979
3. Monthly
4. ISSN 1067-3377
5. Book reviews

6. Federation for American Immigration Reform
   1666 Connecticut Avenue, N.W.
   Suite 400
   Washington, DC 20009

*Industrial and Labor Relations Review*

1. Donald E. Cullen
2. 1947
3. Quarterly
4. ISSN 0019-7939
5. Advertising, book reviews, bibliography, charts, index, cumulative index
6. Cornell University
   New York State School of Industrial and Labor Relations
   Ithaca, NY 14853-3901

*International Migration Review*

1. Silvano M. Tomasi
2. 1966
3. Quarterly
4. ISSN 0020-7993
5. Advertising, book reviews, abstracts, bibliography, charts, statistics, index, cumulative index
6. Center for Migration Studies
   209 Flagg Place
   Staten Island, NY 10304-1199

*International Security*

1. Steven E. Miller
2. 1976
3. Quarterly
4. ISSN 0162-2889
5. Advertising
6. MIT Press
   55 Hayward Street
   Cambridge, MA 02142

*Journal of Legislation*

1. Ronald R. Ratton
2. 1974
3. 2 issues per year

4. ISSN 0146-9584
5. Advertising, book reviews, bibliography
6. University of Notre Dame
   Notre Dame Law School
   Notre Dame, IN 46556

*Journal of Refugee Studies*

1. Roger Zetter
2. 1988
3. Quarterly
4. ISSN 0951-6328
5. Advertising, book reviews
6. Refugee Studies Program
   Oxford University Press, Inc.
   2001 Evans Road
   Cary, NC 27513

*Labor Law Journal*

1. —
2. 1949
3. Monthly
4. ISSN 0023-6586
5. Book reviews, abstracts, charts, illustrations, statistics, cumulative index
6. Commerce Clearing House, Inc.
   4025 W. Petersen Avenue
   Chicago, IL 60646

*Michigan Journal of International Law*

1. —
2. 1979
3. Quarterly
4. ISSN 1052-2867
5. Book reviews, bibliography, index
6. University of Michigan
   Hutchins Hall
   Ann Arbor, MI 48109-1215

*Michigan Law Review*

1. Editorial Board
2. 1902
3. 8 issues per year

4. ISSN 0026-2234
5. Advertising, book reviews, index, cumulative index
6. Michigan Law Review Association
   Ann Arbor, MI 48109-1215

*Migration World*

1. Lydio Tomasi
2. 1973
3. 5 issues per year
4. ISSN 0197-9175
5. Advertising, book reviews, abstracts, illustrations
6. Center for Migration Studies
   209 Flagg Place
   Staten Island, NY 10304-1199

*National Journal*

1. Richard S. Frank
2. 1969
3. Weekly
4. ISSN 0360-4217
5. Advertising, book reviews, charts, illustrations, index
6. National Journal, Inc.
   1730 M Street, N.W.
   Suite 1100
   Washington, DC 20036

*New York Law School Journal of Human Rights*

1. —
2. 1982
3. Twice annually
4. ISSN 8756-8926
5. —
6. New York Law School
   57 Worth Street
   New York, NY 10013-2960

*Population and Development Review*

1. Paul Demeny
2. 1975
3. Quarterly
4. ISSN 0098-7921
5. Book reviews, abstracts, charts, index

6. Population Council
   1 Dag Hammarskjold Plaza
   New York, NY 10017

*Population and Environment*

1. Virginia Abernethy
2. 1978
3. Bimonthly
4. ISSN 0199-0039
5. Advertising, book reviews, charts, index
6. Human Sciences Press, Inc.
   233 Spring Street
   New York, NY 10013-1578

*Population Research and Policy Review*

1. Larry Barnett
2. 1980
3. 3 issues per year
4. ISSN 0167-5923
5. —
6. Kluwer Academic Publishers Group
   Box 358
   Accord Station
   Hingham, MA 02018-0358

*Social Problems*

1. Robert Perrucci
2. 1953
3. Quarterly
4. ISSN 0037-7791
5. Advertising, book reviews, bibliography, charts, index, cumulative index
6. Society for the Study of Social Problems
   University of California Press
   Journals Division
   2126 Berkeley Way
   Berkeley, CA 94720

*Social Science Quarterly*

1. C. M. Bonjean
2. 1920
3. Quarterly

4. ISSN 0038-4941
5. Advertising, book reviews, abstracts, bibliography, index
6. Southwestern Social Science Association
   University of Texas Press
   Box 7819
   Austin, TX 78713

*TransAfrica Forum*

1. Randall Robinson
2. 1982
3. Quarterly
4. ISSN 0730-8876
5. Advertising, book reviews
6. Transaction Publishers
   Transaction Periodicals Consortium
   Department 3092
   Rutgers University
   New Brunswick, NJ 08903

# Audiovisual Aids 6

These selected films and videocassettes present a wide range of information on immigration to America from the colonial period to the present. The selection begins with a number of films and cassettes on immigration in general. These are followed by specific topics on immigration from Cuba, Mexico, and other areas; refugees; and economic and social conditions of immigrants.

The following sources offer films and videocassette in English:

*AFVA Evaluations, 1992.* Fort Atkinson, WI: Highsmith Press, 1992.

*Educational Film/Video Locator of the Consortium of College and University Media Centers and R.R. Bowker.* 2 vols. 4th ed. New York: R.R. Bowker, 1990–1991.

*Film and Video Finder.* 3 vols. 4th ed. Medford, NJ: Plexus Publishing, 1994/95.

*Video Rating Guide for Libraries.* Santa Barbara, CA: ABC-CLIO, various years.

*The Video Source Book.* 2 vols. and supplement. 15th ed. Detroit, MI: Research, Inc., 1994.

The following data are provided for each film:

Title of film

Distributor

Phone and fax number, if available

Data on film

Description

# Immigration

**Immigration**
McGraw-Hill Films
674 Via De La Valle
P.O. Box 641
Del Mar, CA 92014
Color, 24 minutes, sound, ½" or ¾" video, 1967.

Shows how unrestricted immigration became a problem in the United States. Analyzes the change in attitude toward immigrants. Also reveals the great contributions of immigrants to the United States.

**Immigration**
McGraw-Hill Training Systems
P.O. Box 641
Del Mar, CA 92014
Color, 25 minutes, sound, ½" or ¾" video, 1968.

Traces the influx of immigrants to the United States. Stresses their contributions as well as the resistance of several groups to their presence.

**Immigration 1**
Chinese for Affirmative Action
17 Walter U, Lum Place
San Francisco, CA 94108
Phone: 415-274-6750
Fax: 415-397-8770
Black and white, 30 minutes, sound, 1974.

A panel defends immigration service while members of the Neighborhood Legal Assistance Program object, saying that people are still waiting for permanent resident status in the

United States. The film presents two contrasting viewpoints of the Immigration and Naturalization Service and the Neighborhood Legal Assistance Program. The film describes how the Neighborhood Legal Assistance Program is aiding aliens to receive permanent resident status in the United States.

**Immigration 2**
Chinese for Affirmative Action
17 Walter U, Lum Place
San Francisco, CA 94108
Phone: 415-274-6750
Fax: 415-397-8770
Black & white, 30 minutes, sound, 1974.

Film is a question-and-answer session on how Asians are treated by the Immigration and Naturalization Service and how a person from the East can bring a relative into the United States.

**Immigration in America's History**
Coronet/MTI Film & Video
108 Wilmot Road
Deerfield, IL 60015
Phone: 708-940-1260
Toll-free: 800-777-8100
Fax: 708-940-3640
Color, 11 minutes, sound, VHS, Beta, ¾" U-matic, 1960.

Examines historical, economic, and sociological aspects of immigration to the United States by using dramatic reenactments. Examines the major waves of immigrants to the United States from the seventeenth century onward. Shows how settlements developed and discusses major contributions of immigrants.

**Immigration in France and the United States**
Agency for International Technology
Box A
Bloomington, IN 47402
Phone: 812-339-2203
Toll-free: 800-457-4509
Color, 30 minutes, sound, ½" VHS, 1991.

Contrasts immigrant children and their families in Paris and Los Angeles adjusting to new settings. Develops international understanding and geographic literacy for today's students existing in a global environment.

### Immigration in the 19th Century
Films Incorporated
5547 North Ravenswood Avenue
Chicago, IL 60640-1199
Phone: 800-323-4222
Color, 13 minutes, sound, ½" or ¾" video, n.d.

Portrays immigration between 1820 and 1920, when 88 million Europeans immigrated to the United States. Describes the mid-nineteenth century, which saw a stiffening of resistance toward new immigrants. Analyzes possible causes to the problems of new immigrants and their difficulty blending into U.S. society.

### Immigration: New Work and New Rules 1880–1920
Anti-Defamation League of B'nai B'rith
Audio-Visual Department
823 United Nations Plaza
New York, NY 10017
Phone: 212-490-2525
Color, 15 minutes, sound, ½", VHS, 1991.

Explores the daily life of women immigrants shortly before and after the turn of the twentieth century. Includes women from a wide variety of geographic and racial populations and includes historic photographs.

### Immigration of the 20th Century
Films Incorporated
5547 North Ravenswood Avenue
Chicago, IL 60640-1199
Phone: 800-323-4222
Color, 13 minutes, sound, ½" or ¾" video, n.d.

Shows problems created by immigrants that led to the U.S. quota system of the 1920s, which reduced the numbers of immigrants for all but the Nordics and Anglo-Saxons. Discusses the period after World War II when the United States once again opened its doors.

### Immigration Reform: New Obligations for All Employers
American Bar Association
Commission on Public Understanding About the Law
750 N. Lakeshore Drive
Chicago, IL 60611

Phone: 312-988-5000

Color, 85 minutes, sound, VHS, Beta, ¾" U-matic, 1987.

Lawyers advise their corporate clients about new laws regarding hiring minorities.

**Immigration Reform: Part II**
Films Incorporated
5547 North Ravenswood Avenue
Chicago, IL 60640-1195
Phone: 800-323-4222
Color, 60 minutes, sound, ¾" video, ½" VHS, ½" Beta/VHS, 1984.

Presents a panel of the U.S. Court of Appeals. Debates the rights of legal and illegal aliens to employment, medical, and educational services. Part of a 13-part series on the U.S. Constitution.

**Immigration: The Triumph of Hope**
National Geographic Educational Services
P.O. Box 98019
Washington, DC 20090
Color, 25 minutes, sound, VHS, 1992.

Through live action footage, photographs, and interviews, this film relates the experience of immigrants, gives reasons people immigrate to the United States, and discusses how they cope with problems after arrival.

# Immigration Legislation

**America Becoming**
PBS Video
1320 Braddock Place
Alexandria, VA 22314-1698
Phone: 703-739-5380
Toll-free: 800-344-3337
Fax: 703-739-5269
Color, 90 minutes, sound, VHS, ¾" U-matic, 1991.

Looks at history of Immigration and Nationality Act from 1965 to the present. Focuses on lives of both newcomers and long-time residents.

**Work in Progress**
Third World Newsreel
335 West 38th Street, 5th Floor
New York, NY 10018
Phone: 212-947-9277
Fax: 212-594-6417
Color, 14:02 minutes, color, 16 mm, video, 1990.

Documentary shows effects of the 1986 Immigration Reform Act
upon illegal immigrants who could not file for amnesty. The
tape shows the forces—politics, media exposure, Latin folklore,
and culture—that help shape the illegal alien in the United
States.

# Immigrants

**Coming Across**
Pyramid Film & Video
2801 Colorado Avenue
Santa Monica, CA 90404
Phone: 310-828-7577
Fax: 310-453-9083
Color, 46 minutes, sound, video, 1989/1991.

Shows immigrants coming to the United States in search of a
better life. Film depicts a cultural exchange between U.S. teens
and immigrant families from ten countries. The individuals'
hopes, fears, expectations, and differences are revealed in the
film.

**Family across the Sea**
California Newsreel
149 Ninth Street
San Francisco, CA 94103
Phone: 415-621-6196
Fax: 415-621-6522
Color, 56 minutes, sound, video, 1991.

Film shows connection between the Gullah people of South
Carolina and the people of Sierra Leone. Shows how African
Americans kept their ties with their homeland through the cen-
turies in speech, songs, and customs.

## The Immigrant
Cable Films & Video
Country Club Station
P.O. Box 7171
Kansas City, MO 64113
Phone: 913-362-2804
Fax: 913-341-7365
Black and white, 20 minutes, silent, VHS, Beta, ¾" U-matic, 1917.

This silent film with musical soundtrack shows Charlie Chaplin, as an immigrant, falling in love with the first young woman he meets.

## The Immigrant Experience: The Long Journey
Learning Corporation of America
Coronet/MTI Films and Videos
108 Wilmot Drive
Deerfield, IL 60015
Phone: 708-940-1260
Toll-Free: 800-621-2131

New World Entertainment
1440 S. Sepulveda Boulevard
Los Angeles, CA 90025
Phone: 310-444-8100

University of Illinois
Film/Video Center
1325 South Oak Street
Champaign, IL 61820
Toll-Free: 800-367-3456
Color, 28 minutes, sound, ½" or ¾" video, 1973.

Tells the story of the American dream versus the American reality to immigrants, as experienced by one Polish family who came to the United States in 1907. Available from the three sources listed above.

## Immigrant from America
Sterling Education Films
241 E. 34th Street
New York, NY 10016
Phone: 212-262-9433
Color, 20 minutes, sound, 16 mm, n.d.

Compares the different experiences of white immigrants to the United States and black immigrants in the United States. Reveals how differences in education, jobs, and political power gained by other groups have been denied blacks as a result of prejudice, discrimination, and violence. Reveals differences in life-styles between white and black Americans.

**The Immigrant: Journey in America**
New York State Education Department
Bureau of Technology Applications
Room C-7-CEC
Empire State Plaza
Albany, NY 12230
Phone: 518-474-3168
Color, 30 minutes, sound, VHS, Beta, ¾" U-matic, 1980.

Film has three programs—dealing with first contact, life and work, and generations—telling the story of experiences of southern and eastern Europeans who came to the United States in the nineteenth and twentieth centuries.

**Immigrant Novel in America**
NETCHE Nebraska ETV Council for Higher Education
1800 N. 33rd Street
Lincoln, NE 68503
Phone: 402-472-3611
Black and white, 30 minutes, sound, 1969.

Film discusses S. K. Winther's three novels: *Take All to Nebraska, Mortgage Your Heart,* and *This Passion Never Dies.*

**Immigrants and Missionaries**
Anti-Defamation League of B'nai B'rith
Audio-Visual Department
823 United Nations Plaza
New York, NY 10017
Phone: 212-490-2525
Fax: 212-867-0779
Color, 30 minutes, sound, VHS, Beta, ¾" U-matic, 1983.

Discusses work of social reformer Jacob Riis.

**Immigrants in America**
Dallas County Community College District
Center for Educational Telecommunications

Dallas Telecourses
9596 Walnut Street
Dallas, TX 75243
Phone: 214-952-0330
Fax: 214-952-0329
Color, 28 minutes, sound, ¾" U-matic, 1980.

Gives history of first immigrants who came to the United States.

**Immigrants in Chains**
Kent State University
Kent, OH
Color, black and white, 11 minutes, sound, 16 mm, n.d.

Shows how Africans were captured and traded into slavery between 1619 and 1863. Demonstrates the role of the slave immigrant in the labor system.

**Immigrants in the Cities**
Films Incorporated
5547 North Ravenswood Avenue
Chicago, IL 60640-1199
Phone: 800-323-4222
Color, 11 minutes, sound, 16 mm, optical sound, 1972.

Shows how immigrants arriving in the eastern United States provided a labor force for the new industrial economy. Discusses the new wealth created by the immigrants.

**Island of Saints and Souls**
University of California
Extension Media Center
2176 Shattuck Avenue
Berkeley, CA 94704
Phone: 510-642-0460
Fax: 510-643-8683
Color, 29 minutes, sound, video, 1990.

Shows how Catholicism of immigrants has contributed to the cultural features of New Orleans. Depicts a year-long trip through the Crescent City, examining the city, customs, traditions, and feast days.

# Aliens

**Alien Rights**
Chinese for Affirmative Action
17 Walter U. Lum Place
San Francisco, CA 94108
Phone: 415-274-6750
Fax: 415-397-8770
Black and white, 30 minutes, sound, n.d.

Discusses rights of aliens and problems faced by immigrants. Shows how to use the alien registration form.

**Natives**
Jesse Lerner/Scott Sterling
2125 N. Commonwealth Avenue
Los Angeles, CA 90227
Phone: 213-662-8561
Fax: 213-747-8571
Black and white, 25 minutes, sound, 16 mm, 1991.

Presents the struggle of a citizens' group in San Diego attempting to stop the tremendous influx of undocumented aliens.

# Migrant Labor

**Migrant Education**
New Jersey Network
CN-777
Trenton, NJ 08625-0777
Phone: 609-777-5000
Fax: 609-633-2920
Color, 30 minutes, sound, VHS, ¾" U-matic, 1983.

Film documents New Jersey's Migrant Education Program and the computerized system it uses.

**Migrant Farmworkers**
Downtown Community TV Center
87 Lafayette Street
New York, NY 10013
Phone: 212-966-4510
Fax: 212-219-0248
Color, 20 minutes, sound, ¾" U-matic, 1984.

Tells the story of the life of a migrant farmworker. Focuses on illegal aliens as migrant farmworkers, Haitians, cardboard housing, a successful Arizona farmworkers' union strike, and the migrants' hope for a better future.

**Migrant Health**
Great Plains Institutional TV
University of Nebraska
P.O. Box 80669
Lincoln, NE 68501
Black and white, 30 minutes, sound, 16 mm, n.d.

Provides an overview of public health problems regarding migrant farm labor.

**Migrant: Part 1**
National Broadcasting Company, Inc.
30 Rockefeller Plaza
New York, NY 10020
Color, 27 minutes, sound, 16 mm, 1970.

Reveals the story of the economic problems of the migrant workers. Shows how migrant workers lack funds for many necessities such as housing and insurance.

**Migrant: Part 2**
National Broadcasting Company, Inc.
30 Rockefeller Plaza
New York, NY 10020
Color, 27 minutes, sound, 16 mm, film optical sound, 1970.

Talks of the poor working conditions and the poverty of the migrant worker. Points out that the worker lacks insurance, capital, and shelter to improve their situation.

**The Migrants**
Monterey Home Video
28038 Dorothy Drive, Suite 1
Agoura Hills, CA 91301
Phone: 818-597-0047
Toll-free: 800-424-2593
Fax: 818-597-0105
Color, 83 minutes, sound, VHS, 1974.

Film is a made-for-TV adaptation of Tennessee Williams' play about the hardships faced by a migrant family hoping for a better life.

**The Migrants, 1980**
Films Incorporated
5547 North Ravenswood Avenue
Chicago, IL 60640-1199
Phone: 800-323-4222
Color, 52 minutes, sound, ½" or ¾" video, 1980.

Documents the problems of U.S. farmworkers and shows that their living conditions improved little in the 1970s. Shows the grinding poverty of the worker and the low yearly income. Reveals the substandard housing, the presence of illegal aliens, and the use of child labor.

# Refugees

**Refugee**
United Nations
Radio and Visual Services
United Nations
New York, NY 10017
Color, 24 minutes, sound, 16 mm, n.d.

Examines the refugee problems of Africa. Shows the refugee's task of stripping the forest to build huts, the problems of land erosion in raising crops, and pollution of the refugee's environment. Demonstrates life in a refugee camp.

**Refugee Health Problems**
Emory University
Emory Medical Television Network—Department C
1440 Clifton Road, NE
Atlanta, GA 30322
Phone: 404-616-3556
Color, 36 minutes, sound, VHS, Beta, ¾" U-matic, 1986.

Discusses special conditions common among refugees and how they should be treated.

**Refugee Road**
Humanities Resource Center
Capital University
2199 East Main Street

Columbus, OH 43209
Phone: 614-236-6508
Color, 59 minutes, sound, 16 mm, film optical sound, n.d.

Follows a Latvian family from a refugee camp in Thailand to the United States.

**Refugees**
WCCO-TV
Media Service
11th On the Mall
90 South 11th Street
Minneapolis, MN 55403
Color, 23 minutes, sound, ½" or ¾" video, 1979.

Shows the arrival of the Hmong family in Minneapolis. The film shows the difficulties faced by an Asian family adjusting to life in the United States.

**Refugees: An Historical View**
McGraw-Hill Training Systems
P.O. Box 641
Del Mar, CA 92014
Color, 22 minutes, sound, ½" or ¾" video, 1979.

Analyzes the refugee experience by looking at the plight of such immigrants as Jews and other displaced persons from the Russian Revolution, World War I, and World War II. Discusses several solutions to the problem of refugees.

**Refugees in Our Backyard**
First Run/Icarus Films
153 Waverly Place
New York, NY 10014
Phone: 212-727-1711
Toll-free: 800-876-1710
Fax: 212-989-7649
Color, 58 minutes, sound, VHS, 1990.

Tells the story of Salvadorans, Guatemalans, and Nicaraguans who fled their country because of civil wars and economic conditions and came to the United States as undocumented aliens since the early 1980s.

# Regional Immigration

## Hispanics

Hispanic America
Anti-Defamation League of B'nai B'rith
Audio-Visual Department
823 United Nations Plaza
New York, NY 10017
Phone: 212-490-2525
Fax: 212-867-0779
Color, 13 minutes, sound VHS, Beta, ¾" U-matic, 1980.

Stresses increase in Hispanic population due to the upsurge in immigration. Looks at problems and how to solve them. Looks at impact these immigrants will have on U.S. politics and economics.

**Hispanic Americans**
Dallas County Community College District
Center for Educational Telecommunications
Dallas Telecourses
9596 Walnut Street
Dallas, TX 75243
Phone: 214-952-0330
Fax: 214-952-0329
Color, 28 minutes, sound, ¾" U-matic, 1980.

Presents historical viewpoint of Hispanic Americans and has interviews with such Hispanics as Cesar Chavez.

**The Hispanic Culture: Hispanics in America**
Video Knowledge, Inc.
29 Bramble Lane
Melville, NY 11747
Phone: 516-367-4250
Toll-free: 800-532-7663
Fax: 516-367-1006
Color, 60 minutes, sound, VHS, Beta, ¾" U-matic, 1981.

Looks at Hispanic migration into and within the United States. Explores its impact on the Hispanic community and communities in which Hispanics settle. Part of the "Lifestyle U.S.A.—America in the 80s" series.

**Hispanics and Housing: Part 1, the Problem**
New Jersey Network
CN 777
Trenton, NJ 08625-0777
Phone: 609-777-5000
Fax: 609-633-2920
Color, 30 minutes, sound, VHS, ¾" U-matic, 1983.

Shows how federal and state governments, residents, and community leaders study the Hispanic housing problems in New Jersey.

**Hispanics and Housing: Part 2, the Government**
New Jersey Network
CN 777
Trenton, NJ 08625-0777
Phone: 609-777-5000
Fax: 609-633-2920
Color, 30 minutes, sound, VHS, ¾" U-matic, 1983.

Shows how state and federal housing programs affect the Hispanic community.

**Hispanics and Housing: Part 3, the Community**
New Jersey Network
CN 777
Trenton, NJ 08625-0777
Phone: 609-777-5000
Fax: 609-633-2920
Color, 30 minutes, sound, VHS, ¾" U-matic, 1983.

Shows improvements in housing conditions for Hispanics through developments such as Sweet Equity and Villa Borinquen in Jersey City.

# Mexicans
**The Mexican American**
Handel Film Corporation
8730 Sunset Boulevard
West Hollywood, CA 90069
Phone: 310-657-8990
Toll free: 800-395-8990
Fax: 310-657-2746
Color, 29 minutes, sound, VHS, Beta, ¾" U-matic, 1977.

Examines past and current achievements of Mexican Americans.

**Mexican-American Culture: Its Heritage**
Communications Group West
1640 5th Street, Suite 202
Santa Monica, CA 90401
Phone: 310-451-2525
Fax: 310-451-5020
Color, 18 minutes, sound, VHS, Beta, ¾" U-matic, 1971.

Ricardo Montalban relates his own Mexican heritage and mentions contributions made by Mexicans to U.S. music, language, industry, etc.

**Mexican-American Family**
Atlantis Productions
1252 La Granada Drive
Thousand Oaks, CA 91360
Phone: 805-495-2790
Fax: 805-495-0717
Color, 16 minutes, sound, VHS, Beta, ¾" U-matic, 1970.

Tells a Mexican American family's story of adjustments to a new language and society.

**The Mexican American Speaks: Heritage in Bronze**
Encyclopedia Britannica Educational Corporation
310 S. Michigan Avenue
Chicago, IL 60604
Color, 19 minutes, sound, 16 mm, video, U-matic, 1972.

Shows the rich cultural history of Mexicans and how it has been received in the United States in recent years. Stresses that unity and social improvements in the community depend upon the ideals of Mexican youths.

**Mexican-American: The Invisible Minority**
National Educational Television, Inc.
WNET/Thirteen
Indiana University
Bloomington, IN 47401
Color, black and white, 38 minutes, sound, 16 mm, 1969.

Depicts Mexicans' struggle for identity in U.S. society. Presents the problems of the unskilled worker and the difficulties of Mexican children in U.S. schools. Serves as a study of the aspirations of Mexicans to become American and still retain a cultural identity.

**Mexican Americans: A Quest for Equality**
Anti-Defamation League of B'nai B'rith
Audio Visual Department
823 United Nations Plaza
New York, NY 10017
Phone: 212-490-2525
Fax: 212-867-0779
Black and white, 29 minutes, sound, VHS, Beta, ¾" U-matic,
1983.

Examines cultural and economic conditions in rural and urban
Mexican American communities.

**Mexican Americans: Viva La Raza**

Columbia Broadcasting System
383 Madison Avenue
New York, NY 10017
Black and white, 47 minutes, sound, 16 mm, 1972.

Presents a study of the awakening of the Mexican American
community. The film discusses grievances in a Los Angeles
community with the rise of political and religious leaders. The
organization of Mexican workers into unions illustrates these
struggles for economic and social justice.

**Mexican or American**

Atlantis Productions
1252 La Granada Drive
Thousand Oaks, CA 91360
Phone: 805-495-2790
Fax: 805-495-0717
Color, 17 minutes, sound, VHS, Beta, ¾" U-matic, 1973.

Shows the cultural conflict and difficulties Mexican Americans
face in trying to maintain their heritage.

**Mexican or American: An Historic Profile**

Anti-Defamation League of B'nai B'rith
Audio Visual Department
823 United Nations Plaza
New York, NY 10017
Phone: 212-490-2525
Fax: 212-867-0779
Black and white, 28 minutes, sound, 16 mm, 1971.

Traces the history of Mexican Americans from the time of Cortez to the barrios in the Southwest in the 1970s. Shows the Mexican influence on the culture of the region.

## Cubans

**Cuba: Angry Exiles**
Altschul Group Corporation
1580 Sherman Avenue, Suite 100
Evanston, IL 60201
Phone: 708-326-6700
Toll free: 800-323-5448
Color, 14 minutes, sound, ½" or ¾" video, n.d.

Presents a history of the hostilities between Cuba and the United States. Emphasis is placed on the Bay of Pigs through the 1979 Freedom Flotilla. Reveals that some Cubans hope to return to Cuba after Castro loses power.

**Cuba: Refugees and the Economy**
Journal Films, Inc.
1560 Sherman Avenue, Suite 100
Evanston, IL 60201
Phone: 708-328-6700
Toll free: 800-323-9084
Fax: 708-328-6706
Color, 30 minutes, sound, VHS, Beta, ¾" U-matic, n.d.

Focuses on the tens of thousands of Cubans who chose to leave their country.

**Cuba: Refugees and the Economy**
United Press International
800 Broadway
Cincinnati, OH 45202
Color, 25 minutes, sound, video, ¾"U-matic, 1980.

Explores the economic development and political structure of Cuba. Focuses on the great immigration out of Cuba and examines the relations that existed between Cuba and the United States from when Castro came into power up to 1980.

## Haitians

**Haiti: Reason to Flee**
The Cinema Guild
1697 Broadway, Suite 506
New York, NY 10019

Phone: 212-246-5522
Toll-free: 800-723-5522
Fax: 212-246-5525
Color, 27 minutes, sound, VHS, Beta, ¾" U-matic, 1983.

This excerpt from Bitter Cane, a movie looks at Haitian boat people.

## Asians—General
### Asian Power in the Richmond
Chinese for Affirmative Action
17 Walter U. Lum Place
San Francisco, CA 94108
Phone: 415-274-6750
Fax: 415-397-8770
Black and white, 15 minutes, sound, 1975.

Explores the possibility of the Richmond District in San Francisco becoming a second Chinatown. Looks at Richmond Asian Multi Service, Inc.

### The Asianization of America
Centre Communications
1800 30th Street, Suite 207
Boulder, CO 80301
Phone: 303-444-1166
Toll-free: 800-886-1166
Fax: 303-444-1168
Color, 26 minutes, sound, VHS, Beta, 1991.

Looks at role of Asians in U.S. society and how successful they are in business and academia.

### Asians in America Series
Centre Communications
1800 30th Street, Suite 207
Boulder, CO 80301
Phone: 303-444-1166
Toll-free: 800-886-1166
Fax: 303-444-1168
Color, sound, VHS, Beta, ¾" U-matic, 1986.

Three programs describe the journey of Asian people to the United States.

# Vietnamese

**Many Voices: Mother Tongue**
TV Ontario Marketing
Box 200, Station Q
Toronto, Canada M4T 2T1
Phone: 416-484-2600
Fax: 416-484-4519
Color, 15 minutes, sound, video, 1990.

Film explains prejudice and discrimination experience by Vietnames in attempting to adapt to life in the United States.

**S.O.S. Stories of Survival**
Jill Petzall
139 N. Bemiston
St. Louis, MO 63105
Phone: 314-725-1196
Color, 29 minutes, sound, video, 1990.

Shows the story of five Vietnamese adults, refugees from communism, who escaped in boats. Reveals the prejudice they encounter trying to bridge two cultures in the Midwest.

**The Story of Vinh**
Downtown Community Television
87 Lafayette Street
New York, NY 10013-4435
Phone: 212-966-4510
Fax: 212-219-0248
Color, 56 minutes, sound, video, 1991.

Shows the story of the son of a U.S. serviceman and a Vietnamese woman. He immigrates to the United States. In Vietnam, he faced poverty and prejudice. In the United States, he is with a foster family who finds he is more mature than expected. Shows effects of the U.S. foster care system.

**Thanh's War**
University of California
Extension Media Center
2176 Shattuck Avenue
Berkeley, CA 94704
Phone: 510-642-6460
Fax: 510-643-8683
Color, 58 minutes, sound, video, 1990/1991

Shows the story of Thanh, whose family was killed by a grenade thrown by a U.S. soldier. Thanh's throat was torn apart in the explosion. He was rescued and brought to California for treatment and recovery. Shows him returning to Vietnam to marry.

# Cambodians

Cambodian Doughnut Dreams
First Run/Icarus Films Inc.
153 Waverly Place
New York, NY 10014
Phone: 212-727-1711
Fax: 212-989-7649
Color, 27 minutes, 16 mm, 1990/1991.

Shows the story of three Cambodians who escaped the killing fields, came to Los Angeles, and worked in the city's doughnut shops—80 percent of which are owned by Cambodians who are trying to remake their lives in the United States.

Rebuilding the Temple: Cambodians in America
Direct Cinema Ltd.
P.O. Box 69799
Los Angeles, CA 90069
Phone: 800-525-0000
Fax: 213-396-3233
Color, 57:40 minutes, sound, 16 mm, video, 1991.

Cambodians fled for fear of being killed by the Khmer Rouge in the 1970s. 150,000 Cambodians came to United States. Film is a documentary showing influence of Khmer-Buddhist culture on refugees' adjustment to Western life.

# Koreans

The Columbus Legacy: The Koreans, a Middle-Class Migration
The Pennsylvania State University
Special Services Building
University Park, PA 16803
Phone: 800-826-0132
Fax: 814-863-2574
Color, 8:05 minutes, sound, video, 1991.

Examines changes in immigration law in the 1960s that allowed Korean families to immigrate to the United States. Shows Choi, an engineer, who worked in a dry-cleaning business to support his family and educate his children.

# Irish

**The Columbus Legacy: The Irish, Overcoming Bigotry**
The Pennsylvania State University
Special Services Building
University Park, PA 16803
Phone: 800-826-0132
Fax: 814-863-2574
Color, 8:41 minutes, sound, video, 1991.

The Sisters of Mercy started the Mercy Hospital in 1847 in Pittsburgh, Pennsylvania, in response to the poor working and living conditions of Irish immigrants. Tape explores how such sisterhoods helped break down anti-Catholic and anti-Irish bigotry.

# Italians

**The Columbus Legacy: The Italians, a Changing Neighborhood**
The Pennsylvania State University
Special Services Building
University Park, PA 16803
Phone: 800-826-0132
Fax: 814-863-2574
Color, 8:45 minutes, sound, video, 1991.

Documents St. Donato's procession, started by Italian immigrants who came to Pennsylvania in the 1900s looking for work. Describes changes as younger generations move from tiny rowhouses to the suburbs.

# Glossary

**alien**  A person born in or belonging to another country.

**asylum**  A sanctuary or place of refuge.

**bracero program**  A contract program between the United States and Mexico in which Mexico supplied contract agricultural workers to the farms of the southwestern United States from 1942 to 1964.

**Camarioca Cuban**  A Cuban refugee who came to the United States in the Camarioca boatlift and airlift between 1965 and 1972.

**civil rights**  Individual freedoms provided by the U.S. Constitution and the Bill of Rights, such as freedom of speech and religion.

**cultural assimilation**  Refers to the development of a single society from a variety of ethnic groups.  The United States, in reference to its blending of social values, has often been called a "melting pot."

**cultural separatism**  Refers to ethnic groups maintaining the social characteristics of their country of origin, such as language and customs.

**eligible immigrant**  A qualified immigrant who is the spouse or unmarried child of a legalized alien.

**equal opportunity employment**  Refers to an absence of employment discrimination with regard to race, religion, and other social factors.

**295**

**ethnic** Pertaining to a group of persons sharing a common language, religion, or set of customs and traits.

**illegal alien** A person immigrating to a country without admission papers.

**illegal immigration** Entry into the United States without a visa by someone who is not a citizen.

**immigrant** A person who relocates from one country to another.

**legal alien** An alien lawfully admitted for temporary or permanent residence status.

**Marielito Cuban** A Cuban refugee who came to the United States as part of the U.S. policy regarding Cuban immigration from 1980 to 1985.

**migrant** A person who moves from one country to another on a temporary or permanent basis.

**naturalization** The conferring of the rights and privileges of a citizen upon a person from another country.

**passport** A warrant issued to a citizen of a country by appropriate authority, giving permission to travel, protection while out of the country, and the right to reenter the citizen's native country.

**refugee** A person who flees from persecution, such as religious and political oppression.

**sanctuary** A place such as a church or temple where fugitives are free from arrest.

**search warrant** A document provided to a building's occupant to allow authorities to enter the building for the purpose of questioning or searching the premises.

**visa** An endorsement made on a passport by an authorized official representing a country that the passport bearer wishes to visit; this endorsement denotes that the passport has been examined, it has been found correct, and permission to enter has been granted.

# Index

E. Willard Miller is a professor of geography and associate dean of resident instruction (emeritus) at the Pennsylvania State University. He received his A.M. degree at the University of Nebraska and his Ph.D. from the Ohio State University. He is a fellow of the American Association for the Advancement of Science, the American Geographical Society, the National Council for Geographic Education, and the Explorers Club. In 1990, Dr. Miller received the Honors Award from the Association of American Geographers. He has published more than 100 professional journal articles and 30 books. He is listed in Who's Who in America and Who's Who in the World.

Ruby M. Miller is a map librarian (retired) at the Pattee Library at the Pennsylvania State University. She received her B.A. degree at Chatham College and did graduate work at the University of Pittsburgh. She established and developed the map collection at Penn State, and at her retirement the collection had over 250,000 maps and over 3,000 atlases. She is the co-author of 6 books and over 100 bibliographies. The Pennsylvania Geographical Society has honored her with its Distinguished Scholar Award. She is a member of the Association of American Geographers and the American Association of University Women.